"Every patient in psychotherapy wonders, what is my therapist thinking? In this book, Ahron Friedberg, an experienced therapist, shares his thoughts and feelings that arise during psychotherapy sessions with his patients. This is an unusual book. It is not about case histories, nor psychopathology, nor the process of psychotherapy *per se*, although each of these is discussed. Its focus is on the therapist's mind; his thoughts about his patients and their problems; but also about himself, his career, and his life. Friedberg, true to his profession, always tries to understand what these thoughts mean, and how he might use that to help his patients."
Robert Michels, M.D. – Walsh McDermott University Professor of Medicine and Psychiatry, Cornell University

"*Psychotherapy and Personal Change: Two Minds in a Mirror* is a seasoned psychotherapist's gift to the reader, eloquently detailing his own and his patients' inner experience. It expresses our humanity with clarity and courage. For comparison, master clinician-writers such as Irvin Yalom, Erik Erikson and Donald Winnicott come to mind. *Two Minds in a Mirror* is a guide not only for patient and therapist but for us all on our common journey."
Nathan Szajnberg, M.D. – formerly Freud Professor, Hebrew University

"I found *Psychotherapy and Personal Change: Two Minds in a Mirror* deeply enlightening. As someone who has been in psychodynamic therapy for decades, I of course always wonder what it's like from the other side—and now I know. Dr. Friedberg illuminates the analytic process with his usual gentle wisdom."
Andrew Solomon, M.D. – Professor of Clinical Psychology, Columbia University

"I was riveted by two features of *Psychotherapy and Personal Change: Two Minds in a Mirror* – the unflinching candor that Dr. Friedberg turns on himself, and the precise, elegant writing that makes his revelations memorable. I reread some stories a few times, just to dwell in their clearly rendered depths. I never knew that the psyche could be presented so engagingly outside of a novel."
Donald W. Pfaff, Ph.D. – Professor Emeritus and Head of Laboratory, Neurobiology and Behavior, The Rockefeller University

Psychotherapy and Personal Change

Psychotherapy and Personal Change: Two Minds in a Mirror offers unique day-to-day accounts of patients undergoing psychotherapy and what happens during "talk therapy" to startle the complacent, conscious mind and expose the unconscious. It is a candid, moment-by-moment revelation of how the therapist's own memories, feelings, and doubts are often as much a factor in the process as those of the patient.

In the process of healing, both the therapist and the patient reflect on each other and on themselves. As the therapist develops empathy for the patient, and the patient develops trust in the therapist, their shared memories, feelings, and associations interact and entwine – almost kaleidoscopically – causing each to ask questions of the other and themselves. In this book, Dr. Friedberg reveals personal insights that arose as he recalled memories to share with patients. These insights might not have arisen but for the therapy, which operates in multiple directions as patient and therapist explore the present, the past, and the unknown. Readers will see the therapist – like the patient – as a complex, vulnerable human being influenced by parents, colleagues, and friends, whose conscious and unconscious minds ramify through each other. It is a truism of psychotherapy that in order to commit to the process, whatever the reservations or misconceptions, one must understand that therapy is not passive. The patient must expect to become personally involved with the therapist. The patient learns about the therapist even as the therapist helps the patient to gain insight into him- or herself. *Psychotherapy and Personal Change* shows how this exchange develops and how each actor is affected.

Through specific examples, the book raises the reader's understanding of what to expect from psychotherapy and enhances his/her insight into therapy that he or she may have had already.

Ahron Friedberg, M.D., is Clinical Professor of Psychiatry at Mount Sinai Icahn School of Medicine, New York, and served twice as President of the American Society of Psychoanalytic Physicians. He is Editor of American Academy of Psychodynamic Psychiatry and Psychoanalysis Forum, Book Editor of *Psychodynamic Psychiatry*, and a regular contributor to *Psychology Today*.

Sandra Sherman, J.D., Ph.D., was a Senior Attorney in the U.S. government and Professor of English at two major universities. She is the author of four books and over 60 peer-reviewed articles on 18th-century literature and culture and has co-authored several books on neuroscience. She currently works with scientists and physicians to support their research and writing.

Psychotherapy and Personal Change
Two Minds in a Mirror

Ahron Friedberg, M.D.
with Sandra Sherman

LONDON AND NEW YORK

First published 2021
by Routledge
2 Park Square, Milton Park, Abingdon, Oxon OX14 4RN

and by Routledge
52 Vanderbilt Avenue, New York, NY 10017

Routledge is an imprint of the Taylor & Francis Group, an informa business

© 2021 Ahron Friedberg and Sandra Sherman

The right of Ahron Friedberg and Sandra Sherman to be identified as authors of this work has been asserted by them in accordance with sections 77 and 78 of the Copyright, Designs and Patents Act 1988.

All rights reserved. No part of this book may be reprinted or reproduced or utilised in any form or by any electronic, mechanical, or other means, now known or hereafter invented, including photocopying and recording, or in any information storage or retrieval system, without permission in writing from the publishers.

Trademark notice: Product or corporate names may be trademarks or registered trademarks, and are used only for identification and explanation without intent to infringe.

British Library Cataloguing-in-Publication Data
A catalog record for this book is available from the British Library

Library of Congress Cataloging-in-Publication Data
Names: Friedberg, Ahron, 1963- author. | Sherman, Sandra, 1946- author.
Title: Psychotherapy and personal change : two minds in a mirror / Ahron Friedberg, M.D. with Sandra Sherman, J.D., Ph.D.
Description: Milton Park, Abingdon, Oxon; New York, NY : Routledge, 2021. | Includes bibliographical references and index. |
Identifiers: LCCN 2020034343 | ISBN 9780367621988 (hardback) | ISBN 9780367622022 (paperback) | ISBN 9781003108313 (ebook)
Subjects: LCSH: Psychotherapist and patient. | Psychotherapy.
Classification: LCC RC480.8 .F72 2021 | DDC 616.89/14--dc23
LC record available at https://lccn.loc.gov/2020034343

ISBN: 978-0-367-62198-8 (hbk)
ISBN: 978-0-367-62202-2 (pbk)
ISBN: 978-1-003-10831-3 (ebk)

Typeset in Bembo
by MPS Limited, Dehradun

For Eugene
A consummate clinician, master teacher, and loving father

Contents

Foreword   x
Acknowledgements   xii

   Introduction   1
1   Talking and listening   6
2   Trust   30
3   Time and money   49
4   Empathy and relationships   67
5   The present past   85
6   Insight and understanding   101
7   Truth and doubt   122
8   Love and healing   142

   Reflections   160
   Index   167

Foreword

What actually *happens* between a psychotherapist and his or her patient over the course of therapy? How does change *actually* occur where the cause of some difficult symptom (depression, anxiety, unaccountable fear) is buried in the past, and the patient resists facing up to it? Before I read *Psychotherapy and Personal Change: Two Minds in a Mirror*, I wasn't sure you could even adequately address these questions in writing, since they're not just concerned with what each party says, but ... with what they are *thinking*.

By creating a remarkable fugue of interwoven reflections, Dr. Friedberg allows us to enter into the minds of the therapist and patient, revealing what they think as they are thinking it. The immediacy of *Two Minds in a Mirror* makes it a revelation. The candid, up-close-and-personal data provide us a privileged entrée into the private, curtained milieu of psychotherapy. We see the therapist thinking as the therapy unfolds. We see how the mind becomes amenable to restoration.

Specifically, *Two Minds in a Mirror* reveals how "talk therapy" startles the complacent, conscious mind and exposes the unconscious. It demonstrates the intense personal involvement of therapist and patient. It reveals how the therapist's own memories, feelings, and doubts are often as much a factor in the process as those of the patient. Perhaps this aspect of the book will be most astonishing to readers who may never have realized that the psychotherapist's inner life is so entwined with the patient's, much less that any therapist would be willing to expose it.

The book's subtitle is called *Two Minds in a Mirror* because it reflects the therapist as much as it does the patient. In the process of healing, therapist and patient reflect on each other and on themselves. As the therapist develops empathy for the patient, and the patient develops trust in the therapist, their shared memories, feelings, and associations interact and entwine – almost kaleidoscopically – causing each to ask questions of the other and themselves. In this book, Dr. Friedberg reveals personal insights that arose as he recalled memories to share with patients. These insights might not have arisen *but for* the therapy, which operates in multiple directions as patient and therapist explore the present, the past, and the unknown.

But there's more. While *Two Minds in a Mirror* examines how personal change happens, it also demonstrates that the high points and setbacks of the process are a microcosm of human relationships. You'll learn why psychotherapy is "scalable," experiencing first-hand how the ability to develop trust and to listen attentively in the patient/therapist relationship becomes a transferable skill in real life. *Psychotherapy and Personal Change: Two Minds in a Mirror* demonstrates that if you can acquire an understanding of how therapy works, you can apply this understanding in your life.

Once you've read *Two Minds in a Mirror*, you will never think of therapy in the same way. Therapy is not passive or even stream-of-consciousness. The patient learns about the therapist even as the therapist helps the patient to gain insight into him- or herself. So, in that sense, the patient becomes personally involved with the therapist. *Two Minds in a Mirror* shows how this exchange develops and how each actor is affected. If you were to pick up a manual on psychotherapy, you would not encounter this experience, since it would be conveyed in largely conceptual terms. *Two Minds in a Mirror* conveys the ebb and flow of the experience through the minds of both participants.

Finally, I'd like to say that this is a fascinating book. It is entirely approachable, yet deep – and the writing is brisk, elegant, and absolutely clear. I also like how *Two Minds in a Mirror* is arranged with subjects like listening, trust, empathy, insight and understanding, and healing. The immediate give-and-take of a therapy session is set against the wider backdrop of contemporary practice, creating a counterpoint between the highly personal and deeply informed. I think you will be moved by this book and learn a lot.

Arnold Richards, M.D.

Acknowledgements

First and foremost, I want to thank Dr. Sandra Sherman, who helped conceive the shape of this book and is responsible for the clarity of its prose. But beyond her taking on the editorial challenge of *Two Minds in a Mirror*, I want to acknowledge that this book would not have been possible without Sandra's knowledge of the human condition and ability to express it. She was instrumental in bringing these vignettes to life in all their richness and complexity – her influence was transformational.

I especially want to express my gratitude to Dr. Andrew Solomon, who reviewed an early draft of this manuscript and encouraged me to develop it. His own personal honesty and candor (and exceptional eloquence) have been an inspiration for my own modest writing endeavors. Dr. Richard Friedman, whose recent passing was a loss to a generation of psychodynamic clinicians, served as a mentor and guide for the project. His detailed observations and critiques were excellent. Dr. Arnold Richards and others also offered their helpful comments and generous support. Finally, I want to thank Ms. Dana Malefakis, who prepared the citations to books listed as "Further Readings." Her diligence was exemplary.

I am grateful to my patients for displaying resilience and courage. Some of my most valuable lessons have been learned through our work together.

Introduction

What's unique about psychotherapists — compared to most doctors or clinicians — is that we rarely get out of our chair. We do not touch a patient, except perhaps for an occasional handshake or when holding a hand where a patient is bereaved. It's more about eye contact, emotional connection. As a psychiatrist, a doctor trained in medicine as well as different types of psychotherapy, I may order lab tests, but these tend to be for checking medication levels and their physiological effects — usually not for diagnostic purposes. Most healing in psychotherapy occurs through talking and listening. It occurs in our heads. Two people struggle to find the right words, ideas, or emotional connection. Freud's first patient, Anna O, famously dubbed this the "talking cure."

When I conceived this book, therefore, which is about what "happens" during the course of psychotherapeutic treatment, I wondered how to describe an extended, nonlinear, and often inconclusive conversation. Perhaps the patient arrives at some enhanced level of insight into how the past permeates — even distorts — his or her thinking. Perhaps this produces change. Perhaps the psychotherapist — whom we might consider a healer — identifies with the patient, journeying back into his or her own past, to wrestle together with inner demons and vanquish or at least appease them. In an effective treatment, the psychotherapist and patient may meet in the middle, developing empathy, sharing insights, and enabling each other to work through problems.

In any case, there is no disentangling patient and therapist. It is a dyadic relationship. We collaborate and must proceed on trust. The relationship, or rather the process by which it unfolds, is complex, often fraught with miscommunication and missed opportunities. There are often few markers; a discernible pattern can be slow to emerge; there is no typical decision-tree. There are aims and goals but not necessarily an obvious, predictable outcome. Whether the treatment is a time-limited, cognitive behavior therapy or an open-ended, psychoanalytic one, there is no clear roadmap. It may seem like Beckett's *Waiting for Godot*.

To convey this process, I realized I had to emphasize its dynamic rather than give it a particular shape. Freud used the metaphor of the silver screen on which movies used to be viewed. The patient's wishes, fantasies, hopes, and dreams on one side are merged with images of reality captured and projected on the other. The effect was neither dream nor reality, but rather constant shimmering. Furthermore, for Freud the analyst was like a blank screen onto which the patient's innermost thoughts and feelings, past relationships, and conscious and unconscious mental life were projected. They would, necessarily, merge with the psychiatrist's own. Today, we might think in terms of a screen saver with one's favorite photos and images, whose lines and colors merge with and inflect each other, producing nuanced effects and associational patterns. What matters – what actually provides the interest – is the variation of underlying themes.

Accordingly, this book concerns how I try to help my patients to pursue varied, personal versions of understanding and change – with emphasis on the pursuit. A pursuit, by definition, takes time. Much of what is here reflects my notes on patients over the course of a year of psychotherapy. The initial exercise was to capture an incident from each day that remained with me and embodied some element of the psychotherapeutic process. Collectively, and over the course of treatment, these incidents (I hoped) would illustrate the arc of my practice as a psychotherapist and healer.

In his classic *Through the Looking Glass*, Lewis Carroll describes Alice's slipping through a mirror into existential fluidity. The mirror is a portal: Alice initially sees herself, then other versions of herself in alternative realities. Therapy produces a similar effect. Throughout *Two Minds in a Mirror*, there will be stories of courage and resilience, as patients bounce back from difficulties and even severe trauma. Finding a way and the will to heal emotional scars – that is, acknowledging their source and the need to heal – is often an important first step to recovery. There will also be stories of continued disappointment, and – at the opposite end of the spectrum – of defining moments where change is sudden, radical, and astonishing. These stories run the gamut. Crucially, they are not just about my patients, but my relationships with patients, friends, colleagues, and family. So much of what we do as psychotherapists is informed by our own pasts as well as our present lives. Psychotherapists reflect on all their relationships, learning as they go. We are inward, even at times solipsistic, though we talk to people for a living. (As you will see, that is not a contradiction.)

Accordingly, the mirror seems like a natural metaphor for the healing process. That is, even while the healer sees and interacts with the patient, the healer also sees his or her own image and reflects on the reflection. Think of Escher's self-portrait, "Hand with Reflecting Sphere." This self-scrutiny is basic to the conversation of healing. The psychotherapist is both looking out and looking inwards, if not simultaneously then over time, as he or she thinks about the course of therapy. On these occasions, self-doubt is common – Am I some version of this patient? How does that affect our relationship? What can I learn to help him? – but such unease may engender understanding, empathy, and ideally a way forward. This is all premised on my experience – my conviction – that while healing begins in the interpersonal, the realm between two people, it also engages the intrapsychic, both for the patient and psychotherapist. The inner landscape is the lens through which reality is viewed and experienced. The intrapsychic element is as inescapable as the interpersonal.

More broadly, the mirror has been recognized as a metaphor of the mind which reflects the self and others. It abounds in literature, psychology, and philosophy. Think of Narcissus, for example, who in the Greek myth was fatally entranced by his image on water. The mirror is integral as well to the history of science and art, capturing the nature of light and its manifestation of reality. Mirrors in van Eyck's "Arnolfini Portrait" (1434) and Velazquez's "Las Meninas" (1656) raise fundamental questions about the nature of eternity, power, and the role of the artist. The "psyche" of psychoanalysis is a reflection of the soul. What's mirrored back is who we are – our inner and outward aspects.

While no metaphor corresponds exactly to objective reality, the mirror – whose metaphorical valences are so productive of psychic meaning – seems almost part of reality itself. Clearly, it mirrors, so to speak, the intrapsychic explorations depicted in this book. Ultimately, this book *is* a mirror because it reflects – rather than just reflecting on – the connections that I form with patients (e.g., intimacy, empathy) and my reflections on those connections (e.g., the successes, failures, regrets, and ever-emerging self-awareness as a healer).

If this book has any shape, therefore, it is that of one practitioner's mind as he lives his life through a healer's sensibilities, refracted through training and experience. Is this life emblematic of others in the profession? I think so – at least to some extent. And to that end, I hope it is instructive.

★★★★★★★★★★★★★★★★★★★★★★★★★★★★★★★★★★★★★

I practice psychiatry on Manhattan's Upper East Side and have done so for over 20 years. I am a professor at a major New York hospital and belong to an array of professional organizations. Walk down Park Avenue, and you can see a myriad of psychiatrists and mental health professionals with similar profiles. What differentiates one of us from another is, in part, the type of therapy that we practice. Over the years, the profession has branched out into numerous approaches to healing, some highly medicalized, others more psychological and even spiritual. I favor the approach called "psychodynamic psychiatry," which integrates concerns about mind, brain, and body. The psychiatry part is brain and body based. It involves treating symptoms through medication as well as considerations of exercise and diet. The psychodynamic part is a form of depth psychology, whose primary objective is to uncover elements of a patient's conscious and unconscious mental life that may be past but resonate in the present and, through that process, alleviate psychological conflicts and tension. In effect, the patient is helped to have more adaptive defences, greater resilience, and to see him- or herself more truthfully. To arrive at the overall result, psychodynamic therapy relies on the interpersonal relationship between patient and psychotherapist. The art is to integrate the therapeutic approaches to the mind, brain, and body. The whole can be greater than the sum of the parts.

Psychodynamic therapy starts from the assumption that the patient's maladaptation probably arose early in life from troubled relationships, and that it is still causing difficulty. It can play out as dysfunction, for example, where the person may project onto his boss the bad feelings he retains toward his father. In such instances, psychodynamic therapy seeks to reveal and hence resolve the unconscious tensions that underlie the current symptoms. The relationship between psychotherapist and patient is key, as we work through the earlier difficulties, sometimes needing to deal with and confront the patient's past relationships that are carried into that with the psychotherapist – causing possible anger, jealousy, suspicion, or mistrust.

There is no one way to pursue revelations of the past, although the patient usually offers dreams, memories, and associations to identify how the past still occupies, even possesses his life. At its most basic, psychodynamic therapy is talk therapy – a freely flowing conversation that also explores inner conflicts. Over the course of what may become an extended dialogue, trust must develop in both directions. The patient has to trust his own insights and those of the therapist. The therapist has to build trust in the patient and for his own insights into the other person. All this takes time, especially allowing for setbacks as well as successes.

★★

As a composite of my relationships in the practice of healing, *Two Minds in a Mirror* demonstrates that psychotherapy is a microcosm of all our relationships. Emotions that structure ordinary relationships – from anger to empathy to jealousy, vanity, and even fear – also define those of psychotherapist and patient. The difference is that most people are not trained to study their relationships or to stand back and look at themselves in relationship. They may not even really want to, if only out of anxiety or fear. *Two Minds in a Mirror* illustrates how the healing relationship actually unfolds. I will introduce some of my patients, whose stories are woven into the book's chapters. The patients are complex – almost like characters in a novel – and their lives in many instances are permeated by former relationships. One take-away is that transference, the projection onto others of thoughts and feelings from previous relationships, is ubiquitous not only in therapy but also in life.

As you encounter these patients, the effect will seem kaleidoscopic, much as it is in my practice where patients with varied concerns swirl into a day and then days pass into months along with my reflections on them. This effect *is* the story: patients' psychic lives refract through my own and vice versa, as I share with them stories from my own life in an effort to solidify connections and as their shared stories cause me to reflect even further on myself.

It follows that you should expect a type of narrative distinct to therapy: a variegated process rather than a logical progression, where insight, deeper understanding, and personal change can be indirect, incomplete, or sadly fleeting – but also, in rare moments, transformative. There will, of course, be tangents and digressions, but they are all relevant, contributing to the inherent uncertainty that I discuss throughout the book. Within the narratives of *Two Minds in a Mirror*, time is not measured conventionally – an hour can seem endlessly long because it is agonizing. Or a moment can burst into consciousness only to return again and again as its consequences continue to emerge and enlarge. What matters is the interplay of thought and reflection over time. As the narrative proceeds through individual stories, challenges, and insights, it traces an arc through a period in my practice – a period of time that represents the type of growth and falling away of a psychotherapist's practice. The patients are "real" in that their situations are real, though their names and other related facts, attributes, and identifying data have been altered to protect confidentiality.

The stories were compiled over a year of practice, but – with some alterations – they could be exchanged for the ongoing stories of patients who continue to present. In other words, the stories are typical or, at least, the issues that they represent are typical. The point is that while psychotherapy can be inconclusive, both patient and psychotherapist are changed by the process, as their lives entwine in a dynamic ranging from the mundane to the existential.

These stories represent the ebb and flow of the process of therapy: progress and setbacks as the process flows through the participants and then eases off as the patient emerges into greater self-awareness. There are high tides, so to speak, and then low as the participants become less acutely involved. But the process rarely reaches a stasis, since the participants think and rethink it and, sometimes, pick up again after it has apparently concluded.

But no one is ever fully known to themselves, much less secondhand to a therapist. I am reminded of John Ashbery's "Self Portrait in a Convex Mirror" (1972) – his brilliant poem about the distortion implicit in any attempt at self-description and, ultimately, in the process of self-description. The limits of perception extend from patient to therapist and require a steadfast humility. Therapy operates within the range of such humility.

★★★

Two Minds in a Mirror is divided by chapters that represent aspects of the patient-psychotherapist relationship, illustrated by my patients' stories. One challenge in designing this book was deciding what to call each chapter since any name would, necessarily, be reductive in the face of endless nuance. I chose some like "Insight and Understanding," "Time and Money," and "Love and Healing" that seemed to encompass wide swaths of what the book is about. I intend this book for anyone interested not only in how psychotherapy actually happens in its day-to-day practice, but also for readers seeking to learn more about their own and others' psychology. Each chapter illustrates how patients dealt with issues of time and money, work toward insight and understanding, or navigate other issues addressed by psychotherapy. Psychotherapy is a big subject (and human psychology even larger), but it can only be approached through the lives of people – including the therapists – who live it.

1 Talking and listening

The first psychoanalytic patient was Bertha Pappenheim, aka Anna O. She coined the term "talking cure." When she sought treatment with Dr. Josef Breuer in late 19th-century Vienna, she was suffering from hysteria, a condition that converts psychological stress into physical symptoms (e.g., selective amnesia or dramatic attention-seeking). Hysteria was diagnosed primarily in women, especially of the European middle and upper classes. However, by listening to Anna's painful recollections from the previous year (i.e., by getting her to talk about them), Dr. Breuer believed he could relieve her condition and restore her mental health.

Indeed, Anna initially showed improvement. But the "cure" did not last. Within a year, she was in a hospital for treatment of mental disorders. Yet Dr. Breuer's assistant, Dr. Sigmund Freud, recognized that his mentor's approach was revolutionary ... and the famous talking cure was born. The following stories reflect my latter-day experience with the "cure," which has evolved into a dynamic give-and-take between therapist and patient. I show how the therapist's personal, intrapsychic experience (i.e., what doesn't usually make it into his or her formal notes) is as much a part of the story as talking and listening. Some of the stories therefore involve me.

These are not typical case studies, which are far more detailed and usually constitute a retrospective on a long course of treatment. Rather, these stories render moments that stayed with me at the end of the day, and that I wanted to record. They made me reflect on the process of psychotherapy or, rather, they demonstrated how fully therapy is a process that unfolds over time through provocative, individual encounters. Each encounter is somewhere on a trajectory.

In this chapter (and all through Two Minds in a Mirror*), I want to give a sense of therapy's setting, which is at once immediate (e.g., an* *encounter between two people in real time) and historical, as the patient's past ricochets through the encounter and sometimes leaves the participants limp. The effect on the therapist is as tangible as it is on the patient. However, the therapist must also distance him- or herself from the revelations and find in them some useful application to treatment. This can be as ricocheting a process as it was when the patient first offered his memories for consideration. The therapist can be caught up in his own memories and feelings.*

If these stories do not seem to be linear, it is because the process that I am describing is not linear. Talking and listening, like any conversation, is frequently interrupted. It is characterized by digressions, delayed reactions, candor, lack of candor, apologies, and revisions. So, while each of these stories "says something" about therapy, collectively they convey what therapy feels like when it is practiced day after day. These stories also convey how, by talking and listening over time, each party contributes to the patient's growth and change.

Finally, this first chapter is knit together around the concept of taking a "history" (e.g., finding out about the patient in sufficient detail so that the therapist can make a proper diagnosis and design an appropriate treatment). I will intervene between some of these stories to describe aspects of taking a history. The point is to demonstrate that a large part of talking and listening is devoted to the patient's back story, which often emerges slowly as trust develops and the conversation deepens.

Keeping a journal

Beginning a new year, I pause and look back – like looking in a rearview mirror as orientation toward the road ahead. I used to think that the more looking back, the better. But not anymore. While reflecting on the past can enrich our understanding, dwelling in it is a kind of quicksand that pulls you down and under. This is true for both therapist and patient.

We are not very different from our patients. We have dreams, fantasies, pasts, conflicts, and strivings. But therapists make a special effort to look at themselves in a way that allows for increased personal insight and understanding. This heightened self-awareness is part of our skill set. It is the basis of empathy. It gives us a running start on the questions to ask.

This year, I feel that while I *am* my past, I want some evidence of how I have applied this retrospective compendium constituting my identity. How has insight into myself affected my practice? If I have been taking notes on patients, I want to take notes on myself ... or read my notes on my patients as if they were notes on our relationship. So, I will keep a journal. The notes can add up – thoughts, feelings, memories, and realizations about myself or a patient. It is hard to know where the journal will lead, but I will go with the flow in my explorations with patients. Structure emerges, if it does, in looking backward.

Oh, so the "flow" is backward! From my perspective, yes, because while my patients may perceive progress, I want to register moments only once I have realized that they matter.

In this sense, consideration of the past produces the present, shedding light on what my patients and I have worked through. "Working through" is a paradigmatic term in therapy since it implies that there is a lot of Past that has to be exposed before there is solid success. It implies collaboration, a shared project. I want to see and record how it occurs.

I need to cultivate a new discipline: the recall of little impacts or, rather, of moments that are both random and, in retrospect, take on a pointillistic significance in a picture that I cannot perhaps ever fully envision. Sounds something like the Uncertainty Principle (i.e., there is a limit to the precision with which you can ascertain certain complementary variables like position and momentum). But most things are like this if you look long enough. The definition of "narrative" does not require a formal plot – you just need to get somewhere – which is where I am going. (In a picaresque narrative, one incident does not cause the next. Each just happens, and then the next one follows. I think this journal must be picaresque).

> *Psychotherapists are as affected by their pasts, and by what is going on right now in their lives, as are their patients. In psychodynamic treatment, Freud advised therapists to listen with an "evenly suspended attention" (e.g., without interpolating themselves into the analysis). But no therapist fully achieves this state since we all have biases and preconceptions, and we cannot disown what life has taught us right up until today. But we do try be nonjudgmental.*
>
> *Doing so can help a person speak more freely.*
>
> *Nevertheless, before someone even comes into your office, you make certain assumptions. You have their name, which may suggest their ethnic background. From their address, you may learn something of the person's socioeconomic status. A birthdate situates them in one phase of life or another.*
>
> *On meeting a patient for the first time, you make silent judgements – do they seem alert, forthcoming? – because both of you may be travelling together for a considerable time. Is the patient someone you want to work with?*
>
> *Thus, while you try not to be judgmental, you do make judgements concerning the potential course of therapy. These can be subjective, just like therapy itself.*

Taking a history

It is important to take a good history on a new patient. You should get a clear picture, not just of where a person is when they present for treatment but also of how he or she got there. Taking a history is a balancing act because, while you want certain basic information, you also want a person's story to unfold organically. To some extent, they will pick and choose what to tell you, and when. The "facts" can shade off into what someone thinks are the facts, what they remember, and how they interpret the facts. A history can become a hall of mirrors, with all the facts ramifying like they would in a kaleidoscope. The therapist has to make his or her way through them gingerly, going back over to verify, modify, and reinterpret. In a sense, you are never finished taking a history.

Mr. Lauren came from a "good family." His father was a distinguished lawyer, and he had followed his father's profession. His mother was a businesswoman. He described her as "self-involved" when he was growing up. She treated him, early on, as an extension of herself. He had an older sister and a younger brother. His sister had two young children. His brother was recently married.

Mr. Lauren was a newlywed himself. He married an apparently lovely woman, who shared his Jewish faith and values. She was from a traditional family. He said that they loved each other and had a solid foundation of friendship. He found her attractive, and they had a good emotional connection. She had been an excellent friend to him when he had work-related problems.

He was himself tall and good-looking, well dressed, and fit. He made good eye contact and spoke directly about his concerns. He described himself as depressed but still productive. He had difficulty falling asleep and would sometimes wake up with bad dreams. His had no suicidal ideation but blamed himself for the near miss at work that had almost cost him his job. As we spoke, he admitted that previous therapy had been a waste, mainly because he had failed to apply what he learned. "I blame myself," he said. "I'm generally smart, but I can be gullible. I make mistakes because I skip the details. That got me into trouble, and therapy never changed that."

We decided to explore the near miss and to try to understand how it made him critical of himself to the point that he feels depressed. The first step in therapy is to define the problem or, rather, what the patient perceives as the problem. Then we can explore whether the stated cause – e.g., what the patient thinks is the cause – is the source of the symptoms or an aggravating factor. Often, the cause and the problem are the same, and what the patient thinks of as the problem is a way of avoiding the actual problem. In such cases, the patient does not even know that he is avoiding the problem and cannot describe the nature of his resistance. The therapist will have to deal with the resistance even before getting to first base concerning the patient's issues.

But the constituent factors of a problem (and of the patient's resistance to confronting it) can only emerge over time, to the degree that the patient is able to disclose them, and at a pace that allows each side to take in the other. In this sense, therapy is a Chinese finger trap: the harder both sides try, the more they can become stuck. If they ease up, then one side can finally break through and the other can follow.

> *Psychotherapists have different styles. Some say little and may let a patient's story evolve over time, while others are more active. But usually the amount of talking relative to listening is situational. For example, it is hard to keep silent when a patient is being critical of you. As the stories in this chapter demonstrate, however, listening is often as therapeutic as what you say.*

Listening

"Talk therapy" actually requires listening, since the patient talks while the therapist listens. But how does such listening lead to the *patient's* understanding? It is a process. Initially, you want the patient's story to unfold organically, rather than in response to questions or prompts that follow a logic of your own. Such logic may seem careful and inclusive, but it is shaped by your own mind – not the patient's – and ultimately it risks excluding or distorting what you need to hear as the patient would naturally present it. I ask a few relatively broad questions that the patient can interpret. Based on these broad-gauge invitations, I encourage patients to freely associate, even to offer seeming irrelevancies, and to trace a pattern that appears pointillistic … until, finally, I can ask questions that slowly connect the dots.

This type of listening is not passive. Rather, it actively takes in information and cues. It requires the therapist to register data and continually redraw the patient's image, listening for *what* a patient divulges and *when*. For example, a woman's abortion might not come up until well into the course of treatment, at which point it might constitute an important therapeutic moment – signalling, perhaps, the breakdown of shame, the surfacing of guilt, or regret over a lost child. Underneath, there may be jealousy or anger, neither of which would have emerged had the woman just reported the abortion during her medical history.

Patients conceal information. During an initial consultation, Mr. Silver talked about his extensive sexual history prior to meeting the woman that he married. However, it was not until well into the first year of his treatment that he felt comfortable speaking about other aspects of his sexual life. He cited fantasies and experiences from his adolescence and young adulthood. It was part of the therapeutic process and helped him become more comfortable. He reported that this openness translated into his professional life, where he became more personable.

Mr. Silver's case demonstrates that *how* therapists listen informs what they say – we speak from where we listen. If the place we listen from – the attitude we adopt in our listening – is nonjudgmental and open-minded, our responses to a patient will be so as well.

Such listening can be hard since, to a degree, we suspend the biases that inflect how we listen to everyone else. I'm thinking of a patient, Mr. Martyr, one of the few truly mean people that I ever treated. He insulted cab drivers, doormen, and strangers. He attacked me when he felt insecure or on the spot. But it emerged that there were reasons why he behaved so badly. His father beat him as a child. He identified with his aggressive father, which helped him feel bigger and stronger. Beneath the brutishness, he felt weak and insecure.

My being able to tolerate and interpret his anger toward me was helpful to his treatment. I allowed it to erupt in a way that we could step back from it, look at it together, and understand what it was about. We determined that getting angry warded off feelings of depression. He literally practiced anger as a defence against such feelings. It also masked deep feelings of guilt concerning a sibling who had died shortly after birth for which he, in a sense, was a replacement.

In Mr. Martyr's case, listening was more like enduring, an act of generosity that was only minimally reciprocated. But it was also strategic, allowing me to get closer to his motivations. Patients equate intense listening with personal interest, which matters to them as much as (or even more than) professional concern. It encourages them to reveal. They become performers. Resistant patients, who resent the therapeutic process, will open up in spite of themselves because – in the presence of an avid listener – the act of revelation excites them.

There is a kind of dialectic between listening, which therapists do intently, and note-taking, which can distract the patient as well as the therapist. But memory is imperfect, and patients' secretly fear that their details will blur into the next patient's. So, there is a calculus even around the simple act of taking notes. To keep a journal is to take notes.

Taking notes

It's odd work that psychotherapists do. We listen to intimate details about people's lives and note them down. But how we take these notes matters. We might make a mental note of what the patient said and reflect it back as a question. The quick follow-up makes us seem to be listening and thinking in real time. It conveys an active engagement with the patient, an attempt to lock into his or her thought processes.

But too much note-taking at the expense of engagement suggests that we are not listening, not ready to spring spontaneously with a follow-up question or sage aperçu. We should never stop looking the patient in the eye while making notes, whether mentally or on an iPad. That would seem like a deferral of the engagement – of the immediacy – that the patient craves, and would imply that we are a step behind what is happening. Now, in real time. No matter how much depends on history-taking, it is the "fierce urgency of now" that matters to the patient. He or she is not concerned with therapeutic protocol but, rather, is entirely in the moment, where he or she expects the therapist to be.

Note-taking discounts urgency. It's all about later.

Sometimes the details are so scattered that we cannot sort through them until after the session. Afterward, we might fix on a few highlights or – preferably – draw the session into focus. I'll scribble some things down from memory when the patient leaves and then try to reconstruct them at the end of the day. There is a delicate balance between listening and taking notes, depending on the patient's own narrative and, at times, his or her own breathlessness. Generally, I wait until after a session to make notes.

But today the patient talked about a dream that I wanted to make sure I remembered, so I made notes while he recalled it. When he asked what I was writing about, I thought to respond "And what does my note-taking mean to *you*?" But that seemed like such a caricature response, I could almost hear the laughter. So, I just said that I was recording his dream.

Afterward, when I thought about the exchange, I felt like a caricature again, finding a paradigm for my whole practice in a few seconds of discussion. What are we chasing, the telling moment or the slow revelation, and how do we attain either? This seemed to entail the concern for what we take notes on and *when* we should take them. Each note reveals something about the patient but something as well about our process of thinking about the patient.

Caricature aside, however, perhaps I should discuss with this patient how he perceives my note-taking, irrespective of how I use the notes. It could tell me something about whether he feels we are making progress. So, I made a note about note-taking.

With each patient, the balance shifts between listening and taking notes. Sometimes, in the ten minutes between sessions, I frantically note down what I could not while I was listening. If I wait until the end of the day, I lose details – but the advantage is that what remains tends to have made an impact. I actually prefer listening to taking notes because, afterward, I can almost hear the patient's voice in my mind. Also, in some cases, listening is therapy (i.e., it's what the patient needs to see me doing). He or she needs to believe that I am locked into an impermeable duality of only the two of us – not even a pen, much less posterity coming between us.

Listening as therapy

When Mr. Lauren first presented, he was feeling at a loss. He felt guilty about an abortion that his college sweetheart had had. It stayed with him as a source of shame and embarrassment, since he valued life and had been involved with charitable work that reflected this commitment. For Mr. Lauren, being able to say what was on his mind and speak as freely as possible about it helped him feel better.

In Mr. Lauren's case, my listening was tantamount to therapy. When he spoke about his concerns, it felt cathartic. For him, being understood mattered less than being heard. I realize that this is an admission against interest, but I believe it. The acceptance a person feels with being listened to in a neutral and nonjudgmental way can be healing in itself. This is especially true if the therapeutic relationship resonates with a good, caring bond that patient and therapist have created over time.

For instance, another patient was an accomplished businesswoman and successful artist. She had a loving marriage of over 30 years with a wealthy and powerful banker. But she came to me for depression after developing uterine cancer that was metastatic, aggressive, and could not be cured. So how could I help, apart from maybe prescribing an antidepressant? Mostly, I listened to her talk about her life. She had overcome scoliosis as a child through exercise and dance and became highly accomplished. Her husband had seen her dance professionally and became enamored. In turn, she helped promote his career.

It is hard to capture what went on between us. But I was curious about her and her life story. I paid attention. Toward the end of her life, she said that she had come to really value our hours together. I thanked her, but said – only partly in jest – that I was not sure why because I did not feel that I had offered very much. But she disagreed. She said that I listened, and that even though she was dying that helped her feel comforted and understood. It helped her feel alive, if only in the moment.

Unlike in the case of Mr. Martyr, my listening was not strategic. I did not – could not – have a long-term therapeutic objective. I think I provided what a rabbi, priest, or friend might have ... but as her needs narrowed, her need for another person's attentive presence was what she needed most.

Patients frequently prefer the ear of a therapist to that of a friend. They don't want to upset a friend and believe that friends feel obligated to listen, care, and take time. The therapist does not act out of some previously established obligation, but as a participant in an arm's length transaction. The therapist is disinterested in the sense that while he or she cares – in the way any human being would care – there is no risk of encroaching on the therapist, of taking up emotional space to which someone else is entitled. The fact that there are appointments (e.g., limited encounters with definite demarcations) helps the patient to obligate the therapist for just an hour, no more. It's comforting to know that someone will listen and understand but won't feel the pull of a shared, complicated history on their emotions.

Taking a history does not happen all in one session and often occurs sporadically, over several meetings. The idea is to learn what you need to know about the patient, so you can best offer help. In psychiatry and medicine more broadly, this involves a diagnostic assessment of a disorder or condition, which leads to a treatment plan that targets specific symptoms. In psychotherapy, it may involve diagnostic considerations, but the orientation might be more toward determining certain goals and overall aims that you outline and work on together. Since it is the therapist's role to help the person feel better, the first question is often "How can I help?"

The reply is sometimes described as a "chief complaint." It is the reason that the patient has come for treatment. Patients may say that they are anxious, depressed, or traumatized. After hearing about why they think they need help, you might inquire about the "history of present illness" (e.g., how did they come to be in the situation that has brought them for treatment?).

Listening is thus multidimensional. The therapist has to get the patient's backstory even as his or her current situation has to be made clear. Frequently, the dimensions converge, since the past is as "present" for some people as their presence in the therapist's office. Taking a history, therefore, can consume part of every session, as memories ramify into the present as transference, fears, or anxiety. Even when therapists do not set out to take a history, they find themselves taking one anyway. One has to listen for the history that – whether the patient knows it or not – contours to the present.

You try to be curious and ask open-ended questions such as "What brings you here today?" There is often a particular stressor. A job loss or difficulties at work are common. So are marital, financial, and health issues. Identifying the particular concern – if they have been unable to articulate it – can be reassuring.

As a psychotherapist, you want to know facts and details, but you mostly want to give the person a chance to begin to tell their story. We generally set aside at least 45 to 50 minutes for an initial consultation. But this consultation may extend over several sessions as you try to learn about the person and their background.

Are there medical issues that may impact the person's mental state? Over a third of major depressive disorders and anxiety disorders have a medical or biological component. What is the person's past psychiatric or psychological history? Is it the first time a person has sought treatment, or has he or she been in treatment before? What type of therapy or psychopharmacology has the person received in the past, and was it helpful—and if not, why not? Past treatments that have been effective or not can inform your current assessment and choices concerning treatment.

There are different kinds of issues you want to know about, so you can get some sense of the patient's mental health history. Many conditions such as Bipolar Disorder commonly go undiagnosed for years – ten years on average! Developmental conditions like Attention Deficit Disorder generally begin in childhood, although there are adult forms as well. Some conditions like Panic Disorder may have an acute onset and be readily treatable. Others such as a recurrent type of Major Depression are more refractory. We are good at helping with most conditions, and it is important to convey a certain measured optimism.

Listening/reflecting

Breathing helps me to listen. When a patient expresses anger, jealousy, or disturbing fantasies, I take deep breaths. This relaxes me and makes it easier to listen.

I have to think about what a patient is saying and also about what I say next. I am in two time zones, as it were, and the breathing steadies me. The patient may be talking about real, concrete issues like paying bills, running errands, or working. Or maybe there was a dream or resurgent memory. I ask myself why he or she is talking about these things right now. Is it to educate me about what he or she is going through? Or is he or she trying to disclose an incident from the past? Or perhaps the revelation just masks some deeper, undisclosed concern. So, in addition to being in two time zones, I am also on two planes – what is this patient trying to accomplish, and why at this point in the course of treatment?

As if these dualities were not enough, sometimes I also maintain a dual focus that aligns the patient's story with my own experience. I am thinking of Dr. Goodman, a distinguished professor in his 70s. He completed graduate studies at a prestigious university but had never received a degree because of a conflict with his supervisor. Failing to get a degree was a definitive Stop Sign, an inflection point in the course of his life. Though he became an accomplished, well-respected professional, his options were always limited because of not having formally completed training. In and out of therapy, he went on about this obsessively. It resonated because I had also had difficulty finishing my training. I could listen with empathy to how painful it had been for him.

When I respond to a patient, I try to say something that is true from my own experience. I understood the hurt that Dr. Goodman felt and knew what it was like to merit recognition but instead to be passed over. The harder issue, in Dr. Goodman's case and in general, is how much of myself I reveal to justify my empathy. It is one thing to say "I feel your pain," and another to acknowledge the full scope of *why*. The paradox of therapy is that while healers need to seem competent, a genuine display of empathy presumes frailty or failure. I have to decide in the moment how much of myself to reveal so as to keep both elements of that equation in play.

In Dr. Goodman's case, I decided not to reveal myself. There is always the risk that in an effort to explain the grounds of one's empathy, the session will pitch into reverse and become about the therapist. Patients are endlessly curious about the therapist's "personal" side and so even a casual remark can lead to a string of questions. At that point, if you try to steer the conversation back toward the patient, they may take it for evasion. But fortunately, in the following session, another avenue opened up that provided Dr. Goodman some support.

He was an avid collector of old military medals. One day when he was describing an acquisition, his difficult graduate experience (and my own postgraduate one) came to mind. I commented that perhaps he felt he needed a medal so as to be acknowledged. This remark led to his describing the conflict he'd had with his professor in greater detail. Then came a flood of memories about his father and how unacknowledged he had felt by him. Subsequently, and most likely because he was able to draw a connection between his supervisor, his father, and the medals that he bestowed on himself, he was less obsessional about his degree. He was able to have more appreciation for the work he had done.

In effect, the medal had replaced his obsession with failure and became an objective correlative of his excellent work. After he left, I took the *session* as a kind of medal, one of many I could take for sessions where I empathized with a patient based on my own pain, but helped him feel better. I realized that there were several medals that I could claim this way. The next time a patient calls on my own self-doubts and disturbing memories, I will remember these medals and try to earn another.

Listening to negation

Things can come into consciousness by their attachment to words. Freud discovered that anxiety-provoking, upsetting objects can come into consciousness through their verbal negation. Thus, a claim that "this does not bother me ..." or "I'm not scared of that ..." may signal an object of anxiety or fear. It can be useful – in and out of therapy – to listen to what someone is saying from the perspective of what they deny.

One such instance concerned Mrs. Wright when she was discussing her fertility problem. She is a successful businesswoman in her mid-30s. She has a loving relationship with her husband and has been trying to become pregnant for over a year. She had been talking about the possibility, on the recommendation of her fertility specialist, of taking medication to increase her chances. She told me, "I'm not embarrassed, you know," and then went on to recount her visit home over the weekend. There, her younger sister was excited about having had a second child. Their mother encouraged Mrs. Wright to do everything she could to get started. After listening to her describe her visit, I came back to her claim that she was "not embarrassed." Mrs. Wright is psychologically astute and responded by saying how she is, in fact, embarrassed. Actually, that embarrassment – reflecting a sense of physical inadequacy – had prevented her from using treatments that might have been helpful. Finally acknowledging such feelings allowed her to consider those options consciously and carefully.

It is well established clinically that the negation of a thing can allow it to come into consciousness. It provides an opportunity for examination and understanding in the clinical situation. It can also be a source of important information outside of therapy. For example, if a person vigorously denies something is so, this can be evidence for its truth. As Shakespeare observed: "The lady doth protest too much, methinks." Of course, the trick is to determine when a negation is an affirmation and when it is not. Negations in themselves cannot be discounted except in context with a person's larger presentation. It helps to figure out if a person offers the negation as a way of comforting themselves, avoiding embarrassment, or shutting off further discussion and discovery. Maybe they even believe it or, at least, are not consciously trying to mislead. With Mrs. Wright, I was lucky in that when I confronted her, she readily admitted that, for whatever reason, her denial was a dodge. Getting a patient to that point often requires a lot more.

I prefer a patient's negation to silence, since negation is a red flag that you cannot miss. The patient is waving it in your face. At one level, he or she may be asking you to call their bluff – that is, they take comfort in hiding, but not so much that they are unwilling to be found out. Thus, while they cannot bear to feel that they are betraying themselves, and divulging what they have kept from public disclosure, they are not sure how long they can continue in their secret without risking the change that they need. When the patient finally acknowledges a negation, the therapist never acts as though it was a lie or even a breach of the therapeutic contract that demands complete candor. Rather, both parties have some more facts – a new starting point from which therapy can proceed.

I have a lot of practice keeping a straight face, whereas, in other settings, I might have said "Now who do you think you're kidding?"

I keep returning to the difference between therapeutic and social settings. This is because in listening and talking, therapists have a job: to create situations where patients can change consciously, deliberately. In regular conversation, we have no such professional objective. Therapists are not their patients' friends, and, while our conversation may seem friendly, we are always provocative. We use language, like a friend, but we use it differently.

> Before the therapist can listen, much less respond, he or she must decide what to call the patient. The decision is not trivial, since it sets up the nature of the duality that constitutes the therapeutic relationship. I have to be sensitive not to appear condescending or to transgress an ideology – if someone is a feminist, for example, she may resent my using her first name, and may bridle if I say "Mrs." Instead of "Ms." Even if you ask someone what they want to be called, there can be problems – aren't you clued in enough to know what people should be called in a sensitive setting where the power pyramid is already so top-heavy?

Names, my name

A person's name is integral to his or her identity, so how we address someone can influence the course of therapy. The therapist should never prefigure anyone's identity by imposing a name, even if it's meant to suggest fondness or familiarity. I recall a paper which suggested that using a first name was tantamount to a boundary violation – like a physical act. While of course this is silly, I agree that naming is a meaningful gesture that should convey respect. This is especially true given the asymmetry of the situation. I am always Dr. Friedberg, while the patient could be Tom or Mary. I not only have the formality of my last name but also a professional title. The patient might have neither.

Early on, I did not use a patient's name at all. This approach reflected the dogma of classical psychoanalysis to maintain an impregnable distance and to analyze rather than directly respond to a patient's concerns. If I was put on the spot by a patient, I might ask, "What would you like me to call you?" or "Why would you like me to call you by your first name?" I tried to interpret their answers, but I think I was overinterpreting. People hate to go nameless, especially when they seek help. I decided that not addressing a person by name was an affront. It seemed disrespectful, unnatural, and a diminution of their identity.

There was an element of Kafka.

Yet, while first names can seem too friendly, it seems awkward to call a patient by their last name when you may know more about them than a spouse or best friend. So, I usually use first names, preserving the asymmetry that in other respects I try to finesse. After all, I want these people to open up. Thus, while there is a risk of infantilising elderly patients, I usually take it. I might say, "Do you mind my using your first name?"

Sometimes using a patient's first name serves to make a more personal connection or emphasize a point. I remember when a psychiatrist that I was treating decided to drop out of treatment. I tried to help him understand his decision in terms of issues that he had with intimacy and trust. I appealed to him using his first name, as in "You know, Paul ... ." But he objected to what, he said, "sounded like manipulation." He left treatment even more determined.

Another patient was named Moses. On some level, I felt a special kinship, as in Moses and Ahron. But I never told him. I think about myself during therapy, and I did not want to draw attention to that. I called him Moses and wondered whether *he* drew a connection to Ahron.

My point is that deciding what names to use can produce an infinite regress in the therapist's mind which has a likely counterpart in the patient. This is because one's name is *the* most personal possession that one has. How it is used, in any setting, can influence a transaction or a relationship. It stipulates an arrangement, any change in which stipulates another arrangement, hence another possible regress toward multiple possible meanings. It's best, therefore, to determine the therapist's and patient's names up front, even though there may be circumstances where they could change. The fewer surprises, the less likely any potential offense.

Having just said that, I have to make room for a whole other layer of meaning where a patient has a hidden name that they love or hate but cannot escape. It can be immensely resonant and, if you get near it, can open a door to their deepest feelings. For example, a Sandra may have repressed the childhood nickname, Sandy; its recall resuscitates memories of abusive parents or obtuse relatives. But how do you elicit these sorts of names, when all you have to go by is what's on paper? They only emerge as the treatment progresses, and the Sandra recalls a boyfriend who addressed her as Sandy, provoking unaccountable sadness when he meant no harm. If you can explore the memories associated with the name, you may be onto an alternative identity that the patient has made every effort to flee.

> Learning the patient's family history is crucial. Our parents' choices – for themselves and for us – affect us throughout our life. Siblings tend to be underemphasized in terms of psychoanalytic theory, but are important in shaping our experience into adulthood. A relationship with a boss may be based on the template of parent and child and relationships with friends and colleagues with that of siblings.
>
> Sometimes a challenging event that brings a person in for treatment is based on an earlier loss or traumatic event from childhood (e.g., the death of a parent, divorce, sexual abuse, or some other situation beyond normal experience). Even experiences that we may not or cannot remember leave their mark. Eighty percent of premature infants that spend a week or more in incubators suffer from Panic Disorder later in life.

> Family biology also plays a role in a person's psychiatric and psychological history. Anxiety, depression, schizophrenia, attention deficit, bipolar disorder, and many other psychiatric conditions all run in families. Learning about siblings, parents, grandparents, and relatives is a way of obtaining important diagnostic and treatment information about the patient. Early environmental influences such as stress or exposure to drugs and alcohol can have a significant effect.

A family history

Mr. Pierre has started to connect his anxious feelings with a claustrophobic work environment. Things that seemed obvious from my perspective have just begun to dawn on him. He feels "trapped" when, for example, he negotiates a deal, manages his staff, or meets with his boss.

I might have just let him talk about feeling trapped. "What, in general, do you associate with that feeling?" This would be the more classically analytic approach. I find that in treatment, especially early on but also throughout, we educate patients to the process of the treatment itself. *Our questions are a means of education.* While Freud gave the simple instruction to patients to say whatever comes to mind, this is an impossible task. The mind is crowded with feelings, associations, and even irrelevancies like a looming dentist's appointment. From session to session it moves on, somewhat asymptotically, as new associations and slants on associations merge, emerge, and drift into the margins of consciousness. Moreover, you can argue that by the time the patient approaches this Freudian ideal and has said whatever he can possibly think of, the treatment has long since finished, and any resistance to freely associating has been analyzed as well. So, I split the difference with Freud. I asked a boring, clichéd question that had some features of free association – it was very broad – but still focused on Mr. Pierre's family.

The patient looked a little flushed. He said it did not make sense, but that he was thinking about his father and mother arguing. He said their arguments would scare him. He would try to run away, but there was no place to hide. Even in his own room he felt "trapped," since the walls were paper-thin. He made the connection to how his sense of anxiety in certain situations related back to situations from his childhood where he had felt upset and scared but could not leave. We carry our past with us. But it is never the same past as when we first experienced it. It is reimagined and even distorted. The therapist's role is to understand this "new" past and see how it gets in the way. At a deeper level, his or her role is to see how we repurpose the past, perhaps to justify a present that is causing pain. With Mr. Pierre, his ready association of the past with his present unease got me thinking – what is this past really doing? Is it an obstacle to our exploring more deeply the cause of Mr. Pierre's anxiety ("Don't look at me, look at my parents"), or is it a crutch, helping him to explain daily assaults that he feels powerless to stop? I wanted to remain neutral until he could explain more, but I also wanted to offer some suggestions that, in effect, would tempt him to examine his real motivations. I was encouraged by his willingness to dive into the past, and I wanted to question him in a way that would not cause him to turn away.

I realized, however, that merely taking a family history can be misinterpreted by a patient, for example as a signal that you may be willing to shift blame entirely onto parents and siblings when there may still be other reasons for anxiety that the patient would like to finesse. When I take a family history, therefore, I watch for resistance to other lines of inquiry, which can be a tip-off that the patient would use that history as a diversion. I was not sure in Mr. Pierre's case whether even an extensive family history would entirely explain his feeling "trapped" at work. I hoped that taking the history, which was still crucial, would lead to other associations that might further shed light on his anxiety.

But what if it doesn't? When a family history seems not to explain a patient's issues sufficiently, we have to explore more immediate factors. This initiates a balancing act: family history on one side and, on the other, current tics, rivalries, insults, and who knows what else. A person's memory is updated daily. The therapist cannot evade the messiness of the present or the near-present, nor can the patient. Looked at another way, everything becomes history the day after it happens.

Very recent history is sometimes hard to interpret because there is not a lot of subsequent history to provide context. When I tried to explore the recent history of the following patient, and she was not much help, her reticence suggested that while the content of this history would be scant it would also be important. Therapists tend to proceed by closely examining what is barely there.

Mislaid sunglasses

I have been sitting with a patient's sunglasses for two weeks. She left them on her second office visit and then missed her third appointment. Significant? When patients leave things in my office, there often is. The last time a patient left sunglasses, she was dropping out of treatment. Obviously, she had mixed feelings about being in treatment. Leaving her glasses was a way of staying connected to me (howver provisionally).

Mrs. Gottasay presented for treatment because of "worry." She thought she would lose her job to technology. She thought her latest marriage would fail because her husband wanted children and she was 43. Her breast cancer, which had gone into remission two years ago, was still closely monitored and might come back. She talked incessantly.

In a sense, this volubility made less work for me, at least initially, since she was quite open about herself. But I also wondered if she might be defending against other issues with her effusiveness. For example, she mentioned that her father left the family when she was three. But she left her glasses and, when we spoke briefly by phone, she said she had forgotten the next session.

It's a challenge to deal with a patient's ambivalence – one foot in, one foot out the door. I could ask if Mrs. Gottasay had any thoughts about leaving her glasses. But most patients are quick to dismiss such queries with an "oh, I just forgot." Or they may hear the question as a kind of criticism or as too analytic. But if I can engage her in treatment in one way or another, I can keep the question in mind. Perhaps, at some point, I can remind her of the incident, and we can explore its meaning further.

Or, rather, what does ambivalence toward treatment mean? Why would someone worried about her health, her marriage, and her job *not* want to be in therapy? I think Mrs. Gottasay is conflicted about how best to protect herself. One way is to let it all hang out and attempt to deal with it – ouch. The other is not to confront it at all, since that would cause even further pain. She is capable of maintaining both ideas simultaneously, or at least on alternate days. So, if I am to reach her, I have to start with the ambivalence, which the glasses represent. I have to encourage her to come back in, put her sunglasses away, and look steadily inward. If she can discuss her reasons for "worrying," she may be able to put them into perspective and rearrange her life. Or, rather, reposition the worries that occupy so much space in life and probably keep her from approaching things from a position of clarity. Ambivalence just equates to doing nothing, since she keeps cancelling whatever psychological progress she achieves. But she has adopted ambivalence as the course of least resistance. I have to convince her that her course is shortsighted, especially if one of her worries sneaks up on her as a real problem.

A patient can create a kind of instant secret history, designating an event as past and then refusing to discuss it. During the 17th and 18th centuries, before psychotherapy but after Shakespeare plumbed Hamlet's soul, there was a popular genre called Secret History. It was supposed to let readers in on the real backstory surrounding a famous person or notorious event. The authors' actual purpose, in most cases, was to draw attention to themselves – "Look, I have sources that you don't." While they published anonymously, they hoped to be found out. They also sought to shape how history was finally written, since Secret Histories posed as breathless, risky disclosures whose authors had to hide their identity from the public. They created a kind of literary cat and mouse game.

> *I thought of the Secret History when I tried dealing with Ms. Penn's refusal to talk about her dead cat. Except I was the cat and she was the mouse. You try to unearth a patient's recent history but, if she refuses, what do you do? It is as if the patient is setting limits around how much you can help – an affront that is also counterproductive. You are left to analyse the refusal. When I wrote the note that follows, I felt as though the patient had recast therapy as ahistorical or, rather, as partly open to view and partly "secret." Maybe at some point she wanted to be found out, but ... when?*

A cat's tale

The view prevails in insight-oriented psychotherapy that the more we examine a patient's life, thoughts, feelings, and issues, the better. The idea is to be tactful and sensitive, but still to get firmly in our sights what the patient is dealing with.

So, I was in a quandary when Ms. Penn, an accomplished writer, began the session by saying that her cat died. She teared up for a moment. But then she said that she did not want to talk about it again – ever. People are often close to their pets, perhaps especially elderly people without children. This was certainly true of Ms. Penn, who had had her cat for over a decade. It was a little like her losing a child and saying to me she did not want to discuss it again.

Previously, there had been an incident concerning a friend of hers where she had made a similar request to me. I tried to bring it up with her, gently at first and then more directly. I pointed out that the basic contract between us is for her to speak about what's on her mind as freely and openly as she can. She got so angry that she missed the next session and then spent the better part of the following one threatening to leave treatment. I had to realize that this patient's reaction, like Ms. Penn's, was not simply a negation in the mode of Mrs. Wright's, for example an inartful denial when the opposite of that denial was clearly the case. Rather, it was an assertion that something was *so* consequential that its open discussion was unbearable. I thought of how I still cannot encounter stories about Auschwitz or Buchenwald without turning the page, acknowledging their existence, but shrinking from the pain of dwelling on them.

Our patients often know better than we do what they are ready to speak about and when. It is easy to think that our job is interpreting a patient's defences in one way or another. But in psychotherapy as in life, it is not that simple. Sometimes it is better – best even, at least for now – to leave "well enough" alone. Respectful timing is important.

Yet what we refrain from discussing out of respect for a patient may still prey on our minds. I often think about issues that patients refuse to address and can't resist asking why. Was it *just* that the death of a cat was so painful, or did Ms. Penn have associations surrounding the incident that she could not confront? Like Ms. Gottasay, she seemed less than forthcoming, albeit more explicitly. Unlike Mrs. Wright, she was not disclosing by way of pretending not to. She was on a different trajectory, reminding me that each patient's course of therapy opens some doors and closes others – there is no pattern. Perhaps her issues will emerge over time in other discussions. Any refusal to talk leaves open as much as – or more than – it forecloses. In therapy, timing is the correlative of time. If you wait long enough, the context for disclosure may develop, and the disclosure may feel right.

In taking a history, we can uncover real pain. Sometimes we do not realize how close to the surface it is, and we ask questions that are themselves painful to patients, even before they attempt to answer. Pain is often associated with family history which patients try to repress as a means of coping but which questions can disinter. You cannot disavow the need for hard questions, but you have to be ready to show the patient how any revelations will further the course of treatment. Asking a patient to focus on the source of pain may provoke resistance, and then you may have to deal with that.

A father and a boss

Wednesdays are long. I see about a dozen patients. I was not quite ready for my last patient this evening, Mary, wh arrived in a fit of rage. She said she just wanted to kill her boss. Since she is a decent woman, it was surprising to see her so angry.

When I asked what had happened, she described an incident from earlier in the day. She had been speaking with her boss's assistant, when her boss interrupted with something like "Stop wasting your time on that. Go back and do what I told you to." Clearly, he was rude. And he could be obnoxious at times. But he also cared about Mary and had been professionally and personally supportive.

When I suggested that her anger was disproportionate to what he had said, she started in about how I didn't get it. "What don't I get?" "You don't get what it was like for me as a kid." She recalled how her father would cut her off mid-sentence, even on occasion call her a liar and insult her. He was an angry, belligerent alcoholic. The atmosphere he created formed the backdrop to her relationship with her boss. When her boss interrupted her, her relationship with him segued into her relationship with her father, and alarm bells went off.

But there were also a really sickening association. Mary went on to describe incidents from childhood where her father would lie in bed with her and complain about his in-laws, work, and the myriad perceived impertinences that he was obliged to endure. His behavior so enraged Mary that she kept a knife in her drawer by the bedside, "just in case." She said she had wanted to kill her father. When she recalled the flirtatious relationship with her boss, who was married at the time, this history got stirred up as well.

I listened. But at the end of the day, I felt the best I could do was just listen. She thanked me, and I took this to mean she got something from my listening. Yet I also felt that the session was anticlimactic. I should have conveyed that her recollections, and the connection that she drew between a monstrous father and an errant boss, needed further exploration. In a fit of transference, she was projecting her father onto her boss, externalizing anger that she never showed her father while acting out the subliminal sexuality that memories of her father elicited. Obviously, she had to deal with how her father deranged her life. Because of him, she was angry at her boss but also attracted, and clearly resented, her own attraction. Part of her anger at him expressed that resentment. Her feelings were a tangle of conflicting emotion.

Sometimes it is important to scope out a problem, even if we are unsure how to address it. Mary understood the connection between her father and her boss and had some idea of its varied dimensions. But from the perspective of therapy, the drunkenness and brutality would still be easier to address than the sexuality. Maybe Mary would have to leave her job, or at least transfer to another department, before we could adequately work on it. It's hard to deal with a problem if the stimulus persists. And what about the reaction from her boss if she resists his advances? When therapy requires external adjustments, the patient can see it as disruptive. I began by telling Mary that initial changes are sometimes the hardest.

Freud said that love and work were the two pillars of well-being. While relationships tend to take up most people's bandwith, our professional history can play a disproportionate role in how we regard ourselves and navigate the world outside work. It can have a profound effect on our relationships and may, conversely, depend on our ability to carry on relationships.

A person's "success" may be no success at all, at least according to how they measure it. They may hate or fear everyone they work with. They may feel that they themselves are a fraud. Most of the time, they may feel that their financial success is opposite to that of their romantic success. When I consider a person's professional history, therefore, I invariably find it joined at the hip to the rest of their life.

When I take a work history, I look for traits like reliability, attention to detail, and the ability to handle stress. I look for a lot of the same things that HR looks for when they hire people and give them annual

> evaluations. These traits tend to be predictors of success outside of work.
>
> It is interesting how professional historians argue – against their professional interest – that history can be misleading. It gets reinterpreted every generation or so. When I considered Mr. Wordsworth's professional history (below), I had to agree with them. What looked on paper like a success story, was only a narrow version of his ability to navigate the world. He had to correct me.

Work

Mr. Wordsworth appeared distraught today, but claimed that he didn't know why. He thought he should be pleased because he had just won a lawsuit, but he was upset and anxious.

I said "But you do know why. Think." He agreed that he *knew*, but had trouble translating his thoughts into words. "Emotions are another language – at least for me." It emerged that he was sad (the most explicit word he could find) because he was mourning a fumbled relationship. He had puzzled the woman, and she had moved on. Though he was a professional success, he saw himself as emotionally tongue-tied. He could never express what he wanted to say. He could not explain his feelings to the woman and could barely explain his feelings *about* his feelings to me.

I told him I was surprised by the disparity between how disabled he felt and how successful he appeared. I shouldn't have said that since it could only have made him feel worse and since the condition is so common. But his stellar résumé made the disparity seem vast. I realized, afterward, that the danger in taking a patient's professional history is that ostensible "success" can distort or disguise other elements of a person's circumstances. Why? We are still capitalists. We sublimate its tenets into our natural responses. When I catch myself, I cringe.

But Mr. Wordsworth responded to my ill-considered comment by agreeing with it, citing his humiliation at being unable to voice his feelings. His successful trajectory, he said, had to some extent helped to mitigate his handicap. But he had never – at least so far – been able to overcome the sense of being deficient. The affection and attention of beautiful women helped compensate for his feelings, but only temporarily. With this woman, he had lapsed back into them when he stumbled into muteness and could never effect a reconciliation. He said that if he could not succeed with her – an emotionally intelligent women – then he could not expect to succeed with anyone.

In some way, each of us has difficulty giving voice to our deepest feelings, which can become our deepest secrets. Maybe this is partially developmental. That is, we did not have the language to express what we thought, felt, or went through at the time of the experience. Hence, we were never equipped – then or subsequently – to formulate those experiences or reflect on them. A lot of what we keep inside stays there because no one has been around to listen, love, care, and hence elicit our feelings from us. If during therapy a person learns to talk about his feelings, largely by slowly finding the words, he may be able to become less tongue-tied in his other relationships. A person can learn a new language, so to speak, if he can get past the idea that he is unable to learn it. It takes practice, but in therapy there is no humiliation.

Finally, we discussed how all the hard work that he applies to "work" could be devoted to his emotional development. I wanted his success at work to seem less a taunt than an encouragement. Instead of seeing work as an ironic contrast to the rest of his life, I hoped he would see it as emblematic of an achievable goal in other contexts. We set out to practice talking about feelings. I assigned readings such as *Pride and Prejudice* and *Middlemarch* and asked him to describe how the characters' feelings developed and changed. I assigned Pope's *Abelard and Eloise* – no shortage of extreme passion there! – and supplemented it with a couple of romance novels. If he could empathize with others' feelings, I thought he was already in touch with his own feelings and could try putting them into words. A couple of times, I found him paraphrasing a couple of novels, but hey, this was not a class where plagiarism was a crime. It was practice. Mr. Wordsworth had just won a case. Now he had another challenge.

We never sought the ultimate reason for his disability. I felt that it was more important, or perhaps just more expedient, to tackle the problem directly. I felt that taking it on was a doable project. Sometimes, not every problem needs to be traced to its cause. It's enough just to solve it.

Mr. Buck is another version of Mr. Wordsworth – successful but unhappy. Though because he was such a mega success, I found myself in an odd competition for his favor. I have found that it is easy to be drawn into a patient's orbit so that if they are Masters of the Universe, we want to be among the survivors and, if possible, one of their favorites. We empathize when they are troubled, but rescuing them becomes more of a personal test – more a measure of whether we measure up – than it would be with the usual patient. We want to be able to identify with these people and have them identify with us on their level. The whole idea is primitive, but it is no less real.

As I spoke with Mr. Buck and took his history, I kept reflecting on his lofty position. I could not attain parity except, ironically, by serving him well. So that was exactly what I wanted to do. I would have wanted that for any patient, of course, but the meaning attached to it in this case was outsize (like Mr. Buck).

Love & Work, Inc.

Mr. Buck, the head of a major film company, was bright, verbal, and creative. But he was almost morbidly introspective and had a history of serial psychoanalyses. When he was referred to me by an internist, he had been complaining that his life was "meaningless" and that he felt "unhappy." I did not say so, but he reminded me of a Hollywood version of a Hollywood mogul – brilliant, successful, and depressed.

I am always surprised when someone I admire (cf. Mr. Wordsworth) still presents as troubled. Why should I be? I don't believe that conventional forms of success inevitably produce happiness ... and yet I keep wondering when they do not. Perhaps, at some level, I wish I could be one of those mega successes. I would surely know how to handle the glamor and prestige! Of course, I check myself, as I did in Mr. Buck's case. I realize that my "surprise" is a form of envy, lightened up and sublimated.

So, what was the problem? Mr. Buck had three children, all of whom were also highly successful. His marriage was loving. He had money. But one issue I picked up on was that he had just turned 60. His mother had died at that age of a sudden heart attack. He described himself as like his mother in terms of sharing an acerbic wit and sense of style. The similarity was suggestive. Potentially, he perceived his success as subject to physical factors beyond his control. For a man with so much power, the lack of power to control his own body could be disorienting. He said he worked out twice a week, but it was more for appearance than cardiovascular fitness. He didn't think that lifting weights could reverse the effects of stress, gravity, and aging.

Mr. Buck also felt guilty about how he had treated some people in the past. He acknowledged that he enjoyed being "cruel" at times. But when I asked him to elaborate, he gave innocuous work-related examples and was quick to add that he was never violent. I wondered aloud how those tendencies might affect our work together, and he responded that they had been factors in previous treatments. "You know, I'm in a tough business and I just can't turn it off. I realize that we're not competing, but I compete with everyone – those other therapists challenged me, and I got back at them." How long would I last?

I decided, however, that at least for now we had connected. He had been honest, and I was beginning to sense his concerns. Clearly, he felt guilty about aspects of his past and identified with his mother in terms of feeling precarious. At the end of the hour, I gave him my initial impression. I did not think that medication was indicated, which had been one of his questions. I thought the treatment of choice would be an analytically oriented, interpersonal psychotherapy. He understood what I meant and concurred. He mentioned that he would also be seeing another therapist in consultation. We set up an appointment the following week. But I wondered if he would choose me. When you feel that an initial session has gone reasonably well, you resist anticipating rejection – rather, you hope for reciprocity. Where the patient is someone you envy, at least in a way, you *really* hope for reciprocity. You want to be in their league. You want their approval.

When a session is over, I cannot help but reflect on how it leaves me feeling as a professional. Why? I do not feel precarious, certainly not in the way Mr. Buck does, yet I still want affirmation that I am getting through to a patient. Therapy is never one-way. If I make a difference in patients' lives, they have an effect on mine. When therapists lose a patient, we lose a source of self-affirmation, whether or not we tell ourselves that it is their loss. Probably we are afraid of feeling precarious, even becoming so in the future. We toggle between wanting to be in the Big Leagues and fearing a bush-league comedown.

I was feeling something of Mr. Buck's competitiveness. He had made it contagious! He put me in the position of acting the way he acts – if he rejected me, I would feel that some therapist-competitor had beaten me. I understood the ridiculousness of such feelings. I felt as if I had been cast in one of Mr. Buck's movies. Some remake of *The Godfather*. I said to myself "It's just business." But would the joke be on me?

Further Reading

Casement, Patrick. *Learning From the Patient.* New York: Guilford Press, 1991.

Corey, Gerald. *Theory and Practice of Counseling and Psychotherapy.* Belmont, CA: Wadworth, 2013.

Cozolino, Louis. *The Making of a Therapist: A Practical Guide for the Inner Journey.* New York: W.W. Norton & Co, 2004.

Gottlieb, Lori. *Maybe You Should Talk to Someone.* Boston: Houghton Mifflin Harcourt, 2019.

Jacobs, Theodore. *The Use of the Self: Countertransference and Communication in the Analytic Situation.* Madison, CT: Internaitonal Universitie Press, 1991.

Jacobs, Theodore. *The Possible Profession: The Analytic Process of Change.* New York: Routledge, 2013.

Kahn, Michael. *Between Therapist and Client: The New Relationship.* New York: W.H. Freeman & Co., 1997.

Kottler, Jeffrey. *On Being a Therapist.* New York: Oxford University Press, 2017.

Makari, George. *Revolution in Mind: The Creation of Psychoanalysis.* New York: Harper Collins, 2008.

Reik, Theodor. *Listening With the Third Ear: The Inner Experience of a Psychoanalyst.* New York: Farrar, Strauss & Giroux, 1948.

Yalom, Irvin. *The Gift of Therapy: An Open Letter to a New Generation of Therapists and Their Patients.* New York: Harper Collins, 2002.

2 Trust

This chapter examines trust, which in psychotherapy is a belief in the reliability of individuals and processes that affect the course of treatment. There must be mutual trust between therapist and patient, without which there can be little positive change. The patient must also trust in the therapeutic process and not expect instant miracles. Trust is therefore closely aligned with commitment (e.g., with the patient's allowing treatment to proceed notwithstanding digressions, anticlimaxes, and psychological pain). This type of trust is ultimately based on knowledge – not faith – since the patient must assimilate the insights that he or she achieves, registering how they trace an arc of change. Trust develops through expanding awareness.

Therapists trust a patient in a way that is particular to therapy. They do not expect a patient never to mislead – part of being a therapist is figuring out why a patient is reticent, since that can itself be revealing. Rather, therapists want to trust a patient to participate in the process and engage in the real psychological work of personal exploration. A therapist cannot fully trust an indifferent or refractory patient who is simply an observer of his or her own therapy and not a co-participant.

Of course, it may seem odd that a person would spend time with a therapist, and even seek one out, if they are not fully committed to the process. But it happens all the time. A spouse or employer may insist that the person seek treatment. Or he may have a nagging problem but have no idea what is entailed in addressing it. The same conflicts that can motivate a person to seek help can also put a brake on their willingness to participate once the process becomes intense. Patient resistance is a normal part of the psychotherapeutic process but also a barrier to mutual trust.

Thus, I have included instances of successful and failed trust between therapist and patient (e.g., how trust is sustained – or not).

In therapy, trust is always active (e.g., subject to reassessment and conditionality). It is transactional rather than (like love) unconditional. Both parties continually earn it, and it can be lost based on how one party perceives the other (irrespective of whether the perception is accurate). Ideally, when one party feels they are losing trust in the other they should offer an explanation ... and allow the process to heal the breach, if it can. There is an element of what in drama is called "suspension of disbelief," a willingness to allow one's skepticism to abate long enough so that immersion in the train of events can continue unabated. One has to value the process to submit to its potential.

Where the patient is able to sustain trust, the capacity ramifies and can apply to relationships beyond therapy. Trust in the confined, protected space of therapy is thus practice for a wider world, especially for patients who have been so traumatized that lack of trust has hampered their ability to have relationships. Indeed, such "relationships" include those at work – with attorneys or financial advisers or others with whom we share personal information. At the extreme, trust is necessary for the efficient working of any business – if someone is incapable of trust, they become dysfunctional regarding all but the simplest tasks in a complex economy.

There is abundant scientific evidence that the capacity for trust is wired into the neurocircuitry of the mammalian brain. It allows for cooperation and large social networks. One goal of therapy is to clear away the obstacles to trust that a person may be suffering. Of course, no one favors naïve, childlike "blind" trust, but neither can anyone operate when lack of trust is a kind of pathology.

Trust in oneself is crucial to accomplishment. Also, where patients in psychotherapy lack self-trust and project their own lack onto others, these others will never measure up until the patient making all these projections learns to trust him- or herself.

Making up

Once, I told a patient a white lie. I did it in self-defense. When I saw Ms. Steward in an initial consultation, she had a history of forming erotomanic attachments to her therapists. It was early in my practice, and I was concerned that she would form an attachment to me that would interfere with treatment – as it had in the past. I had the naive idea that I could short-circuit an attachment if she thought I was married. So, when she asked, I nodded affirmatively. (Obviously, I am now more aware that transference is not put off merely by one party's legal status.)

Following our initial consultation, Ms. Steward entered into therapy with me. It proceeded well over several years. But in spite of my early demurral, she still displayed signs of erotic transference. I saw it in terms of the erotic relationship that she had had with her father, whom she had viewed as strong and powerful. So, because her erotic attachment to me persisted, I thought that if I talked about my current dating life it would defuse some of her erotic feelings.

"O what a tangled web we weave when first we practice to deceive!" I had forgotten what I said about being married.

Predictably, during one such self-disclosure, she reminded me that I had previously indicated that I was married – so why was I now discussing my dating life? I had to acknowledge that I was not married at the time that I implied I had been.

Unpredictably, however, Ms. Steward said that she knew that already and had known even prior to asking me. When I asked how she knew, she explained that she had researched it through public records and by making "inquiries." I was not sure whether to be impressed, affronted, or embarrassed.

The next time the subject came up, I referred again to my white lie and asked why she had chosen to work with me given that I had not been forthright from the start. She replied that she felt I had been trying to be considerate and to compensate for her history of attraction to therapists. Pointedly, she felt that even though I had not been entirely honest, she could still trust me.

But as I think back on this discussion, I realize that I was lucky. Had the patient not been of an analytic turn herself and not viewed my lying situationally, she would have had grounds to distrust me, maybe even think that I was being manipulative in the interest of keeping a patient whose history of such attachments I already knew. She gave me the benefit of the doubt.

Of course, I also gave her the same benefit. By checking on my marital status without telling me, she was testing me – would I answer truthfully, or fudge? Patients sometimes conduct covert tests. When these tests come to light, sometimes well into the course of treatment, they put therapists in the position of not trusting the patient going forward. Perhaps, this behavior throws into doubt everything that has been said already, a sort of 13th chime on a clock that suggests there is a systemic problem.

My point is that in therapy, trust has to work both ways. When Ms. Stewart disclosed that she had tested me and I acknowledged my white lie, there was a critical situation. She valued the therapy enough and apparently thought highly enough of me to let it go. She let it go because she had developed enough trust in me – contextually, based on all our interaction. Likewise, when I understood that she had tested me, I recognized that she had exhibited enough candor in other respects that I could still rely on her commitment to therapy.

But it was a close call. Would I dissemble again? So far, I have not. But I have not been put in quite the same position where I have been tempted. The strategy of coaxing patients out of proclivities that interfere with therapy is complicated. The therapist wants to protect him- or herself and, concomitantly, advance the course of therapy. That was my starting point with Ms. Steward. But any protective actions can easily pitch into reverse. If today I were confronted with a patient's potential erotic attachment, I think I would address it directly with the patient who, presumably, wants her therapy to succeed. It would be a subject to explore. If the patient is unwilling, then I would try to address the resistance. I know this sounds like an infinite regression into the abyss of feeling and memory, but that is what therapy often is. One hopes, if the effort is accompanied by candor, that the participants can develop a working trust and finally move ahead.

I say "working trust" because trust between therapist and patient is situational and dependent on each other's continual mutual reassessment. Unlike love, which can be unqualified, trust is always subject to re-examination – even between people who love each other – based on the parties' interactions. As a therapist, I have learned to keep away from statements that may seem contradictory or opportunistic. I have also learned to confront the patient who seems to be hiding something out of a less than full commitment to therapy. If a patient's trust in me is beginning to falter, I want to know ... and vice versa. This is the only way to maintain a "working trust."

An initial consultation culminates in a clinical assessment and treatment plan. The recommendation requires a good deal of trust on the patient's part since any treatment entails costs in time, money, and emotional energy. But before outlining treatment, therapists need to ask: Does the person even need treatment? Do they need this treatment? If so, am I the right provider?

A psychiatrist, who is medically trained, is more likely to prescribe psychopharmacology or a treatment that is medically based. On the other hand, a psychoanalyst may be more inclined to recommend analysis, an intensive treatment that can last years. Thus, if a patient is to trust the treatment, he or she needs to have confidence and believe that whoever offers it has candidly evaluated their specific needs and the appropriateness of the therapy. Phobias, for example, are often better treated by exposure therapy – exposing the patient to the source of his or her anxiety without intending to cause harm. Cognitive and behavioral therapies are often helpful for depression and anxiety. While a patient may not know about different treatments, the therapist does not want to lose the patient's trust down the road and should therefore decide – before making a recommendation – whether the course of treatment is likely correct. If it emerges sometime later that a different approach might be better, then the therapist should inform the patient.

Character

There are many ways to define "character" and the qualities that comprise a good character. But we should ignore personality, or the "persona," which is shallower than character and is the aspect of personality that we present to the world. Movie villains have terrific – and deceptive – personalities! Thus, character is based on a person's underlying, enduring traits. These include one's values and ideals, conscience, and other characteristics that help us navigate the world without damaging others. Character is formed based on influences throughout childhood and adult life. A person's parents and siblings, playmates and peers, teachers and mentors affect his or her development. Religion and sociocultural influences are also important. Identification with parents and early childhood experiences can be especially influential.

These factors played a role in the development of Mr. Lauren's character. Some were helpful in the development of his good character, some more problematic. Certainly, his Judeo-Christian values and educational background served him well. He was for the most part ethical, hardworking, and charitable. But some of his identifications with his parents were complicated. For example, he recalled that for his mother "truth" and "facts" were malleable concepts. She would make up excuses as she needed them, frequently dragging young Mr. Lauren into Rube Goldberg-type stories more complicated than they were believable. Thus, if she was late for dinner, she might blame it on how little Mr. Lauren left his clothing at the local Y, and the need to go back to get it. Little Mr. Lauren resented being used in that way, but he also identified with it and grew up with a sense that if he got in trouble, he could finesse his way out of it. But what may seem funny, or perhaps excusable in a child, was not amusing at all as he grew older. As his therapy progressed, he reported that people had trouble trusting him.

As we talked, he became more aware of the factors that influenced his inability to project trust. During earlier analyses with other therapists, these factors remained unresolved and got in the way of treatment. That is, when a therapist recognized his tendency to weasel out of discomfiting situations and tried to mitigate it head on, he felt judged and criticized. He felt that his "character" had been impugned, even though he understood that what the therapist said was accurate and that what the therapist was trying to do was in his interest. His pride got in the way of his treatment.

When Mr. Lauren came to me, the course of therapy was different. I tried to understand the underlying determinants of his character rather than immediately working to correct them. I tried to have him understand them, even though this brought up painful memories of his mother's dissembling. My approach was in contrast to his first analyst who focused directly on eliminating the problematic behaviour. As Mr. Lauren came to terms with the origins of who he was and the deeper influences on his character, he became better able to take responsibility for his actions. He acknowledged who he had been, the first step to becoming whom he knew he had to become.

One of the biggest challenges in therapy is getting patients to realize that they need to accept and eventually disown qualities in themselves that are coping mechanisms and that make life apparently easier. In a certain sense, they have to begin to dislike aspects of themselves, and believe that notwithstanding their attachment to certain characterological tendencies, these are actually counterproductive, even faults. I tried to bring Mr. Lauren back to a point in his life when he viewed his mother's lying as a flaw that caused him pain. Then I said, "Now imagine how someone else feels when you make up stories." He finally got the point. In effect, he had to *transpose* how bad he felt as a child – when he could not trust his mother – to how other people feel when they lose trust in him.

One goal of psychodynamic psychotherapy is to bring the past into the present as information, as data that can be used in the present to produce useful change. We need to trust the past in this regard – perhaps not what "really" happened, the way historians want to present it, but how the patient experienced it. Mr. Lauren experienced the past as painful but also insidiously instructive. We had to undo that instruction by examining how the pain he felt back then could be felt by others now when he put them in similar situations. I did not ask him to relive his prior pain so much as imagine it as a natural consequence in others who would then react, discounting him as a trusted colleague and friend. It was almost like retelling his past in another key. But it got him to reflect on himself and begin to let go of a comfortable, but ultimately counterproductive tendency.

Before recommending a treatment plan, therapists should be clear about what they are treating. That is, are they treating the underlying condition – such as depression – or the symptoms of that condition? For example, a clinically depressed patient may have decreased energy and motivation. They may have changes in sleep and appetite. Often, medication can relieve such symptoms, though it may still be necessary to treat their underlying cause, so as to prevent the patient from becoming even more depressed and to help him or her be personally stronger and more resilient.

One indication for immediate treatment of symptoms is that they are interfering with the patient's functioning. Thus, if the patient has been a good student or employee but the quality of his or her performance has decreased because of poor concentration or less energy or motivation, this may be an indication to treat the symptoms. The same is true for patients who suffered exposure to an unusual event (e.g., war or a personal tragedy), and then felt constantly on edge, avoiding stimuli that recalled the trauma. The Diagnostic and Statistical Manual of Psychiatry (DSM-V) specifies over 500 disorders indicating treatment.

And correct treatments are often varied and multifaceted. They need to be tailored to an individual and his or her needs.

Mr. Lauren was not suffering from a clinical depression or anxiety disorder that interfered with his functioning. But he was clearly in need of help for personal and professional difficulties. While these issues are sometimes helped by medication, they are often more amenable to insight-oriented and other forms of talk therapy, which I recommended. If he needed a medication or more intensive treatment, we could employ such options later on.

A scheduling problem

Mr. Silver was upset with me when he arrived for his session. I thought it might be because of the late hour, which was all I had to offer when he'd asked to reschedule for an earlier day. But what actually bothered him was that I had not returned his call earlier in the week and been more responsive. I was surprised at this and apologized, though from my perspective I had been accommodating – after all, he was still seeing me before his regular appointment.

It emerged during our conversation that my apparent casualness toward a patient, who called out of a sense of need, had breached his trust in me. I was supposed to be there for him. It did not matter that I am supposed to be there for a lot of people, and that I cannot always respond right away to offer an immediate appointment. It occurred to me that patients' trust is often premised on their feeling special, a feeling that develops over the course of therapy as they perceive my care and empathy and become deeply involved in the relationship. When something occurs to undermine that self-induced specialness, they can react intensely. Trust is the first casualty. My apology was beside the point with Mr. Silver, since a curtain had been drawn back, and (in his mind) he saw all the patients that I had treated who had needs equal to – or perhaps greater than – his own. All I could do at that point was proceed with the session and try to build back his trust by listening to the concerns that prompted his call in the first place.

Mr. Silver described a situation from earlier in the week that literally made him sick to his stomach. He had had bouts of gastrointestinal distress and diarrhea directly related to it. The situation was complicated but basically was as follows: He was a trustee on a trust for a handicapped family friend. The sister of the friend, who was the other trustee, had done something illegal with the funds. Mr. Silver had no knowledge of the illegal activity and was actually quite conscientious in carrying out his administrative duties. When he found out about the illegal activity, he confronted the sister. The sister then tried to accuse him of some involvement. He had none. This was apparent to anyone who knew the situation. Mr. Silver consulted a lawyer. A resolution to the situation was devised in which the friend's sister would resign and be responsible for any monies that she had improperly taken.

I was impressed by Mr. Silver's ability to deal with the situation and I said so. That allowed him to be more self-crediting. However, I recognized that my not calling back promptly left him feeling abandoned and without the emotional reassurance he needed to firmly take control of the situation. He had a chronic fear of losing control, in part because it made him sick to his stomach. He said he felt guilty about the trust situation, not because he had done something wrong but because he had not been able to control the other trustee before she had acted illegally. He was being compensated for acting as a trustee and wondered, given what had happened, if he had earned it.

I told him that his final resolution of the issues, which resulted in restoration of the funds, should have reassured him. Ironically, a session that began with a discussion of whether he could trust me, ended in a discussion regarding his own trustworthiness. He saw that. More importantly, he saw that an apparent slip – whether it was a failure to call promptly or a failure to catch a thief promptly – should not be the basis for withdrawing trust in another person. In fact, if the slip is adequately considered, it can be the basis for reinforcing trust. He saw that, too. As he acknowledged the value to him of my explanation of why he deserved thanks as a trustee, he acknowledged that he could repose trust in my good judgement.

At the end of the session, all was repaired, and we were likely in a better place than before the frenzied call and late response. Afterward, however, I thought about the idea of being paid as a fiduciary and therefore having to earn it. In this formulation, the trustee has to keep pace with the payor (e.g., he has to keep trust going no matter what). I hadn't. Thus, since I had lost Mr. Silver's trust, I had to earn it back, which is often harder than earning it initially. When you try to regain a patient's trust in the midst of therapy, you encourage the patient to situate your lapse in context with all the benefits of therapy. You hope that from this perspective, maintaining the relationship wins.

I'm sure Mr. Silver learned from this experience, but so did I. This is often the case during a crisis in therapy. I learned that retaining a patient long term involves the day-to-day attentiveness that patients cherish. You can't rely on patients automatically to place the long-term benefits ahead of slip-ups *that matter to them*. What may seem incidental to the therapist can loom large in the patient's assessment of the therapist. In other words, keeping a patient's trust depends on details that best not be overlooked. If this means treating every patient as special, it may still be easier than backfilling when you don't.

In his theory of personality, the developmental psychologist and psychoanalyst Erik Erikson framed eight stages of psychological development in human beings. Each stage is based on overcoming a conflict or struggle and achieving a developmental attainment central to that phase of life. Erikson coined the phrase "identity crisis" to capture the central conflict at each psychosocial stage of development.

The first and in some ways most basic of these is trust versus mistrust, leading to hope. This stage roughly corresponds to Sigmund Freud's oral stage of development, which covers the period of infancy to around 18 months. During this phase, healthy psychological development not only depends on consistent nurturance but also on the overall quality of the mother-infant relationship. The idea is that the mother, through loving and constant care, conveys a sense of trustworthiness to the developing infant. This helps the child develop trust that carries into relationships other than with parents. So, a child can come to trust other people in the world – teachers, extended family, friends – to support them. Ultimately, a person develops a sense of trust in himself and in his own judgement, which contributes to his identity formation. When this is not present, the world often seems unpredictable and inconsistent, a place to be feared. The person fails to realize that it is their own sense of precariousness that taints the world around them.

Feeling special

Not infrequently, some of the most interesting aspects of treatment occur extra-analytically – before or after the analysis, outside the office. These may or may not be featured in the case presentations, practitioners' notes, or related write-ups.

Some of the most consequential moments of Bobby's treatment, which showcased real growth, occurred after his analysis had ended. He had chosen to attend a prestigious university for an MFA. This put him in a position where, in terms of time and economics, he could no longer continue in a lengthy course of analysis with frequent sessions. We discussed whether this choice implicitly hurt and defeated me as he had wanted to do to his father (whom, he thought, had always stood in his way). He denied that this was his intention and decided to continue with weekly sessions of psychotherapy.

It is important, in therapy, to remember the old saw that sometimes a cigar is just a cigar (i.e., not every action has deep implications). Bobby's decision to cut down on his sessions was *not* aimed at me by way of his father. He just needed more time and money to pursue his degree. Yet even his gesture of support – his interest in continuing in therapy notwithstanding his other obligations – was still a decentering act. It moved our relationship somewhat toward the periphery of his world and, to that extent, reduced my own sense of playing a vital, pivotal role in his life. It's interesting how we trust patients to maintain their level of commitment and, when they do not, we may lose trust or confidence in ourselves more than in them. I realized that I wanted Bobby to continue with the same number of sessions because I felt like we were getting somewhere and I wanted the affirmation.

Of course, that realization made me recalibrate my sense of need and tell myself that I was being myopic. That is, I was doing what Mr. Silver had done, feeling special because I imagined myself at the center of Bobby's world – indeed, its most important inhabitant. Yet if I can now qualify that last statement somewhat (in my favor!), it is in fact routine among therapists to assert that the more frequent and involved the treatment is, the better the result. For neurotic conflicts, which tend to be more nuanced than typical psychiatric syndromes, more intense and longer treatments are seen as more useful, at least in the analytic community. I am not sure that I agree. But in any case, I think there is an element of sublimated self-interest in the claim, whose object is to reinforce the symbiotic trust relationship that I thought about when Bobby became "semi-retired" from therapy.

In any case, I did see advantages for Bobby in his not withdrawing altogether. In psychotherapy, I am able to call him out directly, whereas the process of classical analysis is based on allowing a patient to freely associate until some interpretation emerges. Making the unconscious conscious is a key idea. But sitting face to face with Bobby allowed for a more interpersonal process. I felt better able and inclined to help him deal with the practical realities of his life such as making good decisions about relationships, work choices, and family. I found that in the context of psychotherapy, the decreased frequency of sessions gave each session a more condensed quality. This is not to say that they dealt with more tangible realities. Rather, they worked more like dreams, being distillations of what was on Bobby's mind.

Because they worked well, we developed a new set of expectations – less overall intensity, but an increase in focus within each session. We had to trust the process, as much as each other – a vital component of therapy that is not sufficiently discussed. We had to assume that working together during more compressed sessions drew on each other's ingenuity to make the most of the time we had. We had to be especially candid. We did *not* just go with the flow, but, under the circumstances, we allowed the process to make demands which, in turn, called on our best efforts (as the management consultants say) to improve the time.

I recall one particularly telling incident – in my experience, patients tend to recall incidents from their past that actually become a measure of their present sense of progress. Bobby recalled that one evening, while he was away with his parents and older brother, the two boys were left in the hotel suite with a sitter. Bobby remembers having to go to the bathroom but not knowing where it was. He pooped himself, and his older brother made fun of him. Adding insult to injury, the sitter did not seem sure how to handle the situation and called the parents, who promptly returned and reprimanded him.

So, he was left feeling a sense of shame. Reflecting on that moment from early childhood helped him to lessen its impact and have more perspective on it as a not uncommon childhood experience. Bringing this experience to light from the perspective of adulthood helped him mitigate his sense of shame and doubt.

About a year after we began our new regime, Bobby referred his mother to me. She was depressed about her husband's physical ailments. Though I thought it best to refer her to a colleague, she still wanted to see me and Bobby was fine with it. I was struck by how similar Bobby was to his mother. Here was a key player in his personal past now before me in living color. I had previously been aware of his identification with his mother, but not so keenly. For example, she also saw herself as an artist but could never allow herself to pursue art. She was first of all a wife and mother. Bobby, however, could go for it, and going for an MFA was, in a sense, an enactment of his mother's own desire – a kind of gift to her, albeit a vicarious one.

Because I had a better sense of her from firsthand experience, I was able to make connections for Bobby with greater clarity and confidence. Any notion that he was trying to spite me to spite his father went down the tubes for good. Rather, he was taking up a path that his mother would have pursued herself. If I had ever lacked trust in him, I now had grounds to dispel that feeling. I came to see them both as committed to an aesthetic calling, which Bobby had now trusted to define his career. This proved to be an amazing set of consequences.

Afterward, however, I asked myself why I had needed so much empirical evidence to trust a patient. I realized that trust is fragile, and that we frequently allow our own uncertainties to undermine it. I don't think this is entirely avoidable. Maybe I just shouldn't let my patients know.

Erikson's next stage of development took up the subject of will, roughly Freud's anal stage, in which a young child deals with issues of independence and control. For Erikson, the central conflict to be resolved was autonomy versus shame and doubt. Here, the role of a parent is to instill in the child a sense that he can do basic tasks by himself, which eventually translates into a feeling of self-confidence. Practicing and rehearsing tasks, falling short, and even failing are an important part of the process of learning and becoming self-correcting. If the child does not feel competent, then shame and doubt tend to develop. Successfully navigating this stage leads to self-esteem and trust in oneself. But any such trust is continually vulnerable to experience – if it is battered too often, even as an older child and into adolescence, it will falter. Trust in oneself needs to be reinforced by positive encounters that allow a person to feel successful.

Psychoanalytic training

I listened to a presentation today about supervising a candidate in psychoanalytic training. The candidate had been involved in a case concerning a disturbed patient with childhood trauma. He had done a good job on the clinical work and in presenting his work to his supervisor. However, during one supervision, he told the supervisor that he had been recording sessions with the patient, unbeknownst to both patient and supervisor. His rationale was that he would then be able to present his work in a more clear and thorough manner.

This was seen as an "ethical violation." That is, recording was not allowed in the clinical situation. But why? We make handwritten notes on patients all the time without their consent. Furthermore, if the recordings are for our own personal clinical work, it is not obvious to me that this is a breach of some sort. But the supervisor felt that at the very least, the candidate had shown poor judgment by not making the patient aware of the situation and not obtaining her consent. To her credit, the supervisor handled the matter in a caring, professional manner. She discussed her concerns with the candidate, pointing out considerations of patient welfare and trust that he had overlooked. The candidate then explained to the patient his interest in recording future sessions and obtained her consent. He did not bring his past impropriety to the patient's attention because he and the supervisor felt that this might disrupt the treatment and even harm a fragile patient.

Such caring supervision is not always characteristic of psychoanalytic training. In my experience, the system is draconian and punitive. You can advance yourself by finding fault, even more than by supporting a constructive learning experience. Candidates' work, or even their characters, may be discredited by slight infractions and their careers as analysts negatively impacted. There is no system of checks and balances in place, but only winks and nods. Yet here we saw a different modus operandi, where the supervisor had sufficient trust in a candidate's ability to follow the rules – once their importance was explained – to counsel him rather than apply punishment. In training, trust is based on seeing the professional emergent in the candidate, and crediting his or her potential. This ability to look ahead at the therapist-to-be is crucial if trust is to run both ways during training. Otherwise, there will be a certain condescension in one direction and "fear and loathing" in another. The learning experience will be undermined.

Finally, where there is an atmosphere of trust, candidates will have a sense of freedom, which is necessary if they are to take prudent chances. This candidate did take chances, and when he was reined in, he learned about certain boundaries and why they exist. Ultimately, he advanced his own work, obtaining consent to make future recordings. In the context of therapeutic training, trust amounts to sharing a sense of mission – the mission to produce competent therapists. If defined in this way, trust should come naturally, without having to be earned on the one hand or questioned on the other. This type of trust also prefigures the trust required once the therapist begins to practice and has a series of mentors. The object of training, which carries on through mentorship, is for new therapists to learn when and how to trust themselves (i.e., their developing capabilities to help patients).

> When children have the ability to do things on their own, they take the initiative and develop a sense of purpose. They create their own games and activities. But if this creativity becomes stunted, the child can develop a sense of guilt, possibly because it sees such initiative as competing with the same-sex parent. This also corresponds to Freud's Oedipal stage of development. Within this reconfiguration, a boy's competitive feelings toward his father for his mother's love—and a girl's competitive feelings toward her mother for her father—are a part of childhood development.
>
> However, these feelings may become exaggerated. In Bobby's case, his father began to develop a post-polio syndrome, a degenerative neurological condition, when Bobby was around 5. So, as Bobby's competitive strivings were gearing up, his father was becoming crippled. This added to Bobby's sense of guilt and led to inhibitions regarding his own pursuits. As he explored these feelings in therapy, he gained insight into them and found himself better able to pursue interests with a sense of purpose. He gained a greater sense of trust in his father's support for his endeavours.

Freudian slips

During his session yesterday, Dan said "Keep your enemies close, and your friends closer." He was talking about a friend at work with whom he had a complicated relationship. I knew the quote as "Keep your friends close, and your enemies closer" and, had I heeded its advice, I would have been a better friend. Accordingly, I corrected him.

Dan laughed at his reversal of an old saying, and called it a "Freudian slip." But the slip stung. In fact, Dan was in therapy because he could not trust people with whom he was close. He would question their motivations and put them on the spot over trivia. He could not help himself, even when people pointed out that he was being irrational. When his friends withdrew, he would try to compensate with excessive flattery – making matters worse by topping off his distrust by seeming manipulative.

He had been abused as a child and molested by his father and, while that provided an "excuse" in *his* mind, and would certainly cause a therapist to explore his past, he still could not explain to people that mistrusting everything they said was merely the result of childhood trauma. In matters of trust, people tend to feel that they have earned it on their own terms with their own actions, and that ghosts from the past have no business muddying their integrity.

Since Dan was inured to a constant round of fizzled friendships, the prospect of marriage scared him. Could he sustain the closeness? Would his wife tolerate what he feared would become unremitting scrutiny? He imagined her feeling like a specimen under a microscope with no room to move. Apparently, he loved his girlfriend and wanted to marry her, but they had already had disputes involving his ability to trust. She felt that she could never be good enough for him because marriage required acceptance, and he couldn't accept anyone. He was on his best behavior with her, but still called her out on the silliest things. Moreover, when they were out with friends, she was acutely embarrassed by his sudden fits of obvious mistrust. What Dan needed now, he said, was some way to catch himself in the act – he felt that the motivation to mistrust would never be conquered, but he wanted "techniques" to contain it.

But therapy is not just a fix for noxious symptoms. If it works, if it helps the patient to understand and deal with causes and can provide a cure for underlying problems. In our sessions, Dan talked about relationships with significant others from his past, and I observed that at least with me he had been open and honest. I considered this a good sign because as our relationship developed, his candor was evidence of (at least some) capacity to trust. He had in fact talked about some especially sensitive issues the previous week that he had not discussed with anyone before.

I told Dan to regard me as a test case. If he could continue his candor, and rely on how I responded, then we could create a template for other relationships. He could, in effect, develop transferable skills. That is, therapy could provide a safe space, a place to "practice" and test out desired behavior before going public with it. Patients frequently comment on this phenomenon and say that they appreciate a secure space of confidentiality that is separate from the "real" world. But I tell them, as I told Dan, that therapy is the real world, just one where we work to produce understanding – a less tangible product, perhaps, but as necessary all the same.

Still, I cautioned Dan that transition from therapy to the larger world would not be painless. Just as he had to confront the destructive effects of childhood abuse, he had to stop relying on it to excuse his impulse to mistrust. He did not have the luxury to keep forgiving himself, even with a psychologically plausible explanation, since this only prevented his getting on with life as he wanted to live it. At some point, the instinct for survival kicks in and gets the better of interfering impulses unless we prop them up. Dan's job was to stop interfering with his own vital interests.

Psychotherapists are like tutors, rather than teachers. The psychotherapeutic situation is personalized, where each patient is taught to learn more about his or her thoughts, feelings, and motivating fantasies. By learning to trust in me, Dan became better about trusting other people in his life. He became more open and capable of greater intimacy.

The situation was very different with Blair, whose situation I describe below. Sometimes resistance to therapy overcomes the patient's capacity to trust their own responses to it, or the therapist's capacity to instil any such trust.

Resistance

Blair began today's session by joking about yesterday's session, which she had missed because – she claimed – she had "overslept." But, as it turned out, she had deliberately set her alarm for an hour past when she needed to get up, a feint I had seen with other patients. So, when I thought to ask "Why are you playing games?" I didn't. We both knew what this little ploy meant. She missed yesterday's session for some reason other than catching up on sleep. Was there something she didn't want to discuss?

Blair was settling into a new job and always seemed to be rushed. She had actually missed a few sessions, each time citing work but leaving me to wonder. I tried to find out what was up. As we continued to talk, she indicated that while things were "progressing" with her boyfriend – they were taking trips together – there was no emotional progress. The relationship, she said, was "okay." After a while, I found her idealizing her new job while skirting the central, emotional issue with her boyfriend.

Toward the end of the hour, I observed, "You know, some of the difficulty you've had in deepening your relationship, and the personal issues you had at your last job, relate to difficulties you have in getting close to people. That's true in your relationship with me as well. As soon as we decided that you'd come more often, you began missing sessions." She made some further excuses. I said that more frequent psychotherapy could be an opportunity to work on those issues. She concurred. We agreed again on two sessions per week and set two morning times.

However, just as she was leaving, she said, "Oh, that Monday time conflicts with my personal trainer." I looked at her with an eyebrow raised. "I'll try to rearrange it," she added.

This was anticlimactic. After she acknowledged her problem and her resistance to dealing with it, she fell back into an old pattern of excusing herself from hard emotional work. She knew that her stalled relationship with her boyfriend, like her withdrawal from me, meant that she preferred limbo to actually addressing her issues with intimacy. I needed – we needed – to discover the causes of these issues. But I had no idea if she would return, with or without a commitment to hard psychological work. She was a classic case of sublimating one type of work in another, showing up at the office while skipping the work of therapy.

In such instances, the therapist asks what he or she could have done differently. Blair is not "neurotic," and at one level is entirely aware of her problems. But she hides behind off-putting insouciance and an only partly defensible professionalism. She makes excuses. Of course, excuses are a type of shorthand. My hunch is that if Blair's could be written out, they would reveal a kind of mistrust in the outcome of relationships. She seems not to have developed along the usual lines that lead to trust and self-confidence. This could be one fruitful inquiry, among others. Trust is hard to gauge, but now I have my antennae out.

If I do not hear from her in a while, I will be faced with whether to make excuses to myself: "Well, I tried." Such patients can be maddening because one finds oneself using their language, or at least potentially using it. I will have to ask myself whether I tried hard *enough*. I am tempted to ask Blair since, in thinking about our relationship, she may think again about her other relationships.

It has been my experience, however, that in cases like Blair's the most effective "treatment" is beyond my control. If Blair comes to see that because of a failure to trust she has lost someone's high regard, she may come around. Blair has to experience the consequences of her action painfully ... rather than flitting from job to boyfriend to job without too much suffering. I would never wish suffering on anyone, but sometimes it shakes us out of complacency. I haven't said this to Blair, and she may learn it before I do. It may be hard for her to take in if, somewhere in her past, she has been hurt because she was trusting. Therapy could help her calibrate these two possibilities. However, until she can trust in me, she won't trust the process of therapy. It's going to be a challenge even getting to first base.

Murphy's Law

"Murphy's Law," not exactly on a level with $e = mc^2$, states that "Anything that *can* go wrong will go wrong." It applies mainly to late-night comedy, though sometimes it still has consequences. Its genuinely scholarly counterpart, however, is the High Impact Low Probability phenomenon, which holds that something will be catastrophic in the unlikely event that it occurs. Think airplane crashes or lightning strikes. Yet, for most people, neither of these makes much difference, since their appropriate "risk management" protocol is just to take care and avoid obvious danger.

Mr. Lauren's professional difficulties derived, in part, from an overly trusting nature and an inclination not to be sufficiently careful. Some of our conversations, therefore, focused on his making deliberate efforts to take *more* care (e.g., to slow down, imagine any potential fallout, and then figure out how to mitigate it). I told him to write the future in advance (with all its potential screwups) and then rewrite it so that it came out without his losing his shirt. For this, he had to suspend what appeared to be his basic assumptions that

- Someone else would fix whatever went wrong, and
- He would not be blamed for putting them to that effort.

In other words, he had to take responsibility and, while not overtly distrusting people, still manage situations so as not to force them into cleaning up his messes. He had to calibrate trust in others with trust in himself to do the right thing initially. But finding out how to trust himself – when he had very little experience with it – would be a challenge.

Sound practices that were obvious to his colleagues were not so clear to him. So, we talked about how he might improve by developing a set of best practices and, in general, learning to Think First. We discussed record keeping, consulting with colleagues, and reading the fine print. We discussed slowing down. During the course of treatment, we identified chronic issues and tried to address them before they produced toxic blowback.

Over time, I inquired into why an intelligent and capable man would not be more self-protective. What emerged was a not-too-subconscious wish that his father would save him from life's slings and arrows. This had its basis in his early home life. While Mr. Lauren's mother was dogged in pursuing her own needs and hounded him capriciously, his father would come home at night, humor his mother, and protect him. Mr. Lauren acknowledged a wish to reenact a childhood in which his father reliably intervened for his benefit. At work, he played the role of a child, trusting that he would be delivered from any nasty consequences. If some figures in this recreated world were unkind, others were all-powerful and would take charge of everything. Mr. Lauren could sit back and watch.

As we explored his fixation on his father – the very opposite of Oedipal competition – Mr. Lauren was able to become more adult (i.e., less trusting of others to salvage his mistakes and more trusting in himself to avoid mistakes in the first place). But this was a difficult and challenging process. We had to examine the notion of misplaced trust and how trust can become distorted into an instrument of self-denial. Now Mr. Lauren literally practices where to place his trust and how much to confer on any individual. Concomitantly, he practices how to avoid calling on those he trusts by first calling on himself to do things carefully. He does not undertake tasks that are beyond his competence and is no longer afraid of seeking help with something new. In other words, unsaddled with fantasies of his father, he acts like most people.

Eventually, he will learn to push the envelope of his competence, especially working in teams. In teams, no one has to know everything, but everyone must carry their own weight. But once he is freed of overreliance on others, he will be able to determine the types of teams to join. At no point, however, should he just eschew taking risks. That would be self-defeating and prevent him from learning anything. *It's okay to ask for help when there is a challenge,* just not okay to start out indifferent to the risk environment, on the assumption that it doesn't matter.

Risk management always allows for putting oneself (prudently) in the way of new experience. As I discovered at the start of my career, such venturing out is the best way to develop trust in oneself. The story below is an example.

Getting in touch with myself

Last night at dinner, a young doctor discussed his excitement about being a doctor and now becoming a surgeon. He spoke with such pride about his rotations through a trauma center and the cases in which he had assisted. He loved his medical training and was really into what he was doing.

I felt envious. I have had difficulty fully embracing modern, Western medicine. I'm a doctor, but I tend to think of myself as a healer. I went into medicine partly through playing guitar, which I am not very good at. In college, I used to play for patients in the local hospital one or two evenings a week. I would joke that they were a captive audience and had to listen.

But there was something special, even therapeutic, about those interactions. Between songs, people would talk about what ailed them. A boy talked about his anxiety over not being able to breathe because of a pulmonary condition. Older people brought up their thoughts and fears about death and suffering. Everyone talked about their lives outside the hospital as if to reach beyond its sterile confines. Talking was a way of staying connected and not being isolated by one's medical condition and hospital walls.

These visits were a way of connecting for me, too. The path to healing is a two-way street. It runs through the encounters we make on life's journey. But as I thought about this give-and-take, the act of thinking took on a life of its own. I realized that I wanted to understand the connections that I made as much as I wanted to experience the feelings that they imparted. I wanted to stand outside the connections, not just bob up and down in them. Finally, I realized that I wanted both – the critical distance to analyze the nature of connection as well as the immediacy on which connection is predicated. That is when I determined to become a psychotherapist.

Now, as a practitioner, I realize that some of the most important challenges we face in changing our lives for the better are internal. If connection provides us the wherewithal to come to grips with ourselves, then it is working. I have learned to live in my mind enough to trust my reactions to the world as I perceive it. Going to medical school, becoming a psychiatrist, was an act of trust. I could not have developed that trust – that self-confidence in how I should be in the world – had I not had the series of experiences that led me to my choices. Ultimately, trust in oneself is the product of reflection on a lot of important information. Once we get past childhood, trust building continues, starting with the self and ramifying outward. But it can only come after experiencing life and registering its effect. It does no good to be so self-protective that we do not venture.

Further Reading

Brenner, Charles. *The Mind in Conflict*. New York: International Universities Press, 1986.
Erikson, Erik. *Childhood and Society*. New York: W.W. Norton & Company, 1950.
Freud, Sigmund. *The Interpretation of Dreams*. Translated by A. A. Brill. New York: The Macmillan Company, 1913.
Herman, Judith. *Trauma and Recovery: The Aftermath of Violence – From Domestic Abuse to Political Terror*. New York: Basic Books, 1992.
Hirsch, Irwin. *Coasting in the Countertransference: Conflicts of Self-Interest Between Analyst and Patient*. London: Routledge, 2008.
Kahneman, Daniel. *Thinking, Fast and Slow*. New York: Farrar, Straus and Giroux, 2013.
Kohut, Heinz. *The Analysis of the Self: A Systematic Approach to the Psychoanalytic Treatment of Narcissistic Personality Disorders*. Chicago: The University of Chicago Press, 1971.
Kottler, Jeffrey, and Jon Carlson. *On Being a Master Therapist: Practicing What You Preach*. Hoboken, NJ: John Wiley & Sons, 2014.
Ogden, Thomas. *The Matrix of the Mind: Object Relations and the Psychoanalytic Dialogue*. Lanham, MD: Rowman & Littlefield Publishers, Inc., 1990.
Pfaff, Donald, and Sandra Sherman. *The Altruistic Brain: How We Are Naturally Good*. Oxford: Oxford University Press, 2015.
Phillips, Adam. *The Beast in the Nursery: On Curiosity and Other Appetites*. New York: Vintage Books, 1998.
Searles, Harold. *Countertransference and Related Subject: Selected Papers*. New York: International Universities Press, 1979.
Teyber, Edward, and Faith Holmes Teyber. *Interpersonal Process in Therapy: An Integrative Model*. Belmont, CA: Cengage Learning, 2017.

3 Time and money

Time and money converge in the concept of work. When someone performs work, the money expended to compensate them is calibrated against the value of what they produced during the time expended. In both cases, there is an "expenditure" because <u>both</u> time and money are commodities – not abstractions – that are traded during the course of employment or, in the case of therapy, over the course of treatment. A patient spends time with the therapist and expects tangible results; therapists spend time with patients and expect financial compensation. Psychotherapists do not like to talk about how they are paid, but, in fact, the issue can become a stand-in for the therapeutic relationship – talking about time and money is, in many instances, talking <u>about</u> the relationship.

Of course, therapists counsel patients concerning their relationship to money, which can reflect on how they navigate through relationships where money is an issue. But beyond any simple 1:1 correspondence between relating-to-money and relating-to-people, money ties in with feelings of self-esteem. If you lose a job and have trouble finding another, your sense of self can plummet. Money can be a signifier of who we think we are. It meets up with issues of time when, for example, children yearn for their parents' attention but just receive a check. Children know this is a false equivalence and can carry their resentment into adulthood.

This chapter examines time and money from a kaleidoscope of perspectives. The two commodities emerge as very hard to separate, compounding the complexity of each.

Missed appointments

We had a nor'easter today. The wind, with gusts over 50 mph., blew tree limbs onto cars and into the street. Construction cranes were tied down. It made sense that some patients cancelled appointments. One elderly woman said she was taking a sick day from her volunteer job at a pet hospice and would not be seeing me either. That was fine with me, since I imagined her getting blown off the stairs to my office and taking a fall.

However, other patients cancelled as well, and I became suspicious. Freud said that we have two "reasons" for doing things: the good reason and the real reason. For instance, Mrs. Singh, a relatively new patient, called almost as soon as the National Oceanic and Atmospheric Administration (NOAA) put out an alert for our region. Was this "real"? I have my own alert concerning some patients. I knew that Mrs. Singh had mixed feelings about being in treatment, especially because she came from a culture where discussing problems is perceived as a weakness. Growing up, she felt disadvantaged if she left herself emotionally open and vulnerable. So, while she ostensibly cancelled because of the weather, I knew she was unable to ignore her underlying feelings of shame and embarrassment and, hence, vulnerability about being in treatment.

We had spoken about her initial reluctance to seek therapy and then to let anyone know about it. I tried to educate her that in America the mores of her old culture did not apply and need not stand in the way of getting help. But now, since she did not show up, I think my approach was mistaken. While people emigrate to this country for "opportunity," that does not mean that they can – or even want to – let go of a native culture that they see as part of who they are. Letting go seems somehow a betrayal of their country and themselves. In fact, they cling to their old identity as a shield, a protection from venturing too far into a new, bewildering, and possibly threatening culture. In effect, they are rejecting the freedom to be other than who they are, even if that otherness may also seem attractive. I realized that Mrs. Singh's ambivalence toward therapy was, therefore, an ambivalence about her place in this culture. To antagonize her old culture, as I did, only made her more self-protective, more willing to dig in and resist a very American self-help strategy: psychotherapy. It made her withdraw into an identity that she knew and recognized.

I could also see that by cancelling her appointment, Mrs. Singh resisted spending money on therapy and, thereby, investing therapy (so to speak) with value. In effect, she was treating therapy as an abstraction, something outside the realm of value that she did not have to acknowledge in specific, concrete terms. Therapy could remain an idea, a route to healing that other people pursued but that she could reject *without calculable loss*. If Mrs. Singh does show up to her next appointment, I plan to talk with her about using money – and failing to spend money – as a means of devaluing what is problematic and finessing having to deal with the problem. She may display this type of conduct in an array of difficult challenges as she navigates this new culture, withdrawing to a safe space by holding back on how she bestows value on the new.

As it turns out, it is probably useful that she cancelled her appointment, since she exposed what I think are some coping techniques, or actually avoidance techniques, that we need to address. Ultimately, these may be more significant than the vague uneasiness that she came to see me for in the first place. If she is able to find sufficient will to remain in treatment, we could make some real progress with regard to her integrating into this culture and giving herself "opportunity."

Another patient, Cathy, e-mailed to say that the weather was also the reason for her cancellation. I replied that it was okay, but to feel free to call me before our scheduled hour since the nor'easter was supposed to pass. But she chose not to call. So, when we next meet, I plan to ask why. There may be several "real" reasons, including what I suspect may be sublimated frustration with me. Cathy and I have worked for several years to overcome her shyness and social inhibitions. She has made tangible gains in developing closer relationships with colleagues, fostering a better connection with her family, and even pursuing her dating life more energetically. But she hasn't been able to sustain a committed romantic relationship despite our best efforts. So, I think that cancellation was her way of saying, "I am upset that our efforts did not produce a boyfriend. You wasted my time."

Just as Mrs. Singh measured the value of treatment in financial terms, Cathy did the same in terms of her time. We have been working together for years – so why are we *still* working? In one sense, this is a legitimate question, since the end point of her treatment remains elusive. But in another sense, Cathy is being willful, making demands of the process that are palliative but premature. It's easy to blame therapy, embodied in me, for a personal failure. It is easy to tick off months and years and then call "Time Out!" So, I need to remind Cathy that simply blaming me would be unproductive, even the real waste of time, and that we need to remain focussed on why she still has shyness issues (she is even shy about telling me explicitly that she is annoyed). I will ask her to express her feelings about the value of therapy directly and then carry that forthrightness out into the dating arena. Shyness is ultimately unattractive where it prevents a potential romantic attachment from achieving intimacy. I need to help her understand that if she is concerned about time, she is unintentionally stalling her own romantic ambitions by not displaying her feelings.

Both these patients have problems with directness, transposing onto money and time their "real," deeper reasons for skipping therapy. I wonder if Freud had patients who offered similar excuses during foul Viennese winters. But what matters now is that in asking these women to address why they actually cancelled their appointments they may begin to see that acting out an apparent hostility to therapy was only a short-term fix. In the longer term, they still have work to do … if they are willing to stop blaming the messenger.

People often test one another, consciously or subconsciously, concerning the exchange of time for money. In beginning a course of therapy, the patient may ask him- or herself whether the therapist wishes to help or is just intent on earning a living. While there is, of course, an element of both in our work – as in any professional relationship – I advise residents to keep their eye on the person, not the payment. As mental health professionals, we are by definition in the healing professions, and we should act like that.

Nevertheless, questions arise. For example, when a patient misses an appointment, do you charge for the session? The logic of the relationship says, "Of course, it's my time and they wasted it." But the logic of healing says, "Not so fast ... there could be reasons." Most therapists set out rules in advance and prefer not to get into sticky situations that can produce bad feelings all around. But, since patients miss appointments for all sorts of potentially revealing reasons, it may be best to take an ad hoc approach.

Either way, if you finally do charge, the patient may become upset or angry. It is worth exploring their reaction, since it can expose issues involving their feelings toward therapy and, indeed, toward spending money. If you don't charge, however, that can also be cause for discussion, since the patient may see this as permission to devalue therapy and take it for granted. He or she might do less of the work that therapy demands.

The point is that whatever a clinician does has meaning to the patient, and that may be useful to examine at one point or another.

A scheduling error

I made a mistake today and scheduled two patients during the same hour. This happens every two years or so and leaves me wondering whether I had the type of subconscious motivation that I routinely look for in my patients. Part of the risk in psychotherapy is that it can pitch into reverse, and you become your own patient. In this instance, I cast around for a quick explanation that would stop me from spiralling into my own issues, and I made an executive decision: I had misused the calendar app on my iPad. Mundane, but perfect. Thank goodness for technology, since it is easy to blame and does not try to excuse itself when you would rather not consider alternative explanations. So, I suspect that part of our addiction to technology is that it is a "secret sharer" in our machinations to elude inconvenient outbreaks of self-discovery. It not only takes the blame but, because of its infernal complexity, always provides plausible deniability when we may actually be at fault. I try to use this fallback sparingly ... just to remain in range of plausibility.

But back to my overbooked patients. One of them was new, and I was seeing her in consultation for a second visit. The other, Mrs. Wright, was an established patient who was still ambivalent about treatment. This reflected her mixed feelings about moving forward with other aspects of her life. She had taken several weeks off, and I had scheduled this other patient in what had been her time slot. The iPad might have alerted me to any possible conflict, but it didn't. So, I realized my mistake only minutes before the session, and by that time I could not reach either patient. No wonder, since both of them were in my waiting room with their phones turned off.

Ultimately, I did what I could and decided to use the mistake – which in my own mind I had already explained – to broach an issue with Mrs. Wright that I had been thinking about. I rescheduled the new patient, and Mrs. Wright came in for her session.

I pointed out that when I had made such mistakes in the past, a patient with whom I had an ongoing relationship would recognize my human error and perhaps even forgive me. But now I wanted to examine what happened in terms of our broader relationship and problems she was experiencing that perhaps were undermining it. We began, therefore, by acknowledging that a therapist's mistake can be a learning experience for both parties; a mistake that negatively affects the patient is an early warning sign. She was glad I brought this up, since it relieved her from having to say something or, worse, do something indirectly that could have been hurtful to me.

As I presented it, my mistake may have reflected what I felt to be Mrs. Wright's conflicted feelings toward therapy and may have sublimated my inability to tell her directly that I was resentful. I could see, ironically, that she felt we were finally in sync as I was telling her we weren't. Therapy sometimes makes for theatre – what used to be known as closet drama, to account for the vanishingly small audiences. But in any case, we both knew that after years together our relationship was fraying and that she was ambivalent enough without my purposely substituting another patient in what she still regarded as "her time." A patient can seem carefree or even cavalier about therapy and skip multiple sessions, while still being possessive as to the time in which she could – however hypothetically – receive that unwanted treatment.

I allowed that I was probably annoyed with her. She was struggling with issues involving the next phase of her marriage, becoming pregnant, and letting go of a still-lingering liaison with a former boss. I knew these factors had an influence on her missing sessions, not least because she felt overwhelmed and probably cringed over dredging up what she preferred just to ignore. But I still took her missing sessions seriously and, as we talked, I asked whether I had not helped enough with these matters. She acknowledged feeling that way, but at least we had gotten the issue out in the open. I told her that was a good next step in our relationship, and she agreed. But I assumed that she was still weighing whether the fallout from my mistake represented a new burst of candor or just the last gasp of bathos in a relationship that had run its course.

She may initially have taken my mistake as saying, "I have other patients besides you, even new ones," so that nothing I subsequently said could have persuaded her otherwise. As on many occasions in life, we may have missed our moment, and any chance for reconciliation may have come and gone before this mistake ever occurred. Usually, when we examine psychological meaning, the precipitating factor comes from the patient. Here it was the reverse, and a patient more committed to therapy would readily have accepted that my apparent preemption of her time for another patient's appointment represented a chance to renew our relationship. But there is rarely a perfect setting in which to fall short.

I am interested to see how Mrs. Wright responds. She may decide that with everything that is going on in her life, she has no time for therapy and will therefore relinquish her claim on what has been her "time" with me. As I write this sentence, I have a sense of time's fluidity – how it runs in and out of quotation marks even as it runs from the patient's life into my life as a therapist and a resentful human being. When I see this new patient tomorrow, I will keep my mistake in mind and try to learn from it, not act as if the mistake never happened. But I am going to wonder if they will weigh my mistake in considering whether I was too casual with their time and how that should affect their willingness to spend more of it with me.

It is important to own our mistakes. This is often the first step in learning from them. If you do not acknowledge that you have done something wrong, then it is hard to behave differently moving forward. Sometimes we make a mistake when we don't know better. Sometimes we know better but for one reason or another, conscious or unconscious, we get things wrong. We may be tempted or coerced, but generally it's good to own a problematic act and acknowledge to oneself the reason for what we did.

Mistakes happen in treatment, though some are more evident than others – at least to the therapist, if not the patient. For example, a psychiatrist might give a patient who is depressed an antidepressive medication. Usually, that is an effective intervention. But, on occasion, it might make the patient hypomanic or even manic. We have to ask why. Did the patient have a history of bipolarity? Was he or she aware of that condition in the family? If not, then the mistake may be excusable. On the other hand, if the psychiatrist did not take a careful history, then the fault may lie with him.

In psychodynamic treatments, we may make observations based on limited knowledge or even blurt out an insensitive comment. In trying to be helpful, we can sometimes act without thinking through a case sufficiently. This can occur because we <u>think</u> we know the patient. That is, in the same way that patients have their transference to us as parental or sibling figures, we have our transference to them. This is called countertransference. Growing up, my mother sometimes kept *me waiting – we would be late for an appointment, miss a lesson, or miss a play date. Maybe there was some of my old frustration in how I reacted to Mrs. Wright's missed appointments.*

Criticism

When Mr. Lauren was first in analysis, he felt that he was being blamed for not getting better. In his view, he had done his best and was a conscientious patient. He kept his sessions, spoke as openly as he could about whatever was on his mind, reported dreams and fantasies, tried to listen to what was said, and paid his bill on time. He told me, however, that on one occasion several years into treatment, his analyst told him, "You get two percent out of what you might by coming here." He felt hurt by this remark, especially since his sacrifices to be in treatment – both in time and money – had been considerable. And to add insult to injury, at one point the analyst threatened to "blow the whistle on it," claiming that the process was not sufficiently "analytic" (e.g., Mr. Lauren had not gone deep enough to justify continuing the analysis). To which Mr. Lauren responded, "Who would go all out this way if they weren't into it?"

In all of what Mr. Lauren said, I picked up on his sense of "sacrifice." In his mind, this not only transformed his investment of time and money into something that merited a payback of deference and concern, but also signified a level of commitment which the analyst should have taken into account before placing all the blame on him. In other words, if he had sacrificed so much, maybe some of the blame for his poor response rested with the analyst or even with the process of analysis itself. Indeed, I find this kind of reaction common, in that where the patient gives up spending money or time in order to pursue therapy, he or she feels that criticism based on a poor response to therapy should be mild and slow in coming. "Sacrifice" buys a sense of entitlement which, if it becomes apparent, can infuriate a therapist who also feels that he is performing at his best. So, you get into an entitlement trap where the more a patient sacrifices without measurable results, the more the therapist needs to hold his tongue if he wants to keep the patient.

But this is self-defeating on both counts since *unless* the therapist says something, as I did with Mrs. Wright, the less likely it is that there will be any results. The only solution is to say something firmly enough to get the patient's attention but nicely enough not to cause offence. Of course, since Mr. Lauren felt that he had been doing everything right, and that any failure to respond was not entirely his fault, it was probably necessary to thoughtfully discuss the patient/therapist relationship. This is a hard discussion to initiate for either party – as, in fact, I demonstrated with my own sublimating actions.

By the time Mr. Lauren came to me, hindsight had only exacerbated his sense of having been harshly judged. He kept thinking about what the therapist said, with that typical miserable sense of how he *should* have replied. As I listened to his account of their exchanges, which were still fresh in his mind, I heard drama again, this time an enactment of intrapsychic conflict embedded in the analytic situation. There was an obvious transference, where the analyst assumed the role of Mr. Lauren's hostile mother. Once this hostility became manifest, it took on a life of its own and could hardly be reversed. It would have stymied the flow of treatment – and made criticism seem even more imminently threatening than it was – since Mr. Lauren wanted at least on some level to flee his mother.

The analyst felt frustrated by what was going on in the treatment and would occasionally ask "What's going on here?" as if to invite his patient to explore with him the conditions that were holding them back. Mr. Lauren resented the question, however, since he thought it was only rhetorical and that the analyst had demonstrated incontrovertibly that he thought everything was Mr. Lauren's fault. I didn't hear that in what sounded like a genuine plea for mutual exploration but, without being preceded by an apology, I can see where Mr. Lauren just heard more criticism. I felt that Mr. Lauren wanted me to play Good Cop to the analyst's Bad Cop, virtually asking that I agree with how he interpreted the analyst's request. It is hard being put in that position, however, so I said that it would be most helpful to Mr. Lauren if rather than just dwelling on his previous treatment, we might reflect on it and try to work through some of his thoughts and feelings about it. That comported with our commitment to try again and do better.

However, it was hard for Mr. Lauren to let go of what was on his mind and that, he said, drove him to see another therapist to correct a wrong that had been done him. This time, he felt his sacrifice of time and money should be worth it. I didn't feel as if he was putting a burden on me, but I wondered if perhaps he was excusing himself in advance if the treatment was less than successful. He was returning to therapy after several months, still feeling wounded about how he was treated. He also thought that had he been treated with more understanding, he might have improved – was I supposed to treat him gingerly, or also risk being seen as hostile?

It's hard to create the collaborative relationship that is so important in our work. Sustaining it is crucial, and I felt he was undermining our ability to go the distance by imposing some cost/benefit analysis (better suited to buying a second home, e.g., than investing in an open-ended course of treatment). So, I told Mr. Lauren that in trying to build our relationship, he had to let go of the idea that spending time and money on therapy was a "sacrifice." Rather, he should think of his outlays as investments in or even milestones along the road to recovery. I was not recommending some Pollyanna trick but, instead, that he view his expenditures as the objective correlative of his commitment. He had to start from the assumption that his time and money were well spent on treatment.

In effect, I was asking him to assume my perspective and let go of his. I thought my perspective was justified because I knew more about therapy than he did. If he remained stuck in his way of measuring success against his personal expenditures, he might again become frustrated or even dismayed. I had seen this in other patients and hoped we could get past it.

Yet, I also knew that it's risky to advise a patient to commit to therapy because I am a therapist and strongly believe in it. It could sound self-serving, especially to someone who believes he has been burned. So, I tried another approach, which I hoped we could both "invest" in. This was that his re-entering therapy with me recalled the movie *Rashomon*, Akira Kurosawa's great exploration of how multiple perspectives complicate the past. I could not be certain of what happened between him and his first analyst, even though he seemed to recall it vividly. He could not be certain of whether his analyst was reaching out or just casting more blame. The analyst was probably uncertain of what was "going on," and so asked that pretty amorphous question. Our only course was to start from scratch, where he agreed to leave his old way of measuring progress behind, while I assumed that he was amenable to the hard work that the other analyst seemed to discount. Therapy proceeds through knowledge that patient and therapist establish together as they build trust. He promised to stop putting me on the spot with talk about sacrifice and correcting a wrong and to start building. Perhaps we're on our way.

> I actually knew Mr. Lauren's first psychoanalyst. He was accomplished and well-respected and had made contributions to the field. He even coined the term "enactment," which refers to how analyst and patient engage in a drama where transference and countertransference play out and can come to a head. One transference that Mr. Lauren had to his first analyst was material, such that he experienced analysis as an anxiety-provoking haircut – administered by his mother as he was growing up. His analyst had a younger brother who had also become an analyst, so I wondered whether countertransference may also have played out in moments during Mr. Lauren's analysis.
>
> Generally, as long as patients see that we are trying to help, they will forgive most of our errors. Such occasions provide opportunities where both parties can. There is an idea in the literature called "negative therapeutic reaction," where, ostensibly, the analyst gets everything right but the patient does not get better or may even be worse. But this notion seems a bit self-serving, since if treatment does not produce an overall improvement, we should question ourselves and our approach. Talking over our possible mistakes with patients can provide helpful insights and, ideally, a way forward toward improvement.

Late payments

Mary has not paid her bill for four months, and I'm unaccustomed to a patient's taking such a long payment "holiday" while still receiving treatment. Of course, she insists that she wants to pay, but can't just now because of high expenses – a claim that I may collude in because I hate feeling like some businessman, selling services like computer repair. As I told Mr. Lauren, therapist and patient are in this together, committed to sustaining their relationship over the course of treatment. I want to assume that she will pay. And yet … she is earning more than she has been and recently got promoted. She and her husband just leased a better car and are talking about buying a house.

Mary has chronic problems with money. When she came into treatment ten years ago, she was nearly bankrupt. While she finally paid down what she owed, she now seems to feel entitled to binge or at least indulge on occasion. I may be collateral damage. Ironically, Mary is not in treatment for her spending habits, but, as is often the case, therapy discovers issues as it proceeds. We may, therefore, need to consider her problems with money even apart from agreeing on a payment plan.

I do not want to issue Mary an ultimatum – "Pay me, or else!" – since we have made progress. She has been able to raise a lovely daughter, she vastly improved her family relationships, and she achieved a stable relationship with her common-law husband. But I think that in focussing on the husband, we may get to the root of her current financial issues. Her husband is an actor with only sporadic income. He seems to feel that devotion to Art justifies his being out of work, and Mary has never openly challenged his claim. I have tried to help her understand that her difficulty in confronting him is more about her than him. She believes that telling him to get a job – half of New York's waiters are unemployed actors – will hurt him, just as she felt hurt by her father's rages as a child. Other factors also contribute to her reticence, not least that she is concerned that if she does confront him, he will leave.

It is no secret that one of the main causes of marital breakup is money. Mary is supporting her husband because she would rather suppress her growing rage at his failure to contribute than face his walking out. But I asked her, "What does that say about his love if your husband makes no effort to share expenses while you work your head off?" I added that perhaps, despite his being supported, he will eventually resent his dependence and leave anyway. That gave her pause. Wasn't she just watching as a long fuse slowly led to a meltdown? Her problems with her husband – and with taking care of herself in therapy – had to be addressed together, largely as a single problem that involved her indulgence in immediate gratification without considering the long-term consequences. I could, at least theoretically, walk out on her just like her husband could. So, she had to stop deferring her problems and deal with them.

Today, I gave her a number of options that included putting a hold on her treatment until she could pay down her debt. I did not want to see her stop treatment, and I felt that my own identity as a healer was also on the line. But I felt that the healing process itself required that she come to grips with her issues. Fortunately, she seemed motivated to continue in treatment. She said that she would find the money to pay what she owed and stay current with future payments.

Obviously, if she suddenly now has the money to pay four months' fees, she has had it all along. Her resistance, I think, was based on the fear that she needed a sufficient cushion to keep her from feeling so desperate that she would, finally, confront her husband. The money was a kind of insurance policy against an outburst of candor. But as she also came to understand, her repressed anger was leading her toward neglecting herself and her own best interests in keeping up her payments to me.

I hope that Mary can deal with the situation at home. Her willingness to deal practically with me gives me some hope.

For Mary, psychotherapy was a significant cost, as it is for most people. However, as therapists, we may have our own issues with money. We might see what we charge as reflecting the caliber of our work: a higher fee might appear that we do better work, or a lower one may lessen us in some way. If we're not charging "attorney fees," even though we spend more time training than they do, does that diminish the work? Or what about surgeons, who perform costly, complicated procedures – can we compare to them? While our services may be just as valuable, comparisons are inevitable, since money is a ready and tangible measure of value.

Lately, the trend toward "ethical" investing has popularized the idea that you can do well by doing good. That is, you can have it both ways. Psychotherapists have always proceeded on this notion, so that in helping others we keep our own interests in mind. But we are still in a fiduciary relationship. We have to consider our patients' interests first. We don't suspend our interests but, in every case, we do what is right for the patient. The saving factor is that most patients <u>do</u> pay their fees, and we only rarely face an existential crisis.

Love and money

Mary's session from last week helped to clarify her issues with love and money. For decades, she struggled to get out of debt and, once she had, she found herself with a common-law husband who spent her money without compunction. In effect, she felt that paying her debts on time would leave her with so few resources – for their mutual upkeep! – that she would jeopardize the relationship. There was an obvious codependency that could crack apart if either of them became resentful. But what I wanted to understand was why Mary was so prone to self-indulgent spending, and perhaps why she was initially attracted to someone who even encouraged it.

We discussed Mary's deep sense that her mother did not love her enough when she was growing up. While over the course of therapy, Mary had achieved a better relationship with her mother, she still faulted her for having been self-absorbed when, as an adolescent, Mary needed her. Mary offered, for example, that when her father came home from a binge drunk and roaring, Mary's mother did little to protect her. Instead, she was passive and placating, inclined to protect herself more than Mary. But wait! I saw the connection. By getting into debt as an adult, Mary put herself in a position to need her mother's help. She needed real, tangible help that would confirm that her mother was, finally, at her side. Her being in debt, and literally leaving her mother no choice but to help, would (in her mind) demonstrate her mother's concern on a current basis. It could not repair the past, but it could reenact it positively, for example as a type of psychological score settling where Mary's mother repaid an emotional debt in financial terms. It would not, necessarily, demonstrate love, but it would assure Mary that her mother felt a sense of obligation. She would allow her mother to redeem a deficit in one type of support (protection from a loutish father) by providing support of another type (financial).

The exchange that Mary set up was all too common. It was only mildly surprising, therefore, that her mother had so far gone along with it, perhaps unaware of the deep-seated need for her assistance that Mary's requests represented. Mary had never told her mother why she carried around such resentment, and she lacked the insight to understand how she was using money to reclaim support that she regarded as having been withheld. Her mother, as self-centered as ever, showed no evidence of feeling guilty and never broached the issue of Mary's requests from her own point of view. Thus, as things stood, it was clear why Mary just assumed that her modus operandi could last indefinitely. However, I was less sanguine about the prospects for this arrangement, not least because I felt that it was pathological to fall into debt solely because it triggered a maternal response. I felt that if Mary could see *why* she was so prone to running up bills, and establish a relationship with her mother on firmer grounds, then she might find her way out of chronic debt.

But I had to figure out how to approach the issue. I first alerted Mary to how unfair she was being. Instead of buying her mother's emotional support, she was, ironically, forcing her to display maternal feeling by spending money. This was potentially harmful to someone who needed resources for her own retirement. It was also very destabilizing. I wondered aloud whether her mother would, in time, become resentful enough to withdraw from the relationship, at least on this basis. Mary had not thought that far ahead and, once again, she was thinking dangerously short term. She had indulged her husband's indifference to employment; failed to keep up her payments to me; and now, likewise, she had allowed her relationship with her mother to totter along in the service of a leftover adolescent grudge. She had a knack for creating powder kegs. Thus, when I put her situation in simple, stark terms – and drew her attention to the potential consequences – it was enough to startle her. It began to dawn on her that she had to kick her complacency toward money and start using it like a competent adult.

Recently, I received an e-mail from Mary sharing some of what she had learned about love and money. She elaborated on it further in yesterday's session, offering examples of greater confidence in dealing with her husband and relying less on her mother. Of course, I was gratified. We had worked through some vexing issues, and Mary was able to use what she had learned to make a change. Now maybe she will even keep current with my fees.

> While there were practical issues with paying my fee, my patience showed Mary that our relationship was not primarily about the money. As she understood more about our dynamic, she also became better able to assert herself in terms of being better compensated at work and insisting that her husband be gainfully employed. So far, he hasn't left her.

Turning 50

Mr. Silver was casually dressed when he came for treatment today – a departure from his usual suit and tie. I refrained from commenting, but silently wondered why. My silence was not dissembling. A facial expression or some gesture must have revealed my curiosity, since he quickly volunteered that today was his 50th birthday. I offered best wishes, and he thanked me. A therapist can adopt a neutral and nongratifying stance, but I still think it's useful to acknowledge people's life events and happy occasions. Mr. Silver said that it was indeed a happy day for him since he was taking the day off from work – hence, the casual dress.

He went on to describe an elegant dinner party in his honor that he had attended earlier in the week. It was at a friend's magnificent apartment overlooking Central Park. Ironically – at his own party – he found himself feeling jealous of the man's wealth and success. It bothered him that someone less intelligent than he could "make it so big." He tried to console himself that his wife was more attractive and his children better students. But then his brother came to mind, and he realized that he was trying to convince himself that at 50 he was not the man he thought he should have been. Mr. Silver never saw his brother as a rival, but now suddenly his brother was looming large. I pointed out that if there ever was a rivalry, he had won it, since he had always been his mother's favorite, he was married and successful, and his brother was still trying to establish himself at 46. Nonetheless, he really seemed to want to put himself down and cited two areas where his brother had outshone him: sports and girls. He recalled that when they were growing up, he wanted to beat his brother on both accounts, "scoring" more impressively, as it were.

I pointed out how common it is, when we reach major milestones, to look around and compare our status with others'. I had done the same when I turned 50 and shared with him that I thought I should have published more and been invited to sit on the boards of more journals. So, I "got it." In capitalist societies, let alone in the Learned Professions, the passage of time is supposed to equate with tangible accomplishments. How many rungs of the ladder have you climbed? How many dragons lie slain at your feet? Under this regime, it is always possible to have done more, and so we are always battling relative failure. Even success is itself relative failure, since it could have been greater success. But I also observed that arriving at a milestone is a good occasion to reflect on whether we have achieved enough to make us happy. By happy, I do not mean complacent – "Okay, I can coast" – but, rather, the recognition that in proceeding through life we do not (on average) take more than we give back. We are useful as citizens, parents, colleagues, friends, or however we want to measure utility. We can respect ourselves.

Mr. Silver could respect himself. He acknowledged that in the end material gains were not very satisfying. He joked, "You can't take it with you." So, I asked, "Then why is it so important to you?" My question helped him to see more clearly that his time need not all be billable for him to feel productive and worthwhile. Reflecting on that, he seemed more eager to enjoy the day.

Of course, whether we have "improved the time" is a sticky question when what we value is not so much money, or family, or helping people, but creativity – the intangible production of unique minds. I earn a decent living as a therapist, yet I keep wishing I were a better poet. I know tenured English professors who wish they had written the paradigm-shifting monograph on Modernism, Romanticism, or Geoffrey Chaucer. Creativity leads to a kind of intellectual restlessness that is hard to quell, even at "a certain age." When Mr. Silver left, I thought about whether I could have addressed his concerns so readily if they had not involved rich friends and a sporty brother. I substituted myself and my artistic aspirations for his more mundane worries, and I had to admit that I was still searching for persuasive answers. In cases like mine, there is a role for acceptance. In the end, we can only be who we are. The idea is to be the best at who we are in the time that we have, and leave it at that.

In Erikson's stages of psychosocial development, one's middle years pose an existential challenge: how does one make one's life count? Why should we care about ourselves, and why should anyone else? Erikson frames this challenge as an issue of generativity versus stagnation (e.g., of doing work that is socially valued and personally meaningful). The formulation is relevant not just to work but to family, other relationships, and to one's place in society. It applies to creative work as well as to more conventional productivity. When a person contributes to his immediate or a wider circle through work or, perhaps, raising a family, he feels a sense of accomplishment. Someone who does not contribute tends to feel pointless.

Accordingly, part of having a healthy, fulfilling life during middle age is being able to express oneself through work and relationships. The need for money – and the time to earn it – may constrain one's ability to reach these goals. The issue is how to balance the ideal with what, given our means, we can actually do.

Leasing a car

Today, my wife and I went to lease a car. I have been driving a Jeep with over 100,000 miles on it, and it was time for a change. But at the dealership, we experienced a kind of bait-and-switch. We test-drove a car that we liked and assumed it was the one in the ad because the specs matched. However, as we later learned, there was only one of these cars. The lease for the car that we drove totalled three times the price in the ad. So, we took a pass.

I thought about how when a patient comes for a consultation, the costs that they expect upon entering treatment are far less than the real and final costs. Understandably, people tend to want to keep expenditures – time, money, energy – down. They look for quick fixes. So, I sometimes tell a patient that while I can probably help them feel better pretty quickly (e.g., I can fix or at least reduce the symptoms), personal growth and change take time. That's not what many want to hear, however, and after coming a few times they may simply not return.

Mr. Sterling missed his appointment again on Friday. He called to reschedule but then failed to show again. I know that's a reflection of his ambivalence, but it keeps happening with him. And I have my limits, too. I look at my time as leased in a way. Not in the grand sense that we are all on borrowed time, but, rather, that my time is the patient's time only derivatively. If he fails to use it, he is still responsible for *my* time ... well, at least in principle, since it rarely works out that way in practice. I know that if I told Mr. Sterling that he was responsible for all his missed sessions, he would not return for treatment.

Perhaps Mr. Sterling feels the way other patients sometimes do, that the cost of treatment is more than they bargained for. But in fact, it's not the cost that startles them so much as the length of time that results in the cost. Patients find it hard to imagine that any medical procedure can take years. Or, rather, patients under 60 find it hard. Older patients, with chronic, progressive conditions like macular degeneration and diabetes, understand that regular trips to the doctor and expensive repetitive treatments are a fact of life. For them, cost is associated with not getting any worse, and they're "in it," so to speak, for the rest of their lives. One more such commitment, if they see it as necessary, does not phase them. But other people coming for a consultation want the cost and parameters of treatment to be set out clearly and with boundaries. They want me to define the results and, when I can't with any accuracy, they assume that I just want their money. But if I made promises that I knew I probably couldn't keep I would feel like a car salesman.

The point is that psychotherapists, who offer long courses of treatment, are up against the time value of money. That is, while most other kinds of doctors provide services with quickly visible results – a mended joint, a plumped-up face – our services consume money that could otherwise be *earning* money before any visible results are apparent. Why would you take such a deal, except on faith? And why should you have faith, except on the say-so of the therapist who shrinks (no pun intended) from making promises? It's a hard game, and it's why I need to feel that I am leasing my time to patients responsible for using it.

> *In psychiatry, we are good at relieving symptoms of anxiety and depression through psychopharmacology. But most real change is hard and takes time. Think of the idea, made popular in Malcolm Gladwell's* Outliers, *that to become expert in something takes 10,000+ hours of practice. To become expert in yourself, the way you might become expert in French or computer programming – other complex systems – requires time, commitment, and close observation. You have to be able to understand your psyche in its nuances and in all its functionality, much as you would computers or a language. You have to examine your thoughts and feelings in relation to your personal past. Such deeper truths are often hard to see and can be painful. But really knowing who you are can open the way to growth and change.*

Family meetings

It's instructive to consider the difference between a patient's version of reality and other people's understanding of the same events. Even when patients attempt to be forthright, there is the *Rashomon* problem. We inevitably see what suits us. Part of being a therapist is to discover what accounts for such distortions and concealment and, by exposing it, bring the patient's vision closer to some 20–20 perspective on his circumstances. By talking with other people in a patient's life, a therapist can find the flaws in his or her account of themselves.

I had begun to see Mr. Lewis's sister for anxiety and related alcohol and cocaine use and was treating her with both medication and psychotherapy. I also sent her for drug counselling and to an ENT specialist, who confirmed that she was ruining her nasal septum. But when her mother and brother came to her session this evening, I found their views exceptionally helpful.

I was impressed at how much more clearly her family members, who accompanied her around town, were able to assess the situation. They confirmed that despite Ms. Lewis's insistence that her cocaine use was purely "recreational" – and not addictive – she would walk out of parties and snort cocaine on her own where the drug was not available. She would become indignant when other people refused to join her but, instead, kept their distance. Her family's views not only underscored her addictive behavior but also provided an opportunity to confront her denial. This approach was clearly helpful, and I felt good about the intervention.

At the end of the session, we decided on several further interventions, including a psychopharmacology consultation with an addiction specialist. Her mother insisted on it, and I agreed. I was therefore surprised, when I asked who would pay for it, and her mother exclaimed dismissively, "Let her pay for it." I was not sure what to make of the remark, and Mr. Lewis quickly chimed in to say that he would pick up the bill. But I wondered whether, despite her mother's obvious moral support, there were underlying family tensions involved in Ms. Lewis's addiction.

Who pays for what is often a critical issue in families as children mature. Responsibilities can shift. They become stand-ins, as they had in Mary's case, for simmering resentments that were never adequately explored. Thus, it seemed apparent that while Ms. Lewis' mother was concerned about her, she had expended so much emotional energy on her daughter that she felt no obligation to financially support her – even with regard to a medical consultation that she had insisted on. She was using money as a boundary, telling her daughter that she would go only so far. In effect, she was saying that she had had enough and that love does not always translate into money because *paying someone's debts represents a different kind of obligation than love*. It is discretionary, even for parents. Ms. Lewis's mother probably never came out and said "I've had enough of this aggravation," but withholding her financial support – and telling her daughter to pay for herself – was her way of saying so. Whether her daughter got the message is another issue.

Yet, despite his mother's diktat, Mr. Lewis wanted to finesse what he knew might become a standoff, so he quickly offered to pay. At his next session, I plan to ask why he preferred to keep family resentments from finally being addressed, especially since there had already been a burst of candor concerning Ms. Lewis's addiction. Perhaps he was considering tact and time as well. Immediate disputes about money are openings to long-standing concerns, and I thought we should explore them at some point. But it may also be that Mr. Lewis's reaction reflects his own feelings for his sister and that, ironically, just as his mother seems to feel that she has had enough, he feels that he should do more. Mr. Lewis may feel that he has not done enough for his sister or indeed for anybody and that this is an occasion to begin redressing the imbalance. Money can be a way to make amends for emotional slights or for neglect in general. It is often the easiest way, and so perhaps Mr. Lewis's apparent generosity is actually a kind of cop-out.

It will not be easy to raise this set of questions with Mr. Lewis since they open up so many more. One way or another, questions about money lead back to the time it takes to sort them out ... which, in psychotherapy, leads back to questions about money.

Further Reading

Drake, Pamela Peterson, and Frank Fabozzi. *Foundations and Applications of the Time Value of Money*. Hoboken, NJ: John Wiley & Sons, 2009.

Eliade, Mircea. *The Myth of the Eternal Return: Or, Cosmos and History*. NJ: Princeton University Press, 1954.

Freud, Sigmund. *Civilization and Its Discontents*. Translated by James Strachey. New York: W.W. Norton & Company, 1961.

Grondin, Simon. *The Perception of Time: Your Questions Answered*. New York: Routledge, 2019.

Grosz, Stephen. *The Examined Life: How We Lose and Find Ourselves*. New York: W.W. Norton & Company, 2014.

Hawking, Stephen. *A Brief History of Time: From the Bang to Black Holes*. London: Bantam Press, 1988.

Kinder, George. *The Seven Stages of Money Maturity: Understanding the Spirit and Value of Money in Your Life*. New York: Dell Publishing, 2000.

Lightman, Alan. *Einstein's Dreams*. London: Vintage, 1992.

Plato. *Apology*. Translated by Benjamin Jowett. Vol. 7, *The Dialogues of Plato*. Edited by Robert Maynard Hutchins. Chicago: William Benton Publisher, 1952.

Silver, Tisa. *The Time Value of Life: Why Time Is More Valuable Than Money*. Bloomington, IN: iUniverse, 2009.

Wells, Herbert George. *The Time Machine*. New York: Henry Holt and Company, 1895.

4 Empathy and relationships

Empathy is the capacity to understand what another person feels from that person's own perspective. It is distinct from sympathy, where you may understand someone's feelings, but from your own perspective – or really from anyone's, even just from cable news. (When Bill Clinton famously told an angry heckler "I feel your pain," he got the two mixed up.) This chapter examines the role of empathy in forming and maintaining relationships which, in part, depend on the reassurance that perceived empathy provides.

Psychotherapeutic relationships are based, in large part, in empathy. Of course, while other aspects of this relationship involve knowledge and an experienced outsider's point of view, an ability to listen and respond with empathy is integral to talk therapy. A clinician must be able to tune into what the patient is thinking and feel (e.g., by way of memory) what he or she is feeling. This is crucial to the psychodynamic process.

In general, people with the capacity to empathize do better in relationships. They connect and respond in ways that are felt by the other person. Naturally, a good self-understanding helps you to respond empathically.

The initial interview

When someone comes for an initial interview, I try to get data to inform their treatment. While I listen, I ask myself: Does the patient have a psychiatric diagnosis? Do their psychological problems need treatment? Am I the right person to help? It may be that I can help, but they are looking for a different type of help. Unless there is a good match, the likelihood of healing (according to anyone's definition of help) will be slim.

One of the first questions I ask, therefore, is "How can I help?" Some patients may want relief for a specific symptom (e.g., depression or anxiety). Others may not even be "symptomatic" in a clinical sense, but may still feel troubled (e.g., by loneliness or problems at work). I listen for cues that enable me to decide whether and how we should proceed. I want to determine the depth and nature of the problem, not least from the patient's perspective (even though I may see things differently). This is especially true where the problem may be elusive and, for example, tied up with a sort of general funk in the patient's state of affairs. Freud's prescription for happiness was meaningful work and to love. When work and/or love are unsatisfying, the result is often discontent.

We frequently *become* discontent as we are losing ground. So, I try to get a sense of why someone is seeking therapy *now*. Has something changed that necessitates treatment? Have acute stressors made matters worse? Did someone suggest that "maybe you ought to see someone"? Breaking up with a partner, losing a spouse, and getting fired are common reasons to present for help. But sometimes *good* fortune can trigger a depressive or anxious response as when, for example, a financial windfall sets off a panic attack. Or maybe a promotion entails a sense of guilt and a feeling that such recognition was undeserved. Understanding this kind of paradoxical response can also be an important part of the treatment.

As we begin to talk, I try to form a connection with the person. I'm married, Jewish, a born New Yorker, male, middle-aged – your classic caricature psychiatrist. So how do I jump the synapse, so to speak, with someone who is different from me, with whom I might not even cross paths in "real life"? This week, for example, I saw a new patient, Chrissie, who is single, Christian, and a woman in her 30s from the Midwest. She questioned whether I would understand her problem of being alone in the city with no social network for support. She was quick-witted enough to add that "I wouldn't say that to a surgeon, but this is more personal."

Agreed. But I invited her to talk about how those differences might matter and how therapy could help, assuming that I was the right man for the job. She replied that she hoped therapy could help her find a partner, though she was not quite sure how. I was not sure either, but then she suggested that maybe it could help with the depression that she has off and on when faced with a new challenge, and that if she were feeling "up" she would be more inclined to date.

This was possibly an opening. Was she suffering from depression now? We could certainly treat it. But since she wasn't, there might be something else to help motivate her. I thought to observe that the New York dating scene was famously tough, but she already knew that, and it might not sound empathic. So, instead, I remarked on the difficulty, even scariness of being alone in a big city. It was such a commonplace, almost a throwaway, but its obvious universality reassured her. She felt I understood. We talked for a while more about building up her confidence, and she made another appointment.

The basic fact of psychotherapy is that patient and therapist need to form a bond, since no one – in or out of therapy – will reveal themselves to another unless they feel understood. For the patient, it's an issue of "wavelength" –

does this person get me or am I talking for no purpose? Can the therapist assimilate what I'm saying, so that over time he or she will help me toward change and feeling better? For the therapist, it's an issue of connecting, finding a common denominator – maybe life in the city – and then drawing the patient out behind it. If there is an initial connection, then patient and therapist will develop a level of comfort with each other, ideally permitting each party to perform their roles optimally: the patient will be more forthcoming and the therapist will search his own experience for reasons to empathize. It is a highly nonlinear process, sometimes characterized by breakthroughs. I had a small one with Chrissie, which left us both feeling better.

> When children suffer trauma (e.g., from broken homes or poor parenting), it influences their brain development and also how they form relationships. They may withdraw into themselves and disable their ability to empathize. But in general, humans are wired for empathy. While there are some exceptions, like sociopaths or people with a neurological condition called alexithymia, empathy is a component of human nature.
>
> Nevertheless, extending empathy is an art. It takes practice, since tuning in to another's complex feelings and responses is not easy. In therapy, understanding someone else's feelings – not just intellectually but empathetically – can be crucial.

Dropping out of treatment

Last night, a relatively new patient called to say that he was dropping out of treatment. I was surprised, since we had started off well. He was talking, I was making observations, and he had found the feedback helpful. But there had been warning signs. I was the second therapist he had left. Years before, he had seen someone else for over ten years before deciding that not much had happened. Now he apparently had a much shorter fuse, even though I had taken his return to therapy as a sign that he was willing to keep trying.

Mr. Pauling presented as a single, white, Christian man in his 50s. He complained of anxiety, loneliness, and being obsessed with checking things. For example, he had to examine the walls in a room and all the items arrayed around them. Were they cracked, stable, or likely to topple on him? He had to throw crumpled papers out his office window because, in the trash can, they reminded him of failure. He had a secret fetish about black women, and, at night, he probed the Internet looking for black bondage. He could only date black women, but then went home and masturbated.

I could see why he was lonely, but it was hard to understand the basis for his obsessions this early in the course of treatment. His previous therapy had not made any attempt at all. I knew only that when he was growing up, his parents had employed black housekeepers, which may have been related in some way to his masturbatory fantasies – but how could I tell? When I tried to explore these fantasies, or his other obsessions, he seemed threatened and became angry. I imagined they were a defence against underlying feelings such as rage, but, when I initially brought up rage, he became enraged so I dropped it.

Such reactions among beginning patients are common. They are often conflicted over the therapy they know on some level they need. What was different about Mr. Pauling is that – having once been justifiably disappointed – he could not stick with the process again. I sensed that he felt cornered by it, as if down the road he would have to confront obsessions that pained him but that he could not imagine living without. He was projecting his current state of dependence on these obsessions (for safety, for excitement) onto the future, such that the prospect of change represented deprivation instead of liberation. This was a common reaction as well, since patients starting out in therapy fear that they will somehow be reduced and become a less complex, somewhat rote version of themselves – harmless, socially acceptable, but also boring and a mere simulacrum of their former selves. In these instances, therapy represents a transformational bridge too far that, for all its promises of a "cure," seems to strip away their individuality. It's all concocted, but how do you penetrate such an elaborately worked out rationale? Their stance is more than just typical resistance. It is the creation of a counter-narrative in a parallel universe, which they do not dare to test by letting it play out.

Such complex, negative hypotheses are usually the fruit of high intelligence. Mr. Pauling was, indeed, highly articulate and intelligent. He was in finance. Though he absorbed what I said, and even appeared to appreciate much of it, our sessions felt like rounds in a debate tournament. He had an answer for everything, and he knew how to change a subject that he couldn't handle.

He approached his dating life as he did his other endeavors, very conscientiously. He left no stone unturned on the various websites on which he found women. He also packaged himself as considerably younger (around 15 years younger!) than he was, although he looked his age. He figured he could talk his way out of this one too and was offended when I suggested that he portray himself more accurately. Not surprisingly, over the few weeks he was in treatment with me, several women commented that he did not look like his picture and declined to see him again. But Mr. Pauling had a type of protective arrogance that prevented him from changing. I kept trying to understand more about its origins, but he never let me near it.

After a few sessions, Mr. Pauling was away for a week and, before his next session, he called to say that he was not coming back. I asked if I had offended him, but he said only that some concerns he had had from the beginning of our work were still with him. I was not able to encourage him to come in and talk about them. I suspect that in addition to seeing me as a threat to the status quo of his life, he wondered whether treatment would expose issues of guilt, shame, and embarrassment that he'd then have to contend with.

He may try therapy again, however, since there is a type of serial patient whose fear of his own worst tendencies is equal both to his fear of being cured and the process that it requires. As such patterns continue to be problematic, therapy seems like an option ... for a while. Therapists usually do not refuse to take on such patients, but they do so warily, often trying to elicit some initial insight that they will remain in treatment long enough to give it a chance. I wish Mr. Pauling's next therapist good luck.

> People with a Narcissistic Personality Disorder lack empathy. They see the world only in terms of themselves and cannot take others into account. This may promote their success in some spheres, but limit their capacity to form relationships. This is why some narcissists enter professions – art, for example – where self-absorption is not a hindrance and may even help (Picasso was famously narcissistic).
>
> Of course, there should be a balance between healthy narcissism (i.e., the common self-regard that we all have) and a genuine concern for others. Maimonides, the Early Modern physician/philosopher, posed a series of questions to help one find a right balance: If I'm not for myself, who will be for me? If I'm only for myself, what am I for? And if not now, when? Note that with the first question, he puts himself first. That is, you need to consider and take care of yourself, so you can be there for others.
>
> Anthropologists have found that our natural willingness to extend ourselves toward others is strong where kinship ties are close, and that it diminishes as these ties become more distant. This is not to say that we cannot nurture a willingness to empathize, especially once we learn that empathy is beneficial.

Motivation

Like Mr. Pauling, Mr. Lauren had been in treatment for a long time before consulting me, and had also found it complicated, even at times unhelpful. In his case, he thought it made matters worse. He had entered treatment for depression, and the therapist felt that its causes went deeper than stress. So, he recommended analysis as the treatment of choice ... with pretty disastrous results.

Indeed, things were rocky from the start. During an insecure moment toward the end of the first month, Mr. Lauren put his analyst on the spot, insisting to know what he thought of him. The analyst retorted, "You're obnoxious!" Probably, the analyst saw this demand as breaching classical psychoanalytic protocol and felt justified in revealing his feelings. Or maybe it was just a spontaneous human response to having been put on the spot. Either way, it was out of bounds. Mr. Lauren felt hurt and rejected. He took the man's unbridled candor to mean that he was fundamentally obnoxious, as opposed to being so in that specific, tense moment. When the analyst tried to soften his outburst by suggesting that he could be obnoxious too and it was *just* an outburst – not a carefully considered judgment – the damage was already done. Psychologically speaking, Mr. Lauren never fully came back.

That moment between Mr. Lauren and his analyst is sometimes described as an "enactment," a term actually coined by his first analyst, in which the unconscious of the analyst plays out with the patient in spontaneous and sometimes problematic ways. These moments can be used as opportunities for reflection in the psychoanalytic situation. But it's still not simple.

His analyst later described Mr. Lauren as having had a "negative therapeutic reaction" to the treatment. This term is sometimes used to cover a multitude of outcomes unsatisfactory to the analyst. But it actually means that the analyst got things right, and the patient failed to get better anyway. If you look at Mr. Lauren's case, there were some inflection points during his course of treatment suggesting how the analyst could have proceeded differently. Either way, Mr. Lauren had the sense that his first analyst did not like him, and at times in the course of treatment, his analyst alluded to feeling that way about him.

One distinctive characteristic of Mr. Lauren's childhood were haircuts from his mother that he found humiliating. During these procedures, she was intrusive and judgemental: "Your hair's too long. It looks like a bird's nest." His mother would literally chase him through the household with a clipper, wielding it like a weapon. To Mr. Lauren – and to his analyst – the treatment had the quality of a bad haircut: the analyst positioned behind his patient, the patient in a vulnerable position. When they became aware of this reenactment, the analyst approached it in terms of the transferential and countertransferential aspects of the psychoanalytic situation. That is, the analyst was acting like Mr. Lauren's mother in his critical, probing, and aggressive comments toward his patient, and both patient and analyst experienced it in this way. But while the analyst saw this enactment as an inevitable part of psychoanalytic treatment, Mr. Lauren wanted to mitigate it. By calling him obnoxious (thus raising the specter of his mother's judgments), instead of approaching Mr. Lauren more empathetically, the analyst effectively ended the possibility of an ongoing therapeutic relationship. So the outcome was not *merely* a negative therapeutic reaction. It was hard to analyze the contributing factors.

Mr. Lauren learned a lot about himself during his treatment with the analyst, but he did not feel better. He ended that treatment feeling more deeply scarred, as if the old wounds inflicted by his mother had been reopened and didn't have a safe place to heal. He felt that he had worked with someone for years who never really liked him, a suspicion that he carried concerning his martinet mother as well. He was not able to use the classical psychoanalytic situation, with its supposedly neutral and nongratifying stance toward patients, in a therapeutic way. He did not find helpful a strictly interpretive methodology based in frustrating drives and drive derivatives. During and after the analysis, Mr. Lauren acted out his angers and frustrations rather than finding more satisfying understandings within himself. It is not surprising he felt the treatment had only made matters worse for him.

Sometimes a rigid method of helping a patient can be wrong for them, so it is important to be flexible and open-minded. In insight-oriented therapy, we try to establish a relationship with the patient, testing what works as we proceed. If the relationship frays, we try to repair it. We have to like the patient, but the patient has to like us. If he doesn't like the process, we have to ensure that, at least, he can tolerate it. When we arrive at an inflection point, we do not just keep on keeping on. Nobody would do this in their personal relationships, and there is no excuse for it in the healing professions.

Empathy is not restricted to humans. Primates, dolphins, rodents, and other social animals are aware of one another's feelings. Empathy has a basis in evolutionary biology. Without being anthropomorphic, it is possible to say that empathy makes possible relationships in various species. It facilitates communication, attachment, and care.

The development of empathy is rooted in the infant-mother relationship and is fostered by attachment between the two. It is nourished by siblings and friends, playmates, loved ones, and the community. Some toddlers (age 2) will show concern and care for others. In effect, they empathize and recognize that other people have feelings.

In the psychoanalytic situation, therapists use themselves – their experiences, memories, and feelings – to understand the patient. The therapeutic relationship is the vehicle for the treatment. When the relationship is not empathic, the treatment generally does not progress.

Seating arrangements

In therapy, very little is incidental, even the relative physical positions of therapist and patient. The classic image of the psychiatrist on a chair, with the patient lying on a couch looking up at the ceiling, is rife with asymmetry: the psychiatrist nods sagely while the patient (at some distance) struggles to expose long-festering wounds. The result is not a conversation. The participants' relative positions were not meant to promote spontaneous, let alone intimate, exchange. For some patients, there also is a sense of hierarchy in the situation – the patient deferential, dependent, and even perhaps submissive while the analyst delivers detached observations. The process tends to be long and winding. This was the practice in 19th-century Vienna or, if you are Woody Allen, in the story line of *Annie Hall* (1977). It still prevails in classical analysis.

But in psychotherapy, seating arrangements just take advantage of the size or layout of the therapist's office. An understated mundaneness can be a source of comfort, with Vienna evoked only by an Oriental rug (still the signature artifact of therapists everywhere). Where intimacy is a goal – as it usually is – considerations regarding how to promote it can also play a role. A face-to-face discussion recognizes that participants will be talking, much like in a conversation. The intentional, interpersonal nature of their exchange is signaled by facing chairs or couches. Relative proximity – how close the therapist is positioned to a patient – can also determine the nature of the exchange and can go either way. When the analyst is out of sight of the patient, the process tends to be more intrapsychic, more classically analytic. Sometimes the seating arrangement is also correlated with the frequency of sessions, with fewer sessions leading to less intimacy, more distance.

In my old office, I sat behind a big, cherry wood desk. If the patient came once a week, they would generally sit in front of the desk, looking at me. The arrangement was intentionally clinical, although some patients did not pick up the cues. Dr. Goodman, for example, an elderly man and former professor, saw the desk as distancing, even isolating. He had a chronic pain syndrome that was causing depression. But he also suffered from having grown up with a cold and distant father, who had been a successful businessman. What the father lacked in love, he tried to make up for with money. So even though I was much younger than Dr. Goodman, he would see me – a man behind a big desk – as a father figure, physically and emotionally positioned to deny the love that he was seeking. The physical distance between us re-created the emotional distance between his father and himself. Accordingly, he saw me as cold and distant like his father. When I tried to be supportive and talk about the trauma that his father had unintentionally inflicted, he was still unable to get past what he saw as the unbreachable distance between us. The desk triggered too many old memories, which were reinforced every time he sat in front of it. I asked if we could perhaps find some other seating arrangement, but the desk was so big and imposing that he never got it out of his mind. It would have been experienced like his father offering money instead of love – that is, more of the same, a transparent apology rather than a heartfelt response.

To the side of my desk was a black leather armchair with an ottoman. Patients who came two times per week tended to sit there. Rather than the chairs facing each other, they were positioned at an angle. The seating arrangement conveyed our being on a common journey, like passengers in a car. This was the case with Mr. Young, a businessman from Germany who was preoccupied with contracting lethal infection. When he was growing up, his sister developed a heart condition that left her vulnerable to infection. She was chronically sick, and Mr. Young had been her caretaker. He identified with his sister and imagined that her chronic ailments were also his. I found that by sitting as if we were traveling together, it freed him to talk more about that relationship. He also saw that in our intimate relationship, he remained perfectly healthy, and he slowly began to experience himself as less physically vulnerable and less afraid to venture onto the subway or into crowds where he might pick up something that he feared.

In both these instances, my physical position relative to the patient influenced my relationship to them – one negatively, one positively. I now offer patients some options in how we sit relative to each other, even while trying to achieve a degree of intimacy from whatever position they choose. But I find that offering an initial choice allows the patient to feel that I am not setting up some rigid, unilaterally defined regime that harkens back to a previous therapeutic modus operandi. I want to convey that flexibility and spontaneity will govern our exchanges, starting with how we physically arrange ourselves.

It is peculiar, even quirky, that psychoanalysis developed as a couch-based treatment. Bertha Pappenheim, the first "analytic," would recline with her doctor, the esteemed physician Joseph Breuer, to tell her story of the loss of her father. In the course of a year, her symptoms of hysteria temporarily resolved. Freud recognized this "talking cure," and so psychoanalytic treatment was born on a couch. Nonetheless, Freud himself sometimes conducted his analyses on walks through a park in Vienna. But either from a couch or on a walk, the patient's facial expression may be invisible.

Face-to-face contact – looking in someone's eyes and seeing their expression – is a source of connection in psychotherapy. For some patients, it is a necessary part of treatment. These patients may experience the classical psychoanalytic situation (i.e., on a couch, facing away from the therapist) with a sense of loss and longing that can be hard to overcome. In traditional psychoanalysis, such patients might be deemed "unanalyzable." Of course, the real question is not whether someone is analyzable according to a rigid standard, but what helps a patient to feel better and more whole. When therapist and patient see each other, this may foster a connection – a relationship – that leads to greater and more beneficial change.

On the couch

Mr. Lauren was startled when he went from psychotherapy to classical analysis – that is, when he went from sitting in a chair once or twice a week to lying on the couch several times a week. He had been engaged in insight-oriented psychotherapy for over a year when I made the recommendation for analysis. We talked about it because it is an intensive treatment and because he felt that his first analysis had not been a positive experience. Though Mr. Lauren was an intelligent, hardworking lawyer, he had problems with authority that derived from his relationship with his parents and that affected his professional relationships and surfaced in our therapeutic relationship.

Mr. Lauren saw his father, also an accomplished lawyer, as dispassionate and reserved. He said my observations were like those his father would have made – detached, sharp, frank – even though I did not see them that way (patients often use the term "frank" as a pejorative because they are sensitive to even garden-variety frankness). In the case of Mr. Lauren's mother, there was another disconnect. He saw her as self-involved in that she raised him to be an extension of herself, minimizing and, at times even ignoring who he was, dictating who he should be. In reaction, he experienced my attempts at intimacy as controlling and saw the couch as re-creating the emotional distance that both parents had displayed in different ways toward him. Probably, he would have problems with therapy however it was conducted since regardless of how patient and therapist are arranged there is an inevitable hierarchy that cannot be erased. The patient's only real power is in quitting, which Mr. Lauren had exercised with his earlier therapist.

But before getting further into Mr. Lauren's therapy, I want to note that in the previous paragraph I described what Mr. Lauren "saw" with respect to his parents. As clinicians, we can only see the patient's past through his or her eyes. We have no direct knowledge of their past experience and those involved. Over time, we build a mental picture of the people, experiences, and other factors that led a person to become who he is – or seems to be – right now. As clinicians, and also as people more generally, it may be helpful to keep in mind that these are only impressions, albeit built up over many hours spent with a patient. So as a working hypothesis, I considered that Mr. Lauren had a loving but not very demonstrative father and a self-involved mother who used him as a phallic extension of herself. Mr. Lauren referred to his relationship with his parent so often that, at the very least, I realized that they were central to his self-conception and that – however skeptical I might be – I had to recognize their importance to how his therapy would (or would not) progress.

When Mr. Lauren lay down on the couch, he experienced it as a profound loss. This response had also occurred during his previous analysis, but it had gone unanalyzed. Other patients often find freedom or refuge in the psychoanalytic situation and not having to look at me. But Mr. Lauren experienced it as a loss of contact and connection. It took a while for us to understand what this reaction was about. He found me emotionally distant and restrained. He was upset and frustrated by what he took to be the loss of me, even though he had my undivided attention for several hours a week. I wondered who I was to him. That is, I wanted to understand whom I represented to him in the transferential aspect of our relationship. He often complained about not being able to see me and experienced my attention as being directed elsewhere. At some point, I observed that he experienced me as he had his mother, who could be inattentive and even unsympathetic. His thoughts turned toward a plant in my office that was withering from lack of proper care and attention, and he wondered how I could help him if I could not even care for a simple plant. His thoughts then turned toward the birth of his sister. He was young at the time, but remembered a profound sense of hurt and loss when she was born. His mother's gaze turned definitively toward her, and he said he felt bereft without it.

As the therapy continued, we came to understand the transferential aspect of our relationship. Mr. Lauren saw how he experienced other relationships in terms of loss and longing and how he responded out of hurt and anger. Over time, this recognition helped him to become more confident, more willing to trust connections he had made. Of course, I wondered whether the couch exacerbated his initial negative feelings toward me, and I decided that even though he complained about it, we could use it therapeutically. Had we been sitting face to face, his old grudges would still have come up in one way or another and needed to be talked about and worked through. Some patients just require more work because the therapeutic situation, however it is set up, gets refracted through the patient's past. They see the therapist/patient relationship differently, bent in one way or another based on prior relationships and experiences. The therapist has to straighten that vision out, whether the patient is lying prone, staring at the ceiling, or sitting upright and looking right at him.

No segment of a patient's life can be walled off, least of all the time spent in therapy. The past is present in therapy, and therapy influences what transpires in the future. Therapy can also influence how the patient understands the past, just as what happens in the future can influence how the patient understands therapy. In each case, the goal is not simply truth or even equilibrium, but a type of enhanced knowledge that enables both participants – therapist and patient – to maintain a sense that positive change is possible and that therapy is therefore worthwhile.

When someone is distressed, their words give them away. Another source is the visual. It is ironic that classical psychoanalysis developed a couch-based tradition where not only can the patient not see the analyst but the analyst does not look at the patient; if he does, the patient appears upside down from behind! While this may feel liberating – analysts cite the "revelry" of just listening – it does not promote greater connection. Nor does reducing the contact between two people enhance the intimacy and trust that are part of the therapeutic process. So, patients in this position, so to speak, should not be faulted as "unanalyzable," as they sometimes are.

People connect in different ways; as clinicians, it is our role to be sensitive and sensible about such differences. After all, the question is not whether a relationship is analytic according to some outdated gold standard of treatment, but whether it is therapeutic and helpful to the patient.

Connecting

One of the most important aspects of the psychotherapeutic relationship involves the connection between therapist and patient. Insight and understanding, which are integral to the healing process, ultimately involve the intrapsychic realm, although they are facilitated by the presence of another person. The interpersonal realm deals directly with what goes on between the two participants. The connection that therapists share with their patients – the bond, the relationship – is the means to healing.

Psychiatry today focuses on diagnosing illness and treating symptoms. It has become increasingly medicalized (who has not heard of psychoactive drugs?), turning the psychiatrist's work more toward rationality than emotion. But for some of us, the heart of healing is still in the affective connection we make with our patients, which does not simply involve making a correct diagnosis or implementing the right treatment plan. It involves a unique relationship between two people.

This is an "I and you" relationship, personal, intersubjective, fostered by mutual trust. This does not mean that the therapist should reveal himself on the same basis that the patient will. The relationship is professional and boundaries exist. But using one's life, bringing one's personal experiences to the conversation, is integral to the process and the basis of establishing empathy.

When Mr. Lauren presented for treatment, he had been in a psychoanalytic relationship that was not therapeutic. The affective connection to his analyst was negative. Though he had broached the issue with the analyst, the discussion went nowhere. The analyst said that he was trying to help, which Mr. Lauren found reassuring but not terribly helpful. At least according to Mr. Lauren, his analyst had intensely ambivalent feelings toward him. Put more directly, he felt that his analyst disliked him. But one of the virtues of therapy compared to classical analysis is that there is room for flexibility and sharing (i.e., there are avenues to salvage a flagging relationship by opening up to the patient and seeking to establish grounds for empathy that the patient can recognize). Sometimes sharing an experience from one's own life can reassure the patient and even help him to open up. The message: both of us have been there, done that, so I can understand. To most patients, understanding is tantamount to "liking" them – how could you share similar experiences, have had similar feelings, and not find a reason to work collaboratively. The act of sharing one's personal life may even signify mutual respect.

Nevertheless, it is an uncomfortable fact that therapists should not work with patients whom they do not like, or about whom they cannot find something to like. This is rarely discussed. Dislike destroys the empathy that is essential to the therapeutic process. Proceeding in therapy despite such dislike does a disservice to the patient and ultimately frustrates both participants. The trick is in determining from early on if there's a good fit and, potentially, a working relationship. If there is not, then it may be better to refer the patient to a colleague or another service provider. It's rare that someone would just be boring and not care enough to offer help. Listening to someone tends to trigger interest and generally the concern of one human being for another.

Each individual's experience, as he or she develops toward adulthood, affects how that individual relates to others. There is also a genetic component. The 5-HTTLPR gene, which codes for the neurotransmitter serotonin, determines sensitivity to negative emotional information and, to some degree, resilience. The interplay of "nurture" and "nature" – how we grow up and how we are genetically coded – determines our capacity to form relationships.

Meeting an old friend

I did not hear back from Dr. Rose yesterday after we had agreed to meet. At first, I was disappointed. I took it personally. Maybe he had only limited time in the City, and something else had come up, but at least he could have phoned. I had been looking forward to catching up and reconnecting.

I am not sure why Dr. Rose failed to call. But I suspect it had something to do with his feeling ashamed and embarrassed. These are strong, powerful emotions deep within each of us and based in childhood experiences. Both can play a role in inhibiting a person's pursuit of anything, even a simple meeting, that might otherwise seem enjoyable and worthwhile. I think of embarrassment as being Oedipally based. For example, a son's competition with his father may stir up feelings of guilt, thereby producing embarrassment. Shame, I think, tends to go even further back in childhood to the pre-Oedipal period, involving parental responses to our most intimate, personal connections. Originally, these responses might relate to feelings about fears of expressing oneself in relation to a parent. But as we grow up, they become more generalized. We can feel shame or embarrassment toward people or groups of people around us.

As for Dr. Rose, I have to be nonjudgemental. But I know that a person judges himself in relation to others – if he feels that I am judging him, then he may judge himself. This tendency can inhibit a person from acting in his own best interest as much as the reality of the situation. In fact, they miss the reality of another person's wanting to help. They create an artificial environment that frustrates or even bewilders other people.

Sometimes pointing that out can be useful. Perhaps I may have the opportunity to speak with him and bring it up with him. I thought we had the kind of relationship where that depth of honesty would be possible. But I can also see how it might seem presumptuous, even condescending – how can I really know what is inside his head, especially regarding years past before I knew him?

80 *Empathy and relationships*

Of course, I have felt ashamed or embarrassed, and sometimes I still feel that way. Perhaps I can offer myself as an example and explain how I struggle on occasions. The point is to create empathy and, by sharing or even exposing myself, show the other person that I accept them. I don't think we need to ask *why* someone is experiencing shame – unless we sense that they want to tell us – but we can say that the feeling should not get between them and others whom they assume would judge them if they knew.

As psychotherapists, we try to help people who are, without thinking, projecting their own feelings toward themselves onto unsuspecting others. This is not easy, and it could exacerbate someone's negative feelings – how did you know that I feel so ashamed? Does everyone know? But where you have some background with a person, and think there is an element of residual trust, it can perhaps do a lot of good ... even salvage a friendship.

Mirror neurons are a part of the neural basis of reading emotions in others. Some neuroscientists suggest that, like a "mirror," they become active when we see another person performing an action.

Case presentations

Today, I am making a case presentation to a prestigious group of colleagues at the medical center where I teach. So I've been thinking about the purpose of case presentations. In part, they are vehicles for teaching. They also allow the presenter to learn from his colleagues' responses ... or so the theory goes. But in fact, who really wants to be criticized in a professional setting, especially where, in the hierarchical space of a medical school, everyone's rivalries, vendettas, and egos are on full display? Better, perhaps, just to offer something rote and ritualized, laying out the patient's condition and treatment without venturing too far afield from standard practice. Sometimes when I write up these presentations, and imagine how I could embellish them with forays into the literature – let alone speculations about outcomes – I imagine being a medical novelist. Michael Chrichton was a doctor! Then I could really get into the minds of my patients and present the kind of dyadic dramas (their minds locked in a tussle with mine) that therapists (always on the outside) cannot possibly achieve. Wow! Freedom, liberation, maybe even praise.

But then I come back down to earth. The virtue of a case presentation is that when you are clear, honest, and theoretically grounded, the responses can make you a better clinician. You have to be able to read your colleagues' responses for bias and self-promotion, but, if you can, there is usually something useful in what they have to say. Even their biases are instructive, since they fill out a picture of the general intellectual environment in the field – maybe it's *worth* considering some approach that you may have discounted. Thus, while presentations can be a minefield, you can land on a mine and limp away better able to avoid the next one. You will still have a job after one of these ordeals – though you have to keep telling yourself that you will.

For today's study, I thought about Bobby and how he has matured over the course of his treatment. I should probably say "we" rather than just "he." When he presented for treatment, he was a 29-year-old adolescent. He was getting high daily, had dropped out of college several times, and his life was going nowhere. Oedipal guilt was crippling to him. It had been exacerbated by his father's neurodegenerative condition that literally crippled him during Bobby's childhood. In addition, there was Bobby's relationship with an older brother, who had inherited the father's Oedipal mantle. Bobby was ambivalent about his brother. He hated him for being bullied as a kid but admired him as a writer and for other achievements. He was caught between a succession of male figures whose dominance of his psyche, he said, had made it impossible for him to grow up.

So how do you distill years of rich and complex work down to its essential elements? I would say that early in his treatment, Bobby tended to exhibit a type of passive/aggressive avoidance in dealing with his conflicts. He arrived late for sessions, refused to talk about disturbing subjects, and made choices in his life that could undermine his well-being and our analytic work. But slowly, as we considered many of his psychological defenses, we started to understand his conflicts and he made substantive gains. He graduated from college with a 3.9 average, began to date in earnest, and obtained an excellent job in the arts. He also completed a manuscript and published portions of it. These accomplishments reflected his being able to overcome guilt, inhibitions, and various internal resistances.

For the presentation, however, I would like to explain the factors I saw as responsible for his getting better. That is, in presenting a case, clinicians are often interested in the mutative influences. What about the process helped him better understand himself in the context of our relationship? It can be useful to identify the defining moments of a patient's treatment, but there is an element of uncertainty because what a clinician and a patient consider defining may be quite different – and who's to say, even if the two agree. Nevertheless, there was an interesting moment toward the end of his first year of treatment, when he was about to flunk out of college for not completing his course work. After analyzing what I could regarding his predicament, I said in frustration, "I don't care how you do, just graduate." He stared briefly, as if the possibility were a revelation. Apparently, what I had said distinguished me from his father, a martinet about his academic performance, and showed him that I was a caring (if somewhat aggravated) ally. It opened up the possibility that graduation, irrespective of performance, was a worthwhile, achievable objective. He said he felt liberated. Ironically, he actually graduated with exceptional grades.

What interests me now, however, is that sometimes therapists set themselves up – willingly or not – as perceived opponents of a patient's parents or other authority figures, giving them permission to pursue a course of action that may have seemed forbidden or even unimaginable. We open up common sense alternatives where there had only been strict, even biased demands. Of course, there can be blowback when patients report to parents what the therapist "said I could do," but this never happened in Bobby's case – in part because he was older and finally did so well. It may be, in fact, that set free of his father's demands for top-tier performance, he felt free enough to perform as he would have if left to his own inclinations. Should I cite this possibility in the presentation? Probably not worth the risk (though if I were a novelist ...).

I will not cite the incident when Bobby came in with a bandaged foot and announced he had "driven a nail through it" when actually he had stepped on a nail doing yard work. This led to an exploration of his Christlike fantasies and being sacrificed by his father for some greater good. Very dramatic. But did it lead to actual growth? For presentations, we have to distinguish the drama from the utilitarian, reducing the patient from a person – a personality – to a "case." In this sense, we really switch gears when we move between treatment and making a presentation since, even though treatment is about providing a cure, we are still immersed in our patients' personalities. We display exceptional interest in what they say, even though we know that for purposes of a presentation our colleagues know that we filter out much of what makes our patients unique.

Anyway, I expect that I will enjoy the encounter with my colleagues. If we spar a bit, I will learn something, not least about them.

Acceptance

Poor Mr. Lauren. He tried hard but seemed to gain little traction. After he came through his crisis, he still had chronic problems. He could not insure his practice at a reasonable rate. He had to comply with new rules and ordinances, and he lacked sufficient drive to study them. He was seen as an increased liability, and he agreed that he was.

He had been through difficult times before. During his postgraduate training, some in his group saw him as a loose cannon. He floated novel theories that to them sounded far-fetched. And there had been situations where other groups first accepted but then excluded him, largely on grounds that he was not a good fit.

We had long recognized that he felt deeply excluded from his own family – dropped by his mother when his sister was born. He also understood how his conflictual strivings with his father tended to wreak havoc in his professional life. Now he was, again, facing a challenge.

Mr. Lauren felt demoralized. He knew that he had no one to blame but himself and took full responsibility for his actions. All the same, it was hard for him to accept who he had been, how he had hurt himself, and where he was at in his life.

I identify with Mr. Lauren. I empathize with his frustration, his disappointment, his sense of foreboding. At times, I look over my shoulder and see apocalypse. In "The Imagination of Disaster" (1965), Susan Sontag found this mindset reflected in mid-20th-century science fiction films which, she said, reenacted and distracted us from total annihilation. But Jews have known that the sky was falling since Abraham, even since Adam. We constantly update this idea, personalize it, and even poke Borscht Belt fun at it when we describe WASP-infused parties where we have to make small talk. So, I get Mr. Lauren. I had thought to tell him, quoting Bertrand Russell, that "to conquer fear is the beginning of wisdom" – a fancy way of saying "Get over it." But why go looking for wisdom? Sometimes wisdom is hard to take in, even too much to accept. It can make us see *why* we are in pain and cause us to have to accept difficult aspects of ourselves. It can make problems seem overwhelming and cause us to stop trying to fix them when muddling through may be good enough. I sometimes give myself this advice, since I just don't want to be further challenged with the intrapsychic work. So why not do the same with Mr. Lauren?

In fact, I did, and never quoted Bertrand Russell to Mr. Lauren ... which makes me think: here I am, a purveyor of self-knowledge, and I admit that wisdom can be so painful that it may be best to forego it. Maybe sympathy and support is the best we can muster. Some patients, of course, are willing to face years of therapy and even years of associated pain. But I am not so sure that we should just assume that they all do. Some are more fragile. I have this sense about Mr. Lauren, so I offer him sympathy and we discuss his current issues as if, in time, he will get past them. I decide that this is not a cop-out but a kindness – a palliative – and then I hope for the best.

Empathy promotes a trusting relationship, albeit trust can go too far. In a globalizing world, empathy breaks down cultural and racial chasms. Where we do not literally see the Other, it is necessary to imagine him. We look inward and then project our feelings outward onto everyone else.

Pain

A distinguished psychiatrist gave a thoughtful presentation last night at the psychoanalytic case conference that I host. He summarized his work with a psychosomatic patient who had experienced a traumatic childhood. The patient described a sharp, painful pressure on her chest when she was angry or frustrated, as she often was. The treatment was difficult because of a strong, negative, maternal transference that extended over years. The patient's mother was a pathological liar, so she could never trust what her mother said. This played itself out in treatment with the patient's mistrust of the analyst.

I am not sure whether there was a defining moment during treatment. Rather, it was a slow, arduous process. The psychiatrist helped the patient see that her mistrust of him, and of others, was based in her experiences with her own mother. He helped her see that her need to degrade him derived from her negative feelings about herself, and to see that she had positive qualities. It was interesting that even during the years when she was incessantly negative and hostile toward him, her life improved. She became a successful professional, her relationship with her sister improved, and she made more efforts to socialize. The transference also shifted to a more positive father transference, which seemed to correspond to the resolution of her physical pain.

Of course, the mind and body are linked. We live in our bodies. They manifest our anxieties, conflicts, and woes. The word "hypochondria" means having physical symptoms without evidence of a medical condition. It comes from the Greek hypo + chondra, which literally translates as "under the ribs." That is one place where psychological conflicts often manifest. When psychic reality hits, it sometimes feels like a punch in the stomach.

When I think about relationships between individuals, I sometimes use hypochondria as a model for what can go wrong. Just as the mind and body are linked inextricably, we live in a world where – like it or not – we have to find ways to work things out with others. I don't believe that we have to love everyone. We do not even have to respect everyone – but at least try to treat them with respect. What we do have to accomplish, however, is to find some modus vivendi – some set of protocols, like the body has, where everything works together and things get done more or less the way they are supposed to.

There is this old story where the various parts of the body dispute with each other about which is more important. But the body evolved to work as a whole and function as a unit greater than the sum of its parts. We have to find our unit – our community, our family – and then figure out how to live in it so that we do not merely survive but have the wherewithal to come out pretty well, even excel. Like therapy, this is not easy. Within the confined space of therapy, we can begin to practice, as this psychiatrist's patient clearly did.

Further Reading

Chomsky, Noam. *Problems of Knowledge and Freedom.* New York: Pantheon Books, 1971.
Garfield, Simon. *Timekeepers: How the World Became Obsessed With Time.* Edinburgh: Canongate, 2016.
Goldstein, Rebecca. *The Mind-Body Problem.* New York: Penguin Books, 1983.
La Perriere, Kitty. *Mirrored Reflections: A Memoir.* United States: IPBooks, 2019.
Lowell, Robert. *Life Studies.* New York: Farrar, Straus and Giroux, 1959.
Pinker, Steven. *How the Mind Works.* New York: W.W. Norton & Company, 1997.
Ponsot, Marie. *The Bird Catcher.* New York: Alfred A. Knopf, 1998.
Schafer, Roy. *The Analytic Attitude.* London: Karnac Books Ltd., 1983.
Schafer, Roy. *Retelling a Life: Narration & Dialogue in Psychoanalysis.* New York: Basic Books, 1992.
Scheurer, Maren. *Transferences: The Aesthetics and Poetics of the Therapeutic Relationship.* London: Bloomsbury, 2019.

5 The present past

Our past is encoded as memory, which shapes our life in the present. Sometimes, we are unaware of particular "memories" and can only recover them with effort. Yet such subconscious memories often affect us the most.

Freud famously remarked, "What is not remembered is repeated." Around the same time, the Spanish philosopher George Santayana observed – perhaps more famously – that those who do not remember the past are doomed to repeat it. It's interesting to speculate, therefore, on a late 19th/early 20th-century awareness in Europe of the weight of the past, whether personal or world-historical. There may have been an understanding that the past is not simply out there (detached, inert, finished) but rather a part of the present (intrinsic to individuals and societies, still playing itself out in our affairs). According to Freud and Santayana, the only way to keep the past from warping the present is to actively remember it and mitigate its effect. Freud's model for psychological change was to make the unconscious conscious – we have to confront our memories so that we can deal with their influence on our lives.

Psychodynamic treatments, and in particular the psychoanalytic situation, seek to make the past present and allow patient and therapist to observe, experience, and come to terms with the past. Past relationships are present in the patient/therapist relationship (e.g., their relationship is infused with relationships "transferred" or carried over from the past).

Because the past is ubiquitous, most relationships have an element of transference. Your boss may remind you of your father, and so you act out childhood feelings in the workplace. Your current intimacy-related issues may recall your relationship with a parent of the opposite sex. Until the past is sorted out, it can feel like a broken record.

This chapter concerns the presence of the past and how therapists help patients address it.

A suggestion

Mr. Lauren led a busy life, rebuilding his career while cleaning up detritus from his earlier work. At the end of a day, he had no time – or energy – to be creative. When he looked around, he felt frustrated that he lagged behind his peers and did little that reflected his own unique gifts. He felt caught in an endless round of satisfying but time-consuming cases, getting people out of trouble they never should have gotten into (but for their greed, self-involvement, and lack of common sense).

There is an array of studies on lawyer burnout. It is one of the unhappiest professions, measured by professional satisfaction and quality of life. But in Mr. Lauren's case, his negative feelings stemmed in part from his mother's criticisms of his father, who was also a lawyer and also worked nonstop. Mr. Lauren had absorbed her attitudes concerning the work, doing everything to confirm her negativity by questioning the social value of each case. While he knew that he was helping individual clients, how much did any of this really change things for the better? Moreover, was he making contributions outside the profession that he valued at least as much if not more?

We discussed his dilemma. I empathized, since I work a 60-hour week with little time to write poetry – which I love doing. I can sometimes find an hour and, lately, I have made a special effort. So, I suggested that at least he try to set aside some time regularly for creative pursuits. He liked my idea and said he would take it. He felt that trying to disprove his mother's criticism of lawyers was a way of getting past his past, so to speak, and starting on his own uniquely personal journey. He felt that his life had been a virtual self-fulfilling prophecy of his mother's negativity and that he needed an impetus to restart it in another direction.

Frequently, therapists give patients permission to change the trajectory of their lives, which seems (at least to them) to have been set on course at a time when they had little power to control it. The therapist cannot alter the past and, in some cases, cannot alter the patient's perception of it; they can, however, show patients that the past need not leave the present unalterable as well. That is, we show patients that life is porous in both directions – if the past can penetrate their current reality, and even make a mess of it, then that same reality can be freed of the past to the same extent. It is possible to make things better.

Mostly, moving past the past requires identifying and isolating the factors that are currently causing the problem. This is difficult to do when, at one level, these "factors" are close relatives and friends whom we may love. Patients need to develop a critical distance toward the past so that they can mount appropriate defenses against it ... or, at least, accept it and move on. It is still possible to love difficult or even harmful friends and parents, or at least still accept them, even while disallowing their influence to disrupt our lives' trajectories. Like so much else in therapy, balancing the past and present is a balance between what works and what doesn't. In Mr. Lauren's case, we found a pretty good balance which, over time, he can continue to reset.

Transference is a category mistake: feelings that a person once had for a significant other (e.g., a parent or sibling) are transferred into a present relationship – not least with the therapist. Freud discovered this phenomenon in his case of Dora. She was seduced by an uncle and forced to perform fellatio on him, subsequently developing a hysterical cough which Freud treated with psychoanalysis. But while the treatment resolved the symptom, Dora then developed an erotic transference toward Freud—which he was unaware of at the time—and bolted from treatment. In a famous footnote to the case, he acknowledged what had occurred and so described the phenomenon of transference for a first time.

Quitting treatment

Ms. Steward recently quit treatment. Since I had worked with her for ten years, what bothered me is that she left so abruptly, without explaining why. Partly, I think she was angry at me for suggesting that I could raise her fee, which had remained lower than fees in the rest of my practice. I tried and failed to engage with her on the subject, but she finessed it and talked instead about how her new boss made it hard for her to leave during the day. I pointed out that she was avoiding the subject and offered to see her during the evening. I even said I would consider seeing her at the same fee. But we both knew that she was doing much better economically, which was why I had brought up the issue of her fee in the first place.

I always liked Ms. Steward. She presented as a 45-year-old, single businesswoman from the Midwest. She was pleasant and engaging, but depressed and lonely. Even though she had good social skills, she had been fired from several positions. Typically, she got into negativistic relationships with women in authority and would enact the same kind of relationship that she had had with her mother. She was never able to stop thinking about her mother.

Nor could she stop thinking about her father. For years, she had had an openly erotic relationship with him, and as a child they often slept in the same bed. Not surprisingly, Ms. Steward developed strong, erotic transferential feelings to her psychiatrists. She would become obsessed with them and try to find out intimate details of their personal lives. The erotic feelings were so intense that one psychiatrist considered her delusional and tried to medicate her for the condition. Since he had worked with her analytically, and presented himself as a blank screen, she felt even more intensely that she had to know about him. As her erotic feelings developed in treatment with me, I tried to help her understand them in terms of her experiences with her father and the related feelings and fantasies. But my approach was only modestly helpful.

Ultimately, I tried disclosing myself a little, which short-circuited the transference. By focusing on our real relationship, I was able to help her see that ours was a therapeutic – not an erotic – relationship. When I told her a few months later that I was getting married, she congratulated me. We spoke about whether she would experience my marriage as a kind of loss, and she minimized it. But sometime later, when I suggested that she might be able to pay more for her treatment, she sidestepped the issue and seemed indignant. I think she felt that I was adding insult to injury. Not only had I married someone else, but now I wanted her to pay more for our time together. The issues with her past, which seemed to have resolved, were still real and present in her mind.

What bothers me is that she was unwilling even to talk about my request. I tried to point out some obvious connections, such as between love (i.e., unrequited love) and money, and explore what raising my fee may have meant. But she was unreceptive. The only way to actually resolve the situation would be to have her come in and discuss it, which she apparently is not willing to do. We can only reach the past through the present which, in Ms. Steward's case, is in suspended animation. Some patients willingly remain trapped in cycles governed by authority figures and may never emerge unless they decide to deal with those relationships – and reverse those cycles – for their own reasons. Until they do, it is hard to speak about their "realities" in the present tense, since what is real for them is the past.

> *People normally transfer feelings about parents and siblings onto partners and children, often unaware of the transference. Even where resemblances are slight, the psychological dynamic of the re-created relationship is significant. It may affect marital and sexual choices, career relationships, and other major life decisions. In psychodynamic therapy, when transference is projected onto the therapist, there is an opportunity to examine it, provided the transference is seen as such. Analysis of transference is central to the process of psychodynamic psychotherapy. This is why therapists may be so interested in the meaning of who we are to the patient.*

Motivation

Debbie was an attractive 35-year-old artist from California. She was depressed after ending an affair with a patron of her work, a stereotype alpha male. I treated her with a small dose of an SSRI medication, and she was feeling much better, so she suggested it might be best just to come once a month for monitoring. I doubted it, however, because even though she did well in therapy she did not seem motivated to examine what caused the depression.

I had only a vague idea of her background. Her father was bipolar and a prominent art dealer. The boundaries between him and Debbie were unclear – mostly, she was a mothering caretaker, though once he had tried to commit suicide in her bed. I had no clear picture of her mother except that she hated Debbie's father and divorced him. Debbie married a man whom she described as emotionally distant, and it was only after her divorce that she became orgasmic. She was frank about her personal history, and even good-humored. But she really doubted if more psychotherapy would be useful. She felt she needed to get out more, socialize, and meet someone. Only if things failed to progress as she hoped would she come in to talk.

When I brought up the time sensitivity of some of the issues she was dealing with, she became angry. She said that she already felt burdened enough by her biological clock and did not need me to remind her of it. I then suggested that her relationships with men might be affected by her relationship with her father, but she found this observation too general. Still, she talked about a man she was dating who did not seem like "a keeper." He was nice, successful, and Jewish like her father, but she saw him as bland and boring. Finally, I commented that if a nice guy was available, she seemed uninterested, and this intrigued her. We began talking more about her dysfunctional relationship with her father and, by the end of the hour, I sensed that she might continue in therapy on a more regular basis.

The fact is that I had touched a nerve. I made the past seem as if it had invaded the present and colonized it. The past was keeping her from owning the present. I literally wanted her to confront the past and retake the present. She needed to become self-determining. I told her that the past – her past – was a complex, conflicted place that she had *allowed* to take her over because she was not sufficiently aware of its influence. I said that she ought to become an activist on her own behalf, and that therapy could provide the wherewithal to see her current relationships from a fresh perspective. She seemed a bit startled by the possibility.

As therapists, our arguments are frequently made with graphic, vivid metaphors that startle people into recognition. I imagined the scene in Debbie's mind as the past, dressed not like her father, but as an army that took over her psyche. In this scenario, she would be roused enough to push back.

The therapist responds to the patient based on his own past. This is "countertransference" and it is integral to psychodynamic treatment. When the therapist examines his response to the patient, it can provide insights into what the patient is trying, perhaps unconsciously, to elicit from the therapist. Does the therapist feel hostile toward, or perhaps aroused by the patient? Why? What would the patient like the therapist to think? Therapists' own motivations, desires, and even fears provide insights into their patients' psyches. There is a complex entanglement in the dyadic relationship of psychotherapy (e.g., Two Minds in a Mirror*).*

Impediments to love

Mr. Lauren's mother did not know much about mothering. But she thought she did by virtue of being female. The idea was naive, of course, and an extension of her narcissism. The problem was that Mr. Lauren had his own self-involvement – he claimed that circumstances left him no choice – and so the two found each other insufferable.

Yet, as a child, Mr. Lauren found his mother seductive. Some of his earliest memories involved sneaking into bed with her, watching her undress and bathe. This resulted in Mr. Lauren's getting stuck in an infantile mode of attachment, where relationships were perpetually sexualized without maturing. Intimacy meant physicality. It was a way of bringing women close but also keeping them distant, much the way he had experienced his mother. He tended to see girlfriends as little more than stereotyped sex objects.

The early relationship with his mother was an impediment to adult love. Over time, we tried to understand the residual effects of this relationship, so that he could initiate a healthier, more mature relationship. We got to that point through talk therapy, though not by pursuing the idea – favored by some – that the best way to disown the past is to reject it outright. Therapists should not ordinarily coax someone to hate what they once loved and may still love, since attachment to significant others is valuable, even when people understand the resulting conflicts and pathology. Moreover, if the therapist pushes too hard against a past filled with loved ones, the therapy can pitch into reverse – the therapist becomes the object of hate, not the past. So, I told Mr. Lauren that it was still okay to love his mother, and even to have fantasies about his eroticized childhood. What was not okay, in terms of his own success as an adult, was to allow his sentiments to overtake his present romantic initiatives. In other words, I suggested that his attachment to the past was still part of who he was – it just should not become so predominant that it prevented his further self-definition and intimacy as an adult.

How a child attaches to its mother is crucial to human development and the formation of social relationships. Consistent caregiving makes for a more secure base from which to explore the world. It helps in regulating one's emotions and promotes adaptability and personal growth. But when the mother/child relationship is eroticized, it can lead to issues with separation during childhood, affecting intimacy and trust in adulthood. In terms of emotional well-being, there is no substitute for good mothering—or as Donald Winnicott put it, having a "good enough" mother. Parenting has a steep learning curve.

Perspective

Mr. Wordsworth called early this Sunday morning. Patients understand that I need a day off and rarely infringe except in an emergency. So, when he announced he was on the tennis court at his country club, I was puzzled. What kind of psychological disaster befalls tennis players on a bright Sunday morning?

It turned out that the previous afternoon he had seen the woman with whom he was having an affair with another man. He was quick to add that the man was older and nothing special, but it still upset him. During his treatment, we had spoken about his depressive response to conducting the affair, one of which was that the women came and went as they pleased. He had no control, as he had (or said he had) in his marriage. This brought up issues of his not being able to control himself when, as a child, he stuttered. He did not think about that stutter very much, but was sure that it left him feeling vulnerable, especially because he had been mocked and bullied. I suggested that the prospect of losing a woman stirred up these old feelings.

He agreed and asked if some medication could help him feel better. I pointed out the obvious, that he was on a nice tennis court with a beautiful day ahead of him. I added that exercise and sunlight were good antidepressants. And so why not enjoy the day?

Often, therapists offer simplicity. Patients come in seeking complexity, some miracle molecule that will take away their troubles. But a simple solution is likely the better approach since, ultimately, it requires the patient to use the resources at his disposal and, thereby, to cope. Simplicity teaches coping. It requires the patient to look around, assess his circumstances, and figure out how to make the most of them. As circumstances change, the habit of mind continues, adapting itself to whatever is at hand. If this sounds almost too simple, or even simplistic, it isn't. Rather, it's a kind of soft discipline. It differs from mere acceptance because it requires work. But like discipline, it frees the person from dependence.

So far as I know, Mr. Wordsworth took my advice. Whether he understands its long-term application remains to be seen, but I intend to talk with him about this. Of course, we should probably address, as well, the problem of having affairs, and how they will constantly resurrect past feelings of vulnerability. Does he want to keep feeling vulnerable? Sometimes the best coping mechanism is to stop the conduct that causes the problem ... though therapists are realists, not moralists, and we have to take our own advice about coping.

> Stuttering, like many medical and psychiatric conditions, has both biological and psychosocial dimensions. It affects 70 million people worldwide. While there are different types of stuttering, they can all leave the stutterer with low self-esteem; stutterers feel embarrassed, ashamed, and out of control and are prone to being bullied. If a clinician views the condition as primarily psychological, he would be apt to mistreat it. By understanding the etiology of the condition and the neurophysiology and brain mechanisms involved, he can treat it more effectively. This is true of many conditions that were once the purview of psychoanalytic treatments such as OCD, autism, and bipolar conditions.

Siblings

Time had an article this week about how siblings can significantly affect a person's life trajectory. But this was not just the old truism. Today, the focus is on genetics. The issue is not whether family matters to a person's development but, rather, how to balance interpersonal relations against physiology.

I recalled Bobby's relationship with his older brother, who frequently pummelled him for no apparent reason. It may have involved the guilt he felt as their father progressively declined. But it had a profoundly negative influence on Bobby. He eventually fantasized openly about striking back at his brother. Into adulthood, Bobby remained too traumatized to engage him competitively in writing, karate, or recalling the lyrics to old songs. While his brother became a second-degree black belt, Bobby got injured and dropped out.

It's interesting to consider how we overcome our negative family dynamics and become stronger, better selves. A child relates to its siblings, and parents respond. Siblings identify with aspects of each parent but may also enact the dynamics of their parents' relationship. The therapist has to develop an intergenerational understanding of his patients. At different points in a patient's treatment, various familial relationships will come more sharply into focus, but invariably every relationship is inflected with every other one. Families are kaleidoscopic. Therapists must look in all directions.

I had to dive into the relationship between Bobby's parents if I was ever to understand how he could recover the self-esteem that his *brother* had damaged. The French have a term, *mise en abyme*, which is a technique of placing a copy of an image within itself in a way that suggests an infinitely receding sequence. That is what it's like to examine family dynamics. To understand today, you need to start from the assumption that there are past versions of today – and then you have to examine them. Patients often resist reconstructing these old relationships. So, in a way, the therapist must encourage them to think like a therapist and see the value in enduring the pain of recollection.

Because a patient's relationship to siblings can result in transference, the patient's relationships with peers can be negatively impacted by an adversarial relationship with a sibling. These transferences play out in psychodynamic treatment as well. I often want to know who I am to the person speaking with me – in the sense of who I represent to him. The answer often helps explain what a patient is talking about and informs how I listen.

Connection

Dan came in today, complaining of depression. Over the past several days, he had been *so* depressed that he spent one night on the bathroom floor curled up in a fetal position. He was having suicidal thoughts. Each day was a struggle to get out of bed, and a real accomplishment to go to work. When I asked what the matter was, he said, "She won't have sex with me." When I asked what that meant to him, he said, "We're not connecting."

Dan explained that his girlfriend had been busy with her own life over the past several weeks and did not have as much time for him. This was true. She was opening a restaurant. But I was still surprised by the intensity of his depressive response. He had been doing much better and taking good care of himself. When I asked what he made of being so depressed, he thought back to when his mother had been so preoccupied with her life that she seemed to have abandoned him. He clearly saw his depression, at least in part, as based in this aspect of his history. But his crisis was now, and he asked what he could do.

I suggested that when he's in the thick of it, he could remind himself that such feelings are generally time limited and will pass as they have before. He said he tried to do that but it was hard. I responded that he might keep in mind that his response did not further his relationship with the woman he wanted to marry. He agreed. He needed to be more confident and less in need. I said that sometimes people wished to be needy so that someone would rescue them – a false assumption, since few people want to assume the burden.

Dan looked flushed. He had used that gambit as a child and had tried to elicit rescuing responses from his grandparents when his mother seemed to have abandoned him. We talked about this and were able to see more clearly how those wishes, which may have served some purpose during his childhood, had crippled him now and undermined a relationship he was trying to foster.

What emerged is that childish modes of forming connections will likely backfire in adults. What worked once will not always work later. Moreover, rescue is not love. A child can mistakenly equate the two, but adults should know better. Our conceptions of love needs to grow with us and mature with us. Otherwise, we risk remaining in a fetal position in terms of how we connect to other people.

A dream

At first, I had put it out of my mind, but then it returned. So just before I went to bed, I sat down to record a dream that Mr. Pierre reported earlier today. The night he returned from holiday, he dreamt that he was piloting a plane. He was taking off from New York but could not get the plane to rise. He saw the Twin Towers straight ahead and knew he would crash into one. He awoke in a cold sweat.

Mr. Pierre had long-standing fears of being trapped, so flying had always been a source of anxiety. Thoughts of 9/11 were, of course, still on people's minds, and when he heard our President's speech, he had not felt reassured. But each of us transposes events into the key of our own experience. How something signifies is based in what has significance to us. For Mr. Pierre, the Twin Towers represented his desire for a second child. He noted that one tower was smaller than the other – "younger" as he put it – and he was unsure whether he had the strength to rise above it. In his scheme of signification, he wasn't sure if he could handle a second child. He wondered if he were man enough.

I thought about my Twin Towers of work and love. It can be devastating when an event, perhaps a personal calamity, shatters what one has built. So maybe I avoided writing this evening because I didn't want to piece together signifiers from my own past with the present. I didn't, perhaps, want to interpret their current meaning. I think Thoreau said, "It's good to build towers in the air. That's where they belong. Now put foundations under them." Thinking about the present is the only way to fully comprehend the past, to put it in perspective as markers, and to see that we have not changed all that much from the past, or diverged from the direction in which we seem to be headed. That can be a scary revelation. For all our trying to grow out of those old signifiers, they still signify.

When therapists analyze a patient's past, we inevitably realize – because we are good at analyzing the past, and we find stuff – that we have deliberately neglected to analyze our own. We would as soon not put it together with what we know about our current selves and would like to assume that we have evolved. We play games with ourselves that we do not allow our patients to play. We can always fall back on being too busy, but it's hard to buy into our own excuses when we know the truth.

> *Freud said that dreams are "the royal road" to the unconscious, and his* Interpretation of Dreams *(1899) is a seminal text of psychoanalytic literature. Thus, while contemporary neuroscience may doubt whether dreams have meaning, psychoanalysts and psychodynamic therapists have little question that they do. Freud suggested that the imagery in dreams often contains residue of the day; he called the underlying*

wishes and fears that play out in the dream, "the dreamwork" (which Steven Spielberg adopted as the name for his studios).

Dreams tend to be primarily visual but may have auditory or other sensual components. Significantly, they have manifest content – which can be literally described – and also latent content, which emerges when one analyzes the dream's meaning. Mostly, dreams reflect what is or has recently been on the dreamer's mind, and their interpretation is therefore useful to increasing a person's insight and self- understanding.

Identifications

Today, Mrs. Kennedy talked about how hard it is for her to enjoy life. She takes care of her husband and struggles with her own ailments. But even in her free time, she can't enjoy what she's doing and give herself to the moment. For instance, she very much enjoys gardening. But while she was repotting some plants the other day, she kept thinking that she should be doing something else.

I asked whether doing something she enjoyed was not enough. She said that it was not. Her mother had regularly criticized any form of "amusement" and, when Mrs. Kennedy was a child, even discouraged simple games as "frivolous." Mrs. Kennedy described times when she was excited about something – acting in a play, writing a story, opening a gift – and her mother would respond negatively with "Why would you want to do that?" or "That's a waste of time." Mrs. Kennedy never forgave her mother for what she felt was indiscriminate, sanctimonious disapproval ... but she still internalized that disapproval and applied it whenever she thought to have even a moment's fun (let alone relief from caring for her husband and herself).

She understood that her mother was probably unaware of how completely she had limited her child's right to play. She also believed that her mother would not have wished to blight her right to enjoy life as an adult. Yet, she was still angry, and then turned that anger on herself by shrinking from any sort of sustained pleasure. It was as if she was mad at herself for being mad at her mother and therefore punished herself by reimposing her mother's constraints. The logic was bizarre and self-defeating, but remarkably common. Rather than deal with the past and try to get beyond its effect, she kept the past alive and potent so as to avoid the sticky issue of repudiating her mother's demands. She was afraid that any such repudiation would result in even greater anger at her mother and, thus, a failure to love her mother as she felt bound to do. Ultimately, she was willing to sacrifice her own happiness out of fear that she would let go of or even stop loving a parent – which seemed to her a terrifying prospect, cutting her off from her moorings.

I pointed out the obvious: she relates to herself as her mother related to her. Mrs. Kennedy had been aware of this tendency for some time, but bringing it to her attention gave her the chance to examine it further. She asked what she could possibly gain by it, and I explained what I felt to be her logic – even though her mother was now dead, the prospect of not loving her memory seemed more damaging than anything she could do to herself by imposing her mother's constraints. Initially, the idea that she might "gain" from some negative, punitive aspect of her mother was difficult to process. But as she continued to think about what I had said, she began to come around. We spoke about why her mother may have behaved as she did and, once again, we descended into a *mise en abyme* of endless regress to get some handle on the present.

Mrs. Kennedy said she was glad her mother was dead, but I was not so sure. It may have been that all these years, as she feared a loss of love for her mother, she also felt that applying her mother's strictures was a kind of protection. They kept her from letting go, from liking anything too much. In her current state, even simple pleasures seemed like alluring, possibly addictive temptations, and her mother's dead hand protected her. I am not sure that she will ever emerge from this web of justification – and it is a web, since her fear that she might stop loving her mother is mixed up with the fear that the unhappiness her mother ordained now works to keep her safe. Problems regarding the intractable presence of the past, when compounded with intergenerational crises, are hard to sort out. They depend on the patient's willingness to try, which is often prevented by complex, deep-seated grounds for resistance of which patients may not be aware or don't want to address.

The term "identification" refers to the process whereby a person assimilates an attribute of another, often a parent or significant other from childhood. The process generally occurs subconsciously. Thus, a son might identify with his father as part of resolving the Oedipal phase of development. After losing a loved one, a person may identify, with certain traits or characteristics in the loved one as a way of coping with the loss.

Getting engaged

Blair has been thinking more about getting engaged. Not that her boyfriend has asked yet. But he seems headed in that direction. They spend at least a couple of nights a week together as well as the weekends. They are going on two vacations with his parents in the coming months as well as one on their own. There has been some talk about ring size. So, there is more continuity and shared experience in their relationship.

However, even as they get closer – or maybe because they do – Blair wonders if he is The One. She feels that perhaps there is something missing. This subject came up in a dream that she shared yesterday. As she described it: "I was walking with my brother. I was going to see my boyfriend, but I could not remember his name. I started to say the names of former boyfriends – Ari, Aaron, etc. My aunt was also in the background." Blair's brother had introduced her to her boyfriend, so it made sense that she was looking to him for the name. She recognized that forgetting the name connected with her fear that their relationship was missing something. For example, after almost a year of dating, he had never said "I love you." She felt that their connection was more limited than she would like and wanted to deepen it – to know his name, his essence – but didn't know how. Her aunt had married a man who in some ways was like her boyfriend – friendly but aloof. She saw the aunt as unhappy in her marriage, although her aunt had never divorced.

There was another aspect of the dream too. Blair's college sweetheart, the love of her life, was named "Aaron." The boyfriend that she had dated, who loved her more than anyone else, was named "Ari." Of course, my given name is Ahron and my nickname is Ari. So, I wondered if there might be some connection with me that was holding her back. If she had been in analysis with me, I would have been more apt to make this observation. Given that she was in a one-time-per-week, insight-oriented psychotherapy, I thought that my observation might be farther from her conscious experience and either come off as self-involved or distance her from me. So, I let it go.

But it can be frustrating when a therapist suspects that an element of a patient's past is possibly relevant albeit perhaps beyond reach. In Blair's case, I did not want to make myself (or who I represented to her) the focus of her feelings, or of her treatment, so I risked missing an opening – at least for a while. She understood transferences and how older men could represent powerful father figures. If this turned out to be a key element of treatment, we could always revisit it later. I had to weigh whether I was being ego-obsessed in imagining that an apparent coincidence – Aaron, Ari, Ahron – was not a coincidence and might usefully be introduced into our explorations. I had found what might be a plausible explanation of Blair's unwillingness to commit, and yet – partly out of my own ambivalence, partly to keep her focus reality-based – I tabled it for later. I keep thinking that Blair probably already realized my quandary, maybe even would say "Oh, let's talk about it!" We knew each other well enough for that kind of conversation. So perhaps sometimes I'm a bit too skittish, even to bring up the obvious.

Intimacy

Blair began the session today talking about what to get her boyfriend for the holidays. She knew that what *she* most wanted was a ring, even though she had her doubts about commitment. For her boyfriend, she was considering one of two gifts and wondered whether either might make a difference in getting him to Tiffany's. One gift was a generic dinner theater package; the other was a personal case for his watch collection. Both cost about the same. She saw the first as better because it appeared to cost less and so would impose less of an obligation. The other seemed to display more thought and caring, but fairly screamed, "Hey, I'm interested."

I commented that more intimacy and involvement made her nervous, even though she attributed the emotional restraint to him. This deflection, as it were, is common among people conflicted over a relationship. But she replied that in other relationships she had experienced more intimacy and even love. The first was with her college sweetheart, whom she was not ready to marry. The other was with a boyfriend whom she loved but for whom she felt little passion. When I did not say anything, Blair looked uncomfortable, and I asked what she was thinking. She recalled how as a girl her brother would often punch her when she tried to be pals. They would fight like cats and dogs. For Blair, getting close to a man around her age meant getting hurt. The fact that her brother had since introduced her to her current boyfriend did not change her feeling.

Blair went on to speak candidly about concerns with her current boyfriend. She said that she loved him but felt frustrated that he did not express those feelings in words to her. But as we spoke about her past, and especially her brother, it became clear that she was projecting that old relationship onto this new one, and then blaming her boyfriend in their relationship – not herself – for the lack of intimacy. One way that we try to escape our past is to deny or at least minimize its effects in the present. Blair loved her brother now, and hung out with him, and did not want to burden their friendship with memories of their childhood fights – let alone with examining the effect of those fights on her current relationships with men. So instead, she denied the effect of the past relationship or, rather, just tried to finesse it.

But you cannot finesse the past. It's there and it stays there. You have to admit its relevance – if it is relevant – and then deal with its effects constructively. As Blair began doing that by being honest with herself, she came closer to some stable resolution of the issues that were keeping her from developing mature, honest relationships.

Erikson's theory of personal development frames the first stage of adulthood in terms of love (intimacy versus isolation). Forming real relationships is important during this period. People who feel loved and cared for growing up are more likely to experience intimacy in adulthood. Of course, there are exceptions since life is complex.

Complications

Now that Mr. Block is married, he sounds almost happy. I say "almost" because he tends not to embrace positive feelings. He might say, for instance, that he did not have a particularly unpleasant time with his in-laws.

Over the years, we have discussed this tendency to minimize the pleasure that he takes in things, and to surround even presumably great experiences – like his bachelor party – with double negatives – "Oh, I didn't have a bad time." He has suggested that all this interpolated negativity is perhaps a way to protect himself, and so I asked what came to mind about getting hurt when he described a nominally pleasant situation.

He recalled two instances from childhood. Both involved his older sister, when he was four years old. In one, he described acting in a "play" with his sister and her friends. He was playing the role of a hurt bird. His sister and her friends abandoned him and then came back laughing. In the other, he was excited about getting fried chicken that his sister and her friends had supposedly baked especially for him. But it turned out to be dried dog doo.

We were able to connect these memories of initial excitement and expectant pleasure with letdown, hurt, and disappointment. Obviously, they were humiliating, and Mr. Block said he could recall many more like them. They underscored how our past is like a lens which shapes how we experience the present. By extension, the past conditions how we communicate with others and allow them to understand us. A conversation with Mr. Block is invariably joyless. It lacks grace notes. It can be interpreted as lacking in gratefulness and, hence, to reflect a type of egocentrism.

Yet, once you get to know Mr. Block, you realize that he is hardly egocentric and is capable of gratitude even for the smallest courtesy. *His problem is with expectation.* His early history set a pattern of pratfalls that he has never managed to forget. Thus, while he is actually quite well-adjusted, he keeps imagining that everything will fall apart. He protects himself by discounting happiness in advance – it is all just a house of cards. It's about to collapse, or at least that's what he tells himself to avoid disappointment. His language is part of a protection racket that his memory enforces.

Now we are working on how he can create a disconnect between his early, unhappy memories and the life he leads now. We are going to start on his language – his double negatives – and then work back toward his assumption that what applied when he was four years old does not dictate his existence now. When you say this, of course it sounds so logical and obvious. Yet any therapist will admit that logical, obvious approaches to healing still take a long time. The patient has to believe in the diagnosis and then let it sink in. I think that Mr. Block will, in time, come around, since his nice life is so completely at variance with how he is wont to describe it.

Further Reading

Ashbery, John. *Self-Portrait in a Convex Mirror*. New York: Penguin Group, 1972.
Berger, Jonah. *Invisible Influence: The Hidden Forces that Shape Behavior*. New York: Simon & Schuster, 2017.
Bloom, Harold. *The Anxiety of Influence: A Theory of Poetry*. Oxford: Oxford University Press, 1973.
Cialdini, Robert. *Influence: The Psychology of Persuasion*. New York: William Morrow and Company, 1984.
Darwin, Charles. *The Origin of Species by Means of Natural Selection; Or the Preservation of Favoured Races in the Struggle for Life*. London: John Murray, 1882.
Gardner, Howard. *Changing Minds: The Art and Science of Changing Our Own and Other People's Minds*. Boston: Harvard Business School Press, 2006.
Mitchell, Margaret. *Gone with the Wind*. New York: Macmillan Publishing Company, 1936.
Sheldrake, Rupert. *The Presence of the Past: Morphic Resonance and the Memory of Nature*. Rochester, VT: Park Street Press, 1988.
Straus, Joseph. *Remaking the Past: Musical Modernism and the Influence of Tonal Tradition*. Cambridge: Harvard University Press, 1990.
Ury, William. *Getting Past No: Negotiating in Difficult Situations*. New York: Bantam Books, 1991.

6 Insight and understanding

"Insight" and "understanding" are integral to personal growth and change. But what do we mean by these terms? In psychotherapy, they are not terms of art, with arcane meanings sequestered in some professional dictionary. Nonetheless, in the context of psychotherapy, they apply specifically to the enhanced self-awareness that develops – in both therapist and patient – as the therapeutic relationship deepens and (ideally) produces transformation.

Insight, which has its etymological root in "sight," literally means to see into a person or thing. It penetrates the surface, beneath what is apparent to the eye. For purposes of psychotherapy, insight into oneself is crucial to personal growth and change because, if you don't see who you've been and where you are, it's hard to change course.

However, insight is not the same as understanding, since accurately perceiving reality – even in all its dimensions – does not equate to its proper interpretation. You can see an entire Chinese screen painting down to its minutest detail, but do you know what it all means? Understanding is insight + comprehension. In the context of psychotherapy, understanding involves the ability to mentally encompass oneself, others, or a situation. It may involve empathy or compassion or tolerance. If insight comes in a flash, understanding is more like a light that grows brighter and is, finally, sustained. It's a sacred cow of psychodynamic work – no understanding, no change – although the reality is, of course, more complex. Understanding who you have been can lead to peace of mind and, consequently, a greater ability to change.

This chapter will examine how insight and understanding can develop over the course of therapy.

Being distracted

I've seen Mr. Adman a couple of times. He's bright and creative and works in film and TV production. I was familiar with his work prior to his coming to see me, so I was interested to actually meet him.

He complained of chronic inattention, which he said interfered with his creativity. He could not focus on a project for long and would come up with bright ideas but have trouble pursuing them. Since he met the diagnostic criteria for Attention Deficit Disorder (ADD), I thought to prescribe a medication to see if it helped. But then I thought again.

I remembered how in our initial meetings there was no mention of his father. He had spoken at some length about his wife, son, mother, and sister. But all I knew about his father was that he was a lawyer, so I asked him to tell me more. He replied that his father worked all the time, even when he finally came home. He was the managing partner at his firm and had argued and won landmark cases. In passing, Mr. Adman mentioned that he didn't want to be like his father in terms of constant drudgery.

I called his attention to this remark, noting that he had gone into a creative, less structured industry. I added that he was definitely not like his father in that his father was burdened by too much focus – not too little. Mr. Adman looked flush. He said that he had never thought of that before. We went on to explore other ways in which he was like or unlike his father. I don't know if it will make a difference in terms of his inattention, but the connection to his father started him thinking about why he had ADD in the first place.

Sometimes, insights have to take shape once the initial realization emerges. In the moment, Mr. Adman recognised that he was radically different from his father: his father could focus on a project intensely, while he struggled. This was significant. There is an issue over whether ADD is purely physical – the result of neurotransmitters and brain mechanisms – or whether there is a psychological component that, at the very least, can exacerbate the physical predisposition. In time, as we explore Mr. Adman's relationship to his father, and his dislike of his father's total absorption in work, it may emerge that his ADD is motivated (at least in part) by a negative reaction to and conflict with his father. If this is the case, and Mr. Adman is acting out against his father by avoiding extended professional commitments, then we can work on how he can deal with his own reactions. Maybe he can gradually take on responsibility until he reaches a level that is appropriate – not crazy, like his father's MO, but still suited to making a career in his field.

In therapy, we have to cultivate patience. Insights signal just the start of a path toward change and usually require more insights before that path leads anywhere useful. We have to counsel the patient, after an initial "aha moment," that the process of change has just begun and takes time. Most importantly, the patient needs to realize that it takes hard work – and possibly pain – to gain insight and real understanding. After that, the practical work begins of applying the insight to one's life. It all makes sense as you say it, but when you are very close to the situation, the process seems demanding, complex, and uncertain as to its outcome. But every effort has to start somewhere, sometime, and in Mr. Adman's case it is here and now.

> Many psychiatric conditions such as depression, anxiety, and trauma impact on one's ability to pay attention. While in the case of ADD, the primary symptom is a functional impairment of attention, other symptoms can include motivational difficulty, problems with organization, social impairment, and restlessness. ADD can be readily treated with psychostimulants, which are generally safe. It is remarkable to see a patient with ADD, who has suffered in school or at work, respond to proper treatment. An hour after taking medication, he may report that he cannot remember the last time he was able to focus and so well. Naturally, his work and other areas of his life may also improve.

Oedipus again

Mr. Pierre reported another curious dream: "I was walking alongside a pushcart. A dwarf was lying in it. A horse passed by in the other direction and bit me on the neck. I awoke with a start." He commented that the cart seemed to be heading toward a graveyard, and that he was accompanying it. At first, the dwarf did not remind him of anyone. But when we focused on it, he said his boss actually reminded him of a dwarf – small and thick limbed. He had previously realised that he wanted to "slay" his boss and claim his position. As to the horse that bit him, he remembered waking up that morning with a sore throat, which ached on that side.

Mr. Pierre recalled learning to ride a pony growing up. He found it scary and felt he could never control "an animal." He was told to be very careful in how he fed it lest it bite him. Once he thought it did try to nip him. During his treatment, Mr. Pierre wondered if in response to his murderous wishes, he feared a painful consequence. In this regard, he recalled thinking when he was young that if he became a success, he would pay a price, though he found it difficult to elaborate. He could only say that his father was prone to angry outbursts.

When Mr. Pierre finished recounting his dream, I wanted to "interpret" it. But dreams pose an almost impossible challenge, since the symbolism – if we can call it that – is unclear, and since the patient's memory is unreliable. That is, there is no 1:1 correspondence between a figure or event in a dream and individuals or phenomena in a person's life; nor can anyone perfectly recall the kaleidoscopic unfolding of a dream. The only truth in the patient's version of a dream may be in which elements he chooses to recount – in Mr. Pierre's case, his boss and his father featured prominently. If he was to achieve any insight from the dream, it would flow from his retelling it, which suggests that his father and his boss are significant figures in his life that bear further discussion.

So, we have a place to start. But until there is more context, more actual information about these two figures and their role in Mr. Pierre's life, we will not make much progress. I explained to Mr. Pierre that in future sessions, once we have learned more, we may refer back to the dream ... but at this point, our understanding of it is limited. This is because dreams are frequently illuminating only after we can situate them within a larger knowledge base, sometimes months in the making. We will keep the dream in storage, as it were, for future reference.

> *Dreams have both manifest and latent aspects. In psychoanalysis, there is often intense interest in the underlying or unconscious aspect of the dream that comes to light through interpretation. But the manifest dream, which the person himself describes, is often useful to work with as well. Sometimes our competitive wishes and strivings – as well as other mental content – are apparent and important to consider. You do not even have to scratch the surface to see it.*

Settling down

Bobby loves his girlfriend, but when he talks about marrying her, he refers to it as an "intrusion," an "imposition." His refers to a caveman in his lair and (mixing metaphors) to giving up a bachelor pad. He wants to move ahead with his life but feels anxious about it.

During our last session, there was an uncomfortable silence surrounding the topic of marriage, and I wondered aloud what he was thinking. Bobby replied that he was thinking about his brother. He recalled how, when they were growing up, the brother claimed Bobby's room as a weight room. There was hardly any space left for Bobby to sleep, and though he tried to reclaim the room, he felt powerless to fight back. He found his parents ineffectual as well. So, while he finally just capitulated, he felt enraged at his bother for his "intrusions." He commented that he wanted to punch him and "break his head with a barbell." He saw the obvious connection between his brother's invading his space as a child and taking his next steps as an adult.

Bobby spoke further about his parents' "intrusions" into his life and each other's. He recalled his father's banging his wheelchair on the bedroom door to wake him up on weekend mornings. He described fights his parents had about personal space in a tight apartment, as well as his grandmother's annoying, busybody calls. So, he recognised that a significant part of what he was struggling with did not have to do with his romantic relationship so much as it did with what it stirred up in him.

The question now is how to apply Bobby's awareness. Frequently, "insight" does not apply to – or at least stop at – the contours of a problem but, rather, to how that problem should be addressed. How does Bobby retrain or, perhaps better, come to terms with his associations with his brother and his parents so that they do not distort his desire to settle down? How can he construct defenses that withstand these associations and not let them pervade his thoughts when he even thinks about a life together with his girlfriend? It's like the old joke of telling someone to sit in a room for an hour and not think of a pink elephant. Whatever they try to think about instead of the elephant just seems like an elephant substitute – potent enough to recall the elephant itself.

Bobby will just have to imagine that the real, ultimate defense against these associations is positive associations with commitment. We are going to work on that, drawing on how much fun he has when, for example, he and his girlfriend go away for the weekend. He will have to generalize those good times into a pattern for his life. That is, he will have to believe that such a pattern is possible. Insight often comes when we change what we think, like turning off a negative switch and turning on a positive one. Negative breaks a good human connection, positive makes it. If Bobby can get to that place, he will literally be home.

The importance of Oedipal issues is well established in human psychology. Oedipal urges contribute to conscious and unconscious mental processes that guide the lives of men and women and may even determine specific behaviors. This was famously captured in the Greek myth of Oedipus Rex, in which Oedipus unknowingly kills his father and then beds his mother. The tale has endured because it reflects an essential aspect of the human drama: the competitive striving with the father for the mother's love. Freud famously described this psychological dynamic as the Oedipus Complex, an internalization of the "family romance" conflict, which can later play out in one's life. If normal development is disrupted during childhood, the struggle can become more extreme. Where a father is absent or unavailable, the child may develop guilt, anxiety, and other symptoms that can alter his life. Insight into this central conflict can therefore lead to a more balanced life.

Symptoms

Symptoms indicate a problem that needs to be addressed. Generally, they are a source of acute pain – that's how they come to our notice – but if untreated, they can cause chronic distress. They manifest as obvious, problematic behaviours but also as quiet, persistent calls for help.

Mr. Lauren was certainly symptomatic. He had been troubled by his job loss. Colleagues were aware of it, as were his friends. He had bad dreams and negative thoughts ranging in a stubborn arc from his past to the future. He had difficulty falling asleep, and getting out of bed in the morning was an act of will. Since he did not have to go to work, he tended to linger in bed – a safe haven – as long as he could. He exuded a sense of "woe is me," and he was conspicuously depressed.

In addition, prior to his recent difficulties, he had a history of depressive episodes. The first was when he was in college and away from home. He felt a sense of loss that he could not shake for the months that he was away. His symptoms resolved when he came home, but they left him feeling vulnerable. He had another bout of depression when he was in law school during a stressful semester. He was an average student, and this sense of being like everyone else did not help his self-esteem. His depression was worse in the morning, but stayed with him the entire day. It brought him into therapy for the first time.

At the time, Mr. Lauren responded well to a brief course of weekly, insight-oriented psychotherapy. The experience made an impression on him. He found it remarkable that his depression and other symptoms could be relieved through talking to another person.

Now, however, coupled with his depression (though independent of it) was the intermittent habit of pulling out his hair. The habit was painful, and I noticed a bald patch behind his right ear. The behavior started when he was abroad and had recurred during law school when he was under stress. But, at times, it seemed to have a life of its own, whatever his mood, and follow him around like a bad haircut, so to speak. Why? What did it mean? It might be a common denominator for several conflicts, expressed as anger and self-loathing. He was literally attacking himself, almost as an alter ego (i.e., providing visible *company* for when he was lonely abroad); reminding himself that stress at exam time was counterproductive; and now, berating himself for losing his job. It jibed with feelings of guilt, punishment, and repressed eroticism.

Addressing one or another cause would not necessarily relieve such an entrenched behavior. Where there is a complex of causes, the symptom often has to be addressed on multiple fronts. We started by talking about how he felt about his job loss (embarrassed, inadequate) and agreed to move on to his general dislike of himself and how he reacts under stress. Obviously, we can't substitute admiration in the place of such feelings, but we can attempt to view them from a perspective of neutrality. "Okay, that's what I did, that's how I felt, but now I'm over it." Insight sometimes comes in the form of just admitting that the past is past, and we cannot carry around our toxic reactions to it forever. Insight is sometimes just accepting how things were. If Mr. Lauren achieves this bit of wisdom, he could stop pulling out his hair.

The relationship with one's mother is also important in terms of child development. This earlier phase (i.e., prior to sexual competition with the father) is sometimes called the pre-Oedipal phase – the mother/ child dynamic that is internalized in the mind of the developing child and becomes part of his or her psychic structure. If that relationship is disturbed in some way (e.g., by an absent or overstimulating mother), it becomes a source of psychological conflict. As the child grows up, he may relate to himself in similar ways that the mother used to, which may become a source of depression, anxiety, guilt, shame, and doubt about oneself.

Lost moment

Sometimes it's such an effort to think at the end of a day. The work can be draining. I make a note of each session for my records, but they become a blur. It's often hard to say what is most important in a session, or even remember. Take, for example, my session with Fran.

Fran, an accomplished 80-year-old European woman, presented for treatment with a prolonged grief reaction. She was suffering over the loss of her husband of more than 50 years. They had been very close, and his death left her feeling empty. But she was trying to revive herself. She liked to write, and now with some encouragement from me, she was publishing her first book. She was beginning to tutor at the local community center she had founded. She was deepening her relationship with her sister and even beginning to make new friends.

There was a moment in today's session when Fran made an important connection. But I can't quite recall what it was! She reported being trapped in some kind of repetitive fear or maybe it was that she feared being trapped. I remember I made a cognitive intervention to broaden her perspective on the situation that she found useful. But it did not get at the heart of what she was saying. I asked her if anything came to mind about being trapped. She recalled a memory from childhood. I can't even recall what it was – something to do with her older sister and a trauma as a child. But it came back to her with a clarity and presence that evoked a physical response on her part. She felt a chill and numbness in one of her legs. That's what I remember.

Perhaps she will mention the fear again to me when I next see her. Or I may ask. We have the kind of relationship where she might be surprised but not permanently offended. She might even empathize. Sometimes a patient can understand themselves by seeing their own possibilities in the therapist. If I present to Fran as vulnerable but strong enough to risk her bemusement, she may take up the same attitude as well. In other words, the teaching moment is indirect – not a straightforward insight into herself so much as a deduction from considering me. It is a *Hamlet* moment: "By indirections find directions out." The takeaway for Fran is that if her therapist can recover from a lapse, if he is confident enough to swallow his pride in front of a patient, then why shouldn't the patient go forth and face the music?

I don't even have to make the connection for her. She will figure it out. She will know that I know she will ... because I am that confident.

> *Freud called his first model of mind "topographical," with conscious, preconscious, and unconscious levels. The conscious (most conspicuous) level includes what a person is aware of in a given moment. The preconscious is what can be accessed through memory and self-reflection and is the interface of the surface and what lay beneath. The bulk of the human psyche is what Freud calls the unconscious or, more specifically, the dynamic unconscious. In Freudian psychology, the unconscious comprises psychological conflict and determines much of a person's behavior beyond his or her quotidian, conscious choices. In this model, making the unconscious available to the conscious, through insight and understanding, is integral to the therapeutic process. Unconscious wishes and fantasies are at the core of who we are and how we lead our lives. Shining a light on them enhances our ability to choose how we lead our lives.*

Growth

Mr. Saddington was an athlete in college and had stayed fit until he lost his job. His previous therapist had encouraged him to find a new job, and I thought that it would at least boost his morale if he started working out again. But as time went on, and he still hadn't joined a health club, we talked about why he resisted it. He cited his limited funds, of course, and then said that he felt angry a lot at himself for squandering his life savings on a scam. We discussed his feelings, and I said that beating himself up would only compound his losses, while investing in himself would literally help him rebuild. He agreed and next week joined the health club ... but still has not used it. So, I told him that I could not make him do anything and that on some level his willingness to work or work out had to come from himself. He concurred.

After several weeks, he was working out regularly. The difference in his appearance, level of energy, and mood was remarkable. He had lost 20 pounds, begun to eat right, and also become more social. It helped that Mr. Saddington already had the discipline to get better. We just had to create an internal environment for his abilities to emerge. We had to expose and explore the conflicts that inhibited him, which had contributed to him getting scammed in the first place.

Mr. Saddington's progress sheds light on how personal growth occurs. One way to conceptualize this "how" is to distinguish between the elements of form and structure. Form, as I use it here, refers to internal psychic dynamics including Oedipal issues, sibling rivalries, and basic drives like sex. Structure refers to external aspects of a person's life such as work and family commitments – the real-world scaffolding on which a person builds a life. For Mr. Saddington, this exercise regimen, diet plan, and the like formed structures for his getting better. It was also important to understand his internal state of mind (i.e., his fantasies, conflicts, and underlying psychological dynamic). As we worked on getting both elements of his growth in sync, Mr. Saddington began to improve. His insight was that they had to get in sync.

During Mr. Saddington's adolescence, his mother died of ovarian cancer within a year of diagnosis. He never fully recovered from the loss and, by way of bringing her back, he spent his life wishing for a parent to care for him if he ever needed one. Thus, when he was unemployed, he was puzzled by potential employers who did not "care" enough to hire him. He fell into a scam because he imagined he would be warned by a parent figure who "cared." He inhabited a self-created trap, where his internal psychic dynamic kept disorganizing the external, professional aspects of his life.

As he began to recognize the psychological impediments to his success, in particular his fantasy of depending on an absent parent, he felt increasingly able to achieve success on his own. He contacted colleagues and peers about business opportunities and proposed a business plan to one of them that became a collaboration. In Mr. Saddington's case, insight came in letting go of a wish that was born in grief but had changed shape – and potency – as he matured. Wishes can stay with us, shifting their shape until we can hardly see them. We may have to be coaxed to see them and then see how they continue to guide and upset out lives. This is not easy, however, since disappointment alone is not enough to dissuade us from toxic wishes – it may even reinforce them. Mr. Saddington was sufficiently honest with himself to finally let go.

Psychiatrists want to help people get better. That's our job, and it helps us feel good. But the responsibility in the psychotherapeutic situation when a patient is not getting better is primarily that of the therapist. He should wonder what he is not getting right, not what the patient is getting wrong. The therapist should also ask himself why he himself is mistaken. But such self-reflection is difficult. Sometimes what we require of our patients, we don't even request of ourselves.

Beyond Freud, that is, beyond insight and understanding, other modalities point toward psychological change. For example, Aaron Beck, who was psychoanalytically trained, developed an approach to treating symptoms, called Cognitive Behavioral Therapy (CBT), which looks at a person's assumptions about himself, his situation, and his future. Through questioning those assumptions, CBT allows a person to alter his perspective on life. For example, someone who is depressed tends to have a negative view of the world (e.g., no one likes me), of the future (e.g., that will never work out), and of himself (e.g., I'm bad or worthless). Bringing those assumptions to light, questioning them, and seeing one's reality more clearly can be an effective treatment for depression and anxiety.

Separation

Last week, I received a frantic phone call from Mrs. Wright. Her husband had returned from a trip announcing that he wanted a divorce. When I saw her, she was upset but also scared. She said she loved her husband and could not imagine starting her life over, alone in her late 30s. But I spotted a disconnect. She had demonstrably made work a priority and stayed at the office until 10 every night, so why did she find his decision so shocking? It seemed even stranger that she was trying to get pregnant while her husband wanted to leave.

I saw them both together at their request. Mr. Wright seemed like a kind, intelligent man. He said he loved his wife but had been frustrated with her for some time. He complained that she did not listen to him, especially regarding their spending more time together. In this respect, he seemed more like the typical wife in the relationship. When asked, he said that on balance he would like to try to work things out. Even though he was not a "believer" in psychotherapy, he was willing to give couples therapy a try. I offered to send them to a colleague. But they thought it best to work with me. I scheduled a follow-up appointment. But he ultimately cancelled it.

Mrs. Wright did not keep the appointment either. She called to say that she would not be there and that neither she nor her husband would be coming back. I wondered what was up. When I called to find out why, she was very upset. They had gone away over the weekend, and she said the trip was a "disaster." She was critical of me, and initially I thought her feelings reflected her husband's disapproval of therapy. But it emerged that actually she was angry at me for not saving her marriage. Either way, it was disconcerting for her. For years, Mrs. Wright had been more concerned about work than her marriage and had undervalued her husband. I had discussed this issue with her, but it never sank in. Now her unwillingness to confront the issue had returned like a tidal wave. Her husband had left. She was thinking of going back to Florida. I did not know how I could help her. She did not want my help.

A patient's refusal to understand how they are putting themselves at risk is a major risk to therapists. Often, the problem is not that the patient fails to see a problem but, rather, they refuse to deal with it. This is not a failure of understanding as that is commonly understood, since the patient knows perfectly well what is going on. Rather, it is a failure of will to see beyond the problem to its likely – if not immediate – implications. It is more a disavowal than a denial of the problem. Patients tend to believe therapists when they say, "You have an issue with this or that," but they are less inclined to acknowledge predictions of how that issue – if unaddressed – will likely affect their lives going forward. Part of arriving at real understanding, therefore, consists in thinking through an issue to its logical (or even probable) conclusion. Mrs. Wright had not wanted to do that – maybe because she was scared or maybe because she wanted to think about how she would have to change in order to forestall a terrible outcome.

I wonder if, when I had the chance, I should have been more forceful with her about considering how her total absorption in work could threaten her marriage. She was angry at me now for not saving that marriage but, in fact, I should have tried to save her from herself.

Various methods are available to psychiatrists for helping their patients. For example, as physicians, we can prescribe medication. But some patients wish us to transform their lives, often based in transference. Someone who wants a father to rescue him or a mother to turn her into a dancer will look to us. Part of the therapist's role regarding the "aspiring" patient is to help them understand those transferences, support them in achieving what they're capable of, and still accept their own limitations. That's about the best that mental health professionals – as coach, mentor, or trainer – can do. Thus, while the small differences we make in peoples lives can add up, we are not miracle workers.

A trauma

Cathy could be described as shy, though diagnostically speaking she is actually bipolar. That is, in addition to having had several depressive episodes, she has also had manic episodes during which she became psychotic. She has required hospitalization on three occasions – one of them while she was in treatment with me. She is the only patient in the past six years that I have had to hospitalize.

Her personal history is painful. Her mother had a drinking problem, and her father had a bipolar condition that was either unrecognized or poorly treated. The most shocking event in her life occurred at around eight years old, when her mother shot and killed her father. Ostensibly, it was in self-defense. Because the family was well-known, the matter became public. The mother was tried for murder and found innocent. Cathy had to deal with this profound trauma and its consequences. Her mother's drinking problem worsened, and she squandered the family's significant wealth. The mother, Cathy, and her sister then moved in with her uncle. He sexually molested and abused Cathy while her mother turned a blind eye.

Over the years, Cathy has discussed these matters at length and worked through their devastating impact on her. To her credit, she has fostered family relationships and friendships. She has a fine work history as a classical musician. She is a nice person with good values.

She is also currently angry with me. She feels that I have only been able to help her in limited ways – which, of course, is true. For months she has been saying that she would like to discontinue her therapy and just come monthly for psychopharmacology. I have tried to demonstrate the usefulness of continuing in therapy as evidenced by the significant personal gains she has made. But right now, despite my best efforts, she feels that I am not very understanding of how difficult a life she has led. She does not see any point in continuing therapy. I don't know what will happen. But I give her a lot of credit for coming as far as she has.

Nonetheless, I think that psychopharmacology – pills – provides Cathy with an excuse of sorts, which justifies her not continuing to do the hard work of therapy. She knows that she has made progress, but she ascribes it largely to the pills and finesses the need for continued effort. She conflates taking pills with her ability to avoid rapid mood swings. Accordingly, she minimizes the deeper gains she has made due to the insight that we have achieved together. Ironically, if I were to point out that medication management is not a substitute for insight, she would probably agree; bipolar conditions have a strongly biological basis and often require treatment with medication. But what's necessary is not necessarily sufficient.

Yet, despite her slacker mentality, Cathy is perhaps in tune with current practice, which is oriented toward symptoms relief and quick fixes. Patients want to feel better fast, and the profession has complied. Is this wise? In response to patient arguments and, indeed, to the movement of treating symptoms rather than causes, I once thought of writing an article called "The End of Insight." Most patients see the difference between medication and talk therapy, but some who can benefit from pills would rather expedite the process. The two approaches can go hand in hand, which is a virtue of psychodynamic psychiatry. I wrestle with this issue whenever I prescribe a medication, and I think that patients need to consider it as well. Both dependency and insight are ongoing – so which sounds like the better choice?

Psychoanalysis has a long history of being misapplied to conditions that could better be served by other treatments. We now recognise that one-size-fits-all approaches do not work. Refractory major depression and severe personality disorders like Borderline Personality Disorder are better handled by psychopharmacology and other therapeutic protocols, which may usefully include a psychotherapy element. Some conditions require an ongoing role for medication management and/or psychotherapy – or sometimes issues can be addressed with short-term treatment and care. A clinician has to assess the problem and implement an effective treatment, modifying it as required. A correct approach to treatment and care can sometimes make a tremendous difference in a person's life.

Defining moments

My talk went well today, and I enjoyed presenting my clinical work to my colleagues. They are all well-trained, seasoned clinicians. They asked good questions. One member asked if there was a moment in the treatment that I considered especially defining. It was hard to formulate a response, however, since the treatment had extended over six years, and there were several periods that seemed significant.

The whole idea of a defining moment seems anomalous in the context of therapy – while change is a slow process, "defining moment" suggests that treatment can crystallize around a specific, instantaneous insight. Suddenly, everything comes to a head. There is a phase change: Ice deliquesces into vapour. Of course, there are such moments in therapy, but they are rare. Usually, change occurs in modest increments and, if you're lucky, generally in the right direction.

But I did think of Bobby. When he reported having "driven a nail through his foot," he finally acknowledged that – actually – he had stepped on a nail while doing some yard work. Through exploring his accident, what emerged was a deep-seated fantasy about being Christlike and needing to suffer to access his father's love. This led to our exploring his relationship to pain and suffering, and he was able to let go of more of his need for self-punishment. We also explored other of his father/son dynamics, such as his fantasies about Abraham and Isaac's relationship. Obviously, his own life experience with his father had dramatically influenced his intrapsychic life.

So, when I responded to my colleague, I cited the moment when Bobby acknowledged that his story of driving a nail into his foot was part of a much more mundane event but *also* part of his fantasy life in a quest for love from his father. This was a defining moment, and a string of insights followed from it. My takeaway is that while insight may come in a flash, what follows from a moment of clarity lies in the work required for fantasies to become truth and segue into reality. Insight is waiting to unfold in these cases and needs only a rush of candor.

> Sometimes insight comes from providing a missing piece of information or making an observation or deduction that results in better understanding. In psychodynamic work, we are primarily interested in insight into the self. This is based in introspection or self-reflection and, ideally, there is a kind of eureka moment or epiphany. In Gestalt Psychology, rather than an associational learning process, the idea is to see a problem or situation in a new way, which may release a past experience that creates a larger and more coherent context.

Sensitivity

I used to wonder whether psychological issues in mental health professionals occur more frequently than in the general population. Now I am virtually sure of it. Of course, it could be that our problems just stand out more – like the shoemaker's child without shoes. But I actually think that people with psychological struggles are drawn to this field. They want to become expert in their own demons, not necessarily to slay them so much as to live with them at a higher, more elevated level of understanding. Perhaps the bravest of us write about them. We may choose to expose ourselves in writing not to advance the profession but to satisfy some need to explain ourselves to the world. Those who do not explain their troubles to the public may sublimate them in helping to address the troubles of others, finding satisfaction in that their enhanced self-knowledge allows them to explore the Mariana Trenches of other people's psyches.

People in this profession train themselves to be sensitive, to pick up on cues that would go right by someone else. Everything is grist, to be ground and reground, considered from many angles. Nuances loom large, the way they might for a lawyer drafting a 100-year lease. No possibility is too small. But the question that I ask myself is, "How can I best help others?" Or perhaps more personally, "How can I be true to myself in the world?" Am I a type of intellectual narcissist, prone to inordinate excitement over each personal insight that I stumble into? After all, I am writing this book, full of my own insights – or what I think are insights – and I want to keep generating them. I *do* want to help my patients, and many *say* that I do, and yet there is this urge to explain myself beyond the confines of the therapeutic relationship. At the very least, my experience of myself is that I have become increasingly sensitive to how I affect people, how they affect me, and how these reactions continue to construct the psychological profile that I am defining for myself in my head.

In this regard, I have become more sensitive to sensitivity in other people.

I run a conference with a colleague, Dr. Freund, a fine clinician and a decent man. He is also quite sensitive, as I determined from watching him with other people. Once, when he gave a presentation to the conference I presented at, he was offended when a colleague greeted him with an unusual heartiness that exceeded the profession's rather prim decorum. Did Dr. Freund think he was outside the bounds of the usual constraints? I could see Dr. Freund flinch at the possibility. When we were at dinner following the conference, and Dr. Freund was introducing the society's president, the colleague made Dr. Freund wait a moment before delivering his remarks. Dr. Freund apparently found this condescending, enough to make a joke about it – almost as if to say "Well, if I can joke about it, it probably wasn't meant to be what it seemed to be." Most people, I think, were embarrassed for his embarrassment, since they would have just brushed it off.

I am not suggesting that Dr. Freund is among those of our profession who cultivate hypersensitivity. But I do mean to convey that I am attuned to it, and that it is prevalent among psychotherapists. Of course, "sensitivity" is a many-pronged term, and we have to be clear about what it means in context. Dr. Freund is sensitive in the sense that he picks up on even the smallest slight. One has to be careful with such people. In general, therapists are sensitive to what patients say in that they try to situate these statements within a framework of what they know about the patient, and they approach the implications from a widely informed therapeutic perspective. Such "sensitivity" entails intense thought, ideally leading to some insight that helps the patient to heal. It may come full circle, of course, when it links up with how the therapist reflects on him- or herself, leading to empathy on the one hand and an enhanced narcissism on the other.

Nothing is simple in therapy, least of all the language that we use to describe it.

I knew that I would have to be especially considerate in my collaboration with Dr. Freund. Still, at each turn, I think I offended him – not consulting him before sending out invitations, not being sufficiently responsive when he requested information, and questioning how our involvement in another conference might impact our co-leading this one. Dr. Freund was always cordial toward me, but he ended up causing me to doubt myself. This is the boomerang effect of hypersensitivity – everyone is walking on eggshells. If I gained any insight in working with Dr. Freund, it was that if someone is *really* sensitive about slights, then people who work with them must develop corresponding defenses to avoid always second-guessing themselves. But I have to combat the wish to make so many of my colleagues my patients ... maybe an insight, too.

The idea of Emotional Intelligence was popularized by Daniel Goldman, an author and science journalist. It is typically associated with empathy and the ability to connect with others. It can be measured by emotional quotient (EQ) as a corollary to intelligence quotient (IQ). Both are important to success. People with high EQ have better job performance and leadership skills as well as mental health. While some

> people have a greater natural endowment, EQ can also be developed. Open-mindedness, extroversion, and conscientiousness are positively correlated with a higher EQ, and inversely with alexithymia (an inability to identify and verbally describe feelings) and neuroticism. Being in touch with one's own emotions also helps one to be more sensitive to others.

Leaving home

Mrs. Kennedy started her session today by saying that she was excited to begin a writing project. She had joined a workshop at a local university, and her first assignment was to write about what "home" meant to her. She began her essay with a memory of how, when she announced her engagement, her mother decided that her fiancé was "a cripple" and banished her from home. So, the day that Mrs. Kennedy announced her engagement, she gathered up two shopping bags full of clothing, got into her fiancé's car, and never returned.

The night after starting her class, Mrs. Kennedy dreamt that she was back in the kitchen of her parents' house. A knife and gun were on the kitchen table. The body of a woman lay in a pool of blood on the floor. A black man was standing over it. I listened to her associations, which included thoughts about her mother, writing, and a black man she knew growing up. I observed that she saw writing as an aggressive act in which someone would get hurt. She looked astonished, as if someone had revealed a secret or some deep truth about her.

Mrs. Kennedy then went on to say how much better and lighter she was feeling. She had been impressed that such emotion could be stored up for all those years. I was impressed as well. But what we ultimately realized was that over the years she had not made the association between writing and weaponry, she had been looking for a weapon to retaliate against her mother – one that would not physically harm her, but could bring her into a new awareness of how she had hurt her daughter. Frequently, a patient's insight comes with how they can induce insight in others and make them understand what has been impossible to voice in the normal course of a relationship. Mrs. Kennedy never felt she could tell her mother, "Look, you've hurt me," but the essay externalizes her feelings. It is a surrogate for Mrs. Kennedy, so that even if she never confronts her mother with it, it still says what she would have said in person if she could have.

Insight is not, therefore, just about self-understanding, but about how to formulate one's feelings and express them so that they are available in however wide an arena one wishes them to fill. In Mrs. Kennedy's case, she contemplated an audience of one ... but that is a huge step up from zero, that is, from not being able to say anything to her mother because she lacked the means. Now Mrs. Kennedy knows how to say what she wants to. Whether she actually confronts her mother is secondary to an understanding that she does not lack the means.

Generally, the goal is not just to achieve insight and understanding but to apply the understanding to one's life – which takes work. There's a line from a Jewish text called Ethics of Our Fathers *which says "If your wisdom exceeds your deeds, your wisdom will not endure. If your deeds exceed your wisdom, your wisdom will endure." I try to keep in mind what I've learned about myself and others as I do my best with each day.*

Resistances

Yesterday, Mr. Sterling called to apologize for not getting back to me when I had phoned to reschedule the appointment he missed. He asked if I could see him during his lunch hour, and so that's when we met.

He jumped right into talking about his affair with a coworker. He had so much to say that he didn't even know where to start. But I stopped him, suggesting that we first discuss ground rules for his treatment. He agreed and said that it had been hard for him to attend sessions because of his work. When I raised an eyebrow, he got the message and said there was more to his not coming.

He said he was confused about his affair and thought that talking about it would be difficult. At one point, he meant to say that the situation was "ambiguous" but slipped and called it "ambivalent." I listened for a while and then called the slip to his attention. Despite his vigorous pursuit of the affair, did he also feel ambivalent about it? He protested, but admitted feeling guilty, as if he were betraying what he said was a loving marriage. I pointed out that his ambivalence about the affair was passively expressed by his not coming for treatment and avoiding his conflicts. Often, conflicts in one area of a patient's life will ramify into conflicts about therapy, since therapy requires that the patient deal with a conflict they do not want to address.

Patients go through the motions of therapy because they know they have a problem, even as they avoid the pain of dealing with the problem. They fear coming to grips with the motivations that are causing the problem and the steps they may have to take to correct the problem. They will themselves into a state of protracted conflict which, as they experience it, is still preferable to the work of changing their lives. In these situations, insight is hard to achieve, since the patient does all that he can to maintain a kind of psychic stasis. It was only Mr. Sterling's slip that got us moving in some sort of positive direction.

Once we got started, he spoke more openly about how hard it was to give up the relationship because he felt his manhood and self-esteem were bound up in satisfying the woman. But I pointed out how this was more about him than about her, and how his wife was entirely left out of the equation. I also noted that if the woman had heard his justification, she would think that she was being used as an extension of his ego. This got to him.

I do not normally confront or shame patients into insight, but this time it seemed appropriate. Mr. Sterling knew that his actions made him feel "guilty," but he persisted nonetheless because his tenuous manhood was at stake. Why didn't he try to satisfy his wife if he were so worried? His logic was faulty (to say the least), and he knew it. I am not sure if he will return, but I think he went away with a different paradigm for considering his affair. Maybe he will try it out.

Motivation

I saw David again today. He was late, however, and missed about half his session even though we had previously discussed his coming on time. He began by addressing his lateness and asked if he had "blown it" so totally that I might now discontinue his treatment.

I could easily have spent the rest of the session on his comment. In fact, I did observe that he was already trying to create a negativistic relationship with me similar to what he had had with his father. He was also testing me – waiting to see how far I would go when, inferentially, he put me in the position of his uncaring father. If I took the bait, I would be firing him and he would not be quitting me. But I was familiar with this dodge from other patients, so I did not take the bait. I told him, "No, you haven't blown it although that thought might be something for us to consider." He responded by saying that in his first treatment the analyst had seemed so judgmental that every session ended in frustration all around. I said that if he felt frustrated with me – and I thought he would from time to time – to let me know so we could talk about it. That seemed to reassure him.

Sometimes patients have ulterior motives – like avoiding the real problem – and it is useful to call these motives out for discussion. Other times, you choose to let things go to be considered later or even not at all. When the issue is clinically significant, such motives need to be outed. In David's case, I could see that he did not even want to talk about his father, just about the vagaries of scheduling. So, I finally said, "Look, we can talk about whatever you want, but the main thing is for us to help you get better." That seemed to register – at least a bit.

David's initial insight, finally, was that while I was not going to be judgmental, like his first therapist, it did not make sense to waste his time or mine. He was in therapy for a reason, possibly multiple reasons, and it was in his best interest to deal with his problems honestly. That I put his integrity into play made a difference, I think. He knew he was playing games, but had not seen this as holding him back. When he did see it, he agreed to put aside scheduling issues and to open up for real.

One aspect of psychodynamic work is, ironically, to analyze resistance to the work. When a patient comes late or does not come at all, there are reasons. Sometimes they are reality-based (e.g., a traffic jam, a phone call that ran late). But even when they are real, there may still be internal resistance. This is because it is hard to look at difficult or conflicted aspects of oneself. And on top of that, to pay for it! So, a wealthy person, whose finances are not an issue, might nonetheless complain that treatment is unaffordable. Moreover, the rewards of the psychotherapeutic process are not always evident, especially right away. It's like dieting. You know it's good for you but don't really want to do it. Resistance can be a signal that something is coming up in treatment that should be addressed. It's like when you look into a mirror and notice a few extra pounds. Analyzing the resistance to treatment is an important part of the process. It's not the psychotherapist being self-interested but, rather, doing his job.

Making it

Mr. Stevens has been anxious about his finances, even though he is pretty well fixed. True, his wife lost her high-powered job, but she would still receive a year's salary. Their expenses were significant – two children in private school, a new apartment to renovate – but he still had *his* high-powered job, and they had money in the bank. His wife's family also had money and were willing to help out if necessary.

So, where did this anxiety come from? He even raised the possibility of needing to stop treatment and had missed a couple of sessions. I thought about an issue with Mr. Stevens' father that had occurred during his senior year of high school. His father had taken a risk in his business that did not go well. He did not have other backup and support. After a while, he could not pay his mortgage, the house was lost, and he had to work pumping gas. I reminded Mr. Stevens of this incident, which was a source of shame and embarrassment but, as we discussed it, emerged as a significant source of his anxiety as well.

He understood that when we compare our lives to others', especially those who have made an imprint on us, we tend to assume that the circumstances are continuous across multiple lives and over generations. If somebody lost a job and suffered inordinately, then that could be us. Yes, it could, because anything is possible. But if you look more closely at the circumstances, and see that they are radically different, you realize how unlikely that possibility is. As we spoke about all the resources that Mr. Stevens had, and all the others he could call on if he needed them, the picture became clearer. He understood that he had not been thinking realistically, but just reacting. He realized that he had to be financially prudent, but that withdrawing into fear was imprudent and could prevent him from taking measures that could be useful relative to his actual circumstances. Facing reality, while often challenging, is the best and most prudential way.

Next steps

Dan has decided to move forward with his life and get engaged. He is now in good shape financially and opening up an art gallery while maintaining another job. He and his fiancée are shopping for apartments. She's thrilled about the idea of marrying him. He's a nice man with a winning personality.

But as he's moving forward, his sex drive has moved in the other direction. He is still able to perform, but his desire has waned. Dan's open in discussing his inner life. He talked about how a big turn-on for him was always getting and then pleasing the woman. Now that he has her, the challenge is no longer there.

He also revealed more about his sexual experiences as a young man, when he often watched his uncle in sexual encounters with women. He took voyeuristic pleasure in watching. Creating scenes in which he was his uncle was a turn-on for him. Now, as the only man in a monogamous relationship, he could no longer avail himself of fantasized pleasure. So, in moving forward with his life, he felt conflicted.

Whatever stage of life we're in, we have to deal with the issues that find us. An adolescent going off to college may be ambivalent about becoming more independent; a woman trying to get pregnant may want a child but wish to remain childlike and pampered. Dan was conflicted about sex with a woman he would see day after day and with whom he could not experience the rush of fantasy. I told him that if he wanted the joys and commitment of marriage, he had to accept that marriage was with a real human being. He could have fantasy women, but not in marriage.

Giving up the past usually requires that we make trade-offs. In Dan's case, the past was a source of fun but also of frustration. I suggested that the frustration far outweighed the potential fun, and that marriage would ultimately prove a greater source of joy than masturbation. Put that way – as an adolescent versus being a man – he recognised that clinging to the past was self-defeating. He couldn't bear the thought of further stunting his own development.

I think that my allusion to masturbation made my point graphically. I have learned that speaking directly to patients, in fair but clear, even at times graphic terms, is sometimes the best approach. Assuming that a patient will not just become alienated, the point is to help a person awaken to the truths about himself and the fact of the world around him. In Dan's case, I think it worked.

Further Reading

Hammond, Claudia. *Mind Over Money: The Psychology of Money and How to Use It Better.* New York: HarperCollins, 2016.

Iacoboni, Marco. *Mirroring People: The New Science of How We Connect With Others.* New York: Picador, 2008.

Johnson, Sue. *Hold Me Tight: Seven Conservations for a Lifetime of Love.* New York: Little, Brown and Company, 2008.

Kottler, Jeffrey A. *On Being a Therapist.* San Francisco: John Wiley & Sons, 2010.

Nichols, Michael P. *The Lost Art of Listening: How Learning to Listen Can Improve Relationships.* New York: Guilford Press, 2009.

O'Hanlon, Bill, and Sandy Beadle. *A Guide to Possibility Land: Fifty-one Methods for Doing Brief, Respectful Therapy.* New York: W.W. Norton & Company, 1997.

van der Kolk, Bessel. *The Body Keeps the Score: Brain, Mind, and Body in the Healing of Trauma.* New York: Penguin Books, 2014.

Weiss, Andrew. *Beginning Mindfulness: Learning the Way of Awareness.* Novato, CA: New World Library, 2004.

Yalom, Irvin. *Love's Executioner and Other Tales of Psychotherapy.* New York: Basic Books, 2012.

7 Truth and doubt

"The truth will set you free" (John 8:32). The statement is a motto – a rallying cry – wherever the ability to speak and learn are valued as avatars of change. The idea is political. If epistemological obstacles stand in the way of progress, they are vulnerable to reality-checking. So, go ahead, knock them down. In the smaller, more intimate precincts of psychodynamic work, the principle is comparable. Knowing your personal truth allows you to live unhampered by old limits and misconceptions. For example, a traumatic experience from the past might be repressed. When you see and accept it, this can be psychologically liberating, allowing you to move on. If you are conflicted about your sexuality but then become aware of and accept yourself, this can be liberating as well. By "liberating," I mean that you are free to make the most of who you actually are. Your self-conception is in sync with your reality.

But human nature is complex and multifaceted. One's past – as memory – is open to doubt. Memory is a reconstruction. It can be fallible and even false. It is not objective and is warped by wish and emotion. Actually, reality itself is not "fixed." For example, if you look at the physical nature of the world, what seems straightforward is less clear than meets the eye. Light has a dual nature. In some experiments, it seems like a particle, a photon, with a specific energy and dimensions. In other instances, it appears to have a wave nature. Furthermore, as the German physicist Werner Heisenberg discovered, dogged examination will not wrench the nature of reality into focus. The more precisely the position of some particle is determined, the less precisely its momentum can be predicted from initial conditions, and vice versa. So, doubt is intrinsic to any observation.

> Accordingly, truth and doubt are inextricably connected. In therapy, it is important to get as close as possible to truth but to accept the ever-present, concomitant element of doubt. That's the best any of us can do.

A dream

Tim, a new patient, missed a few sessions. But he came in this week and talked about taking his small daughter to the beach last Sunday. She had never seen the ocean and loved it. He also mentioned watching football later that day, when the New York team lost. Then he reported a dream. He was playing baseball where he was the first baseman. A runner on first base was well on his way to second, and Tim threw the ball to get him out. But he threw poorly, and the ball landed in the outfield. The second baseman, who he mentioned had a goatee, started yelling at him. They fought and tried to punch each other.

Tim associated the runner with his daughter. When he saw her running toward the water, he was scared that she would be in danger and out of his reach. He associated the fight with the second baseman with fights he would have with his father for infractions like being late for dinner or getting a bad grade. The goatee, however, was not his father's, but came from a close friend who used to play baseball with him. He also said it was like Freud's, whom he remembered as having a goatee.

I thought to make an observation about his seeing himself as being in a fight with me. I considered tying it in with his missing his session. But I remained silent. Maybe I will bring it up next week. What strikes me now is how fluid these associations are – the same figure who represents his father also merges into a friend, Dr. Freud, and even me. His daughter is a runner in a baseball game where all these characters converge. I think it is hard to sort through what these kaleidoscopic interpretations mean. But what they tell us is that psychic "truth" may not have any single, univalent meaning. Truth may be in the convergence. If I am mixed in with his father and Dr. Freud, as well as with a friend, then the nature of Tim's relationship with me – and his objectives in seeking therapy – may be tangled up with settling old scores, so to speak. It may be that his missing a session is about besting me, showing me who is boss and who can win at the game (called Therapy) that we are playing.

In therapy, truth is always relative, since there are always multiple ways of looking at the same issue. My perspective will not be Tom's, and both our perspectives can change as treatment continues. In therapy, truth is neither singular nor static. The question is always whether we can find some workable truth that increases the chances of a patient's betterment and, perhaps, full recovery. I posed a workable truth in Tom's case, which starts from an assumption of why he missed a session. It could collapse, since such truths are still – and always will be – hypotheses. But now at least we have a starting point. We are, as it were, on first base.

> *In dreams, the rational aspect of the mind goes off line while the associational aspect (with its own logic) emerges. A boss is connected to a father who is connected to me as a psychotherapist. A baseball bat has a phallic valence. The same is true in therapy. As you begin to more freely associate, you become more comfortable with underlying thoughts and feelings. That can help you to connect with other people as, over time, you develop shared associations. It is a kind of intimate shorthand.*

Honesty

It's hard to let people in on one's secrets since honesty can have consequences. It poses a dilemma: is the truth worth the risk? For example, when Mr. Lauren presented for treatment several months ago, he had been entangled in conflict at work and, after a struggle, he decided to tell his potential employer all the relevant details. Fortunately, his candor made an impression, and he was hired. But it could just as easily have sunk him.

Mr. Lauren ultimately came around to the idea that the consequences of dishonesty are often worse than what could happen if you tell the truth. If he had lied, he might have gotten the job only to be fired later when the truth was discovered. This could have tainted his career forever. So, he weighed that against the possibility that if he told the truth, he might be turned down for the job but still have the chance for something else – and the truth won.

But what struck me was that he was bothered by how he reached his decision. He had been primarily utilitarian, weighing possible outcomes and choosing the less dangerous or problematic. He said his decision reminded him of Truth or Consequences, the New Mexico town with a name that suggests that lying *inevitably* produces a bad result. Of course, lying only ups the ante on risk – unless you want to assume that the real risk is to your integrity, in which case there is, in fact, the inevitable risk. Mr. Lauren said he felt embarrassed that he had not factored morality, and hence self-esteem, more fully into his decision and had proceeded primarily in terms of his more immediate, utilitarian concerns. I told him that what he did was understandable, but that it was good to go back over his decision now, as a survivor, to see how he might have thought it through from multiple perspectives.

When we weigh whether to tell the truth, we are weighing more than that. We are weighing all the potential outcomes that can result from people's reactions to what we have revealed. Sometimes, those outcomes may be damaging, not just to oneself but to others. Truth is therefore embedded in a matrix of concerns. We can end up feeling like custodians of the facts, revealing and hiding them based on how we calculate the effect of what we say. In Mr. Lauren's case, the only person who might have suffered from his telling the truth was himself, which in his view was another reason why he should not have hesitated to be honest. In his meticulous, lawyer-like way, he was beating up on himself for doing the right thing for the wrong reasons, though I could see why.

Mr. Lauren was someone who often found a reason to be angry with or critical of himself. If there was no reason at hand, he would create one. He needed to feel that he owed the world an apology, that he was always making up for some original sin that he could never efface. He was looking for personal truth, a right relation to the word that transcended whether he told the truth on one occasion or another. This personal truth – which was endlessly elusive – meant that he could tell the truth and still not be a truthful individual. When I asked how he would ever be satisfied with his moral position, he responded that this latest episode had only set him back. When telling the truth and being honest morphs into a need for moral rectitude (however that is defined), every lie is a mark of one's own immorality. I finally just added that nobody is perfect, which is a total cliché but still has merit. Mr. Lauren said that it still mattered where we fell on the spectrum – a lawyer's answer, but an honest one.

When a parent is honest and sets a good example, the child tends to identify and the behavior becomes part of his or her character. In his structural model of the mind, Freud pointed to an aspect that he called the superego and described it as heir to the Oedipus complex (which, of course, bears on the child/father relationship). When the child emulates the father rather than competing with him, his behavior (i.e., that aspect of the father's character) becomes part of his superego. Teachers, religious figures, and other authority figures can have a comparable influence. Later psychoanalysts have disagreed somewhat over this critical and judgmental aspect of the ego and called it the ego ideal.

Motivation

Mr. Lauren was clearly motivated and genuinely tried hard. But, in many ways, things kept getting worse. He did his best to change – to grow personally and better himself – but despite his best efforts he kept having more difficulties.

His most recent episode was the worst. It was why he lost his job. Years before entering treatment with me, he had taken on a client critically in need

126 *Truth and doubt*

of help. The man was indigent and in dire straits – not at all the kind of client typical of Mr. Lauren's practice. But Mr. Lauren saw himself as a caring professional. The client was referred by a senior partner at another reputable firm, so he offered to help on a pro bono basis.

That client did well under Mr. Lauren's care. His problems were handled professionally, his life improved, and he seemed appreciative. Over time, he sent Mr. Lauren other clients who had similar problems, and they also did well. The hitch was that Mr. Lauren was unaware that some of them were involved in illegal activities. When their situation was uncovered, he was implicated, and it took months for the police to sort through the evidence. When he was ultimately found innocent of any wrongdoing, the damage had already been done – both to his reputation and to his sense of himself as a competent lawyer.

He acknowledged that not only had he been careless, but he had also been swayed by a need to justify his professional life by doing good in the world. He had a chronic sense that no life is fully "justified" except by continued reaffirmation of one's highest and best impulses. It was a prescription for exhaustion, hastiness, and unwise attempts at saving everyone around him. At bottom, it was an extreme, highly personal application of the Jewish idea of *tikkun olam*, saving the world.

We explored the roots of this extreme view of charity and good works. I suggested that it reflected a low self-esteem which, left unchecked, could precipitate self-defeating or even self-destructive consequences – in this case, going overboard to help several apparently needy clients without first checking their backgrounds. Thus, he had to work on his self-esteem and keep it from falling any lower in view of his recent behavior. He had to forgive himself and then work toward self-acceptance. I pointed out that instead of assuming that one good deed just cleared the way for another, he should view his good deeds as cumulative, slowly accruing into an edifice, a more objective correlative of his own self-worth.

But could he accept this view of himself? Where someone exhibits perpetual doubts about their own value, it is hard to just change their self-conception. Doubt is a powerful weapon against the self since there is always *something* to throw up against any counternarrative. I did not suggest that Mr. Lauren reach for the opposite of doubt – certainty – since that would be unrealistic. I do suggest that he strive for equanimity, doing the best he can at a pace consistent with self-preservation and out of a conviction that he is already "justified."

The German philosopher Martin Heidegger said, "Learn backward, live forward." A person may spend a vast amount of time punishing himself for a mistake, but he can't reverse it. He can learn from it, correct its lingering effects in the present, and try to do better going forward. In

Christianity, a related notion urges us to look toward the future: no good deed goes unrewarded, that is, you can earn your way into heaven. Psychoanalytically, it comports with notions of sublimation and deferred gratification.

But the flip side of these essentially positive notions is the snarky idea that no good deed goes unpunished. It has some truth in it because any generosity necessarily comes with a cost. Other people may be selfish and take advantage of a kindness. So, a person can be too giving for his own good – even and sometimes especially because when being generous, we need to take care of ourselves and our own best interests.

Obsessions

Mr. Silver, a Texas money manager, originally presented with obsessive thoughts about a dying client. He was concerned that her children would transfer her assets into their name, notwithstanding that she wanted a large portion to be set aside for charity. He worried that since she had dementia, she would be deemed incompetent to rewrite her will and protect her assets. His obsession eased once the matter was resolved, but he still kept thinking about the situation, and I saw his inability to let go as an expression of deep conflicts.

Mr. Silver always wanted to do the right thing. The foundation of his ideas about right and wrong – truth and lies – was his Christianity. He was not raised in a religious household, but was "born again" in his early 20s. Prior to that time, he experimented sexually, so that while he had dated girls in high school, he had several homosexual liaisons during college and graduate school. In response to desires that he considered gross – and from which he felt he needed protection – he adopted Christian rules as a compass, indeed, a way of life.

He is genuinely happily married and has a good sexual relationship with his wife. But homoerotic thoughts have recently reemerged, and they trouble him. So, his continued, near obsession about doing the right thing for his client could be seen as a defense against his not wanting to do the right thing sexually. His obsessive behavior sublimated his concern about unwanted desires and the welfare of his marriage, so that protecting his client from predation signified his ability to hold off homoeroticism and the threat that it posed to his well-being. It was a form of reassurance that he had the strength not to backslide. It was a correlative of his Christian sexual values.

Mr. Silver is concerned if not terrified that his wife will find out, perhaps when he just does not feel like sex. He fears he will blurt out his whole history, right up to his current thoughts. Mostly, he fears that his wife will be so hurt that she will be unable to cope. He thinks she could see their whole marriage as having been a sham. Long ago, he decided that if he still had homosexual thoughts but didn't act on them, then he wasn't lying. His wife couldn't accuse him of lying on top of being gay. It's just that when he pictured his wife, and actually thought about her reaction, he couldn't be sure that she would see things his way. Maybe she *would* think he was a liar even if she didn't think he was actively gay. He was tormented by doubt.

I explained to Mr. Silver that his elaborate defensive structure had protected him so far, even if it did motivate him to worry about a client who no longer needed him to worry. Now he had to honestly gauge whether broaching the subject with his wife would, in fact, risk his marriage. He carried around too much fear. Of course, it was precisely this fear that kept him from accurately assessing whether he could tell his wife. He said she was a very sympathetic woman, but that you never really know how people will respond in the moment, even those with whom you are intimate. In such instances, the truth may be a casualty ... the lesser casualty since, at least, you have protected yourself.

> *The British pediatrician and child psychoanalyst Donald Winnicott proposed a distinction between the true and false selves. The true self is who we are inside, with private/personal thoughts and feelings. The false self is how we portray ourselves to the world, that is, "false" in an adaptive, practical sense. A false self might be a heterosexual family man facing outward toward a religious community, but with private homosexual thoughts and feelings. He might be an alpha male to the world of Wall Street but submissive in bed. A woman might be a savvy politician but yearn to be a homemaker. It is hard to be truly ourselves in the world because it demands that we make compromises and even sacrifices for family, community, and society at large.*

Myself an example

In the course of treatment, psychotherapists put themselves to use – not just as experts on human nature, but as humans. We start from the proposition that our lives, apart from our learning over years in training, can edify a patient and affect the therapeutic outcome. More than any other healing profession, we expose ourselves, hoping that a shared experience may jolt a patient into awareness of his own motivations ... and potential for recovery. We cite ourselves, rather than textbooks, to create empathy, even at the risk that personal revelations will diminish our authority. It's worth it. What the patient gains, perhaps at our expense but to the benefit of the treatment, is an understanding that nobody is alone – if the therapist has "been there done that," then maybe no behavior is so off the charts that it cannot be fixed.

This week, I had another session with Irene, and I used myself as an example to buck up her courage. Irene is a businesswoman who is trying to pass a licensure exam. She has failed it twice. If she fails again, she goes on probation at her job and could be fired. The stakes are high, and she's stressed. Up until this week, I had said nothing about my own experience, but now I decided that I should. I never just spill my life, but save such revelations for when they could have the most impact, and I thought that now they would. Patients don't expect their therapists to have similar frailties, and when it turns out that they do, the effect of the surprise can be dramatic. It can shock them into rethinking their own issues. Thus, I told Irene, calmly but with obvious pain, that I had also faced problems in getting through training and had once found myself in a cycle of panic and despair. "Forget despair," I said. Despair induces passivity, so once you realize how pointless it is you can work your way out of it. The trick is to get past the panic, which has negative physiological effects. She said, "Doesn't panic just make your work harder?" I responded that I knew, from my own experience, that panic can cause you to freeze, to forget what you know, and to lose confidence. That did it. The fact that I *knew*, viscerally and not just because I had read it, that panic was a downer, got her attention. She became interested in how I proposed to tackle her panic.

The last time she took the exam, her sense of panic got in the way. She hadn't until now accepted that, but after hearing my story she did. She was willing to take a low dose of propranolol, a beta-blocker, which would short-circuit the physiologic anxiety response and hopefully increase her performance. We also discussed various study strategies, including setting aside more time, taking a review course, and focusing on the areas where she was weak. The point was to reduce her panic which, up until I had "outed" it with my own example, she had dismissed as a reason for her failure.

Irene still has a lot of cognitive dissonance about passing the exam. She saw it as a step on a career path to crunching numbers, which she did not want to do. So, another part of our work was to separate out her passing the exam from its consequences. It was clearly in her best interest to pass because she would then have more freedom to choose the best way forward. Recognizing this aspect of the situation seemed to help quiet some of her conflicts and facilitate her studying. I noted that few of us, myself included, know exactly how we are going to end up as practitioners – psychotherapy has more branches and "schools" even than finance. The point is to get to the place where you can make your own decisions. To Irene, that seemed right. In offering myself as a practical example, I provided a relatable truth. I stood in as a verifiable instance of what I had claimed. My expertise came down to myself, but for that very reason it was persuasive.

Sometimes it is helpful when therapists share themselves. Of course, sharing oneself should not be a self-indulgence or narcissistic. But it can be helpful to a patient when the therapist uses him- or herself as an example.

> *I'm not sure that I ever used it as an example in a session, but my first memory was of choking – or at least that's what I thought. I was less than 3. I was at dinner and seated to my father's right. We were eating chicken and peas. Suddenly, I couldn't breathe. My mom saw my distress and called out, "Gene, he's choking, he's choking!" She stood me up and started pounding my back to dislodge the food. I remember my dad disappearing and wondering where he was. Then I recall being given some medication. In a few minutes, I felt woozy but better. The moment passed and then I went off to sleep.*
>
> *Years later, I recalled the experience to my own psychoanalyst as an example of how I thought my father could at times be passive or even not sufficiently present when I needed him. But in that moment, I realized that he left the scene to get medication because he knew that I was not choking but having an allergic reaction – as it turned out, to green peas. So, my father had actually been very effective in the situation, perhaps even saving my life! In that instant of psychotherapy, an event that had given me doubts about my dad was reversed and gave me certitude about his effective presence. That was an important recognition and allowed me to reassess other times he was quietly and effectively present.*

Telling it how it is

Last week, Lynn had a consultation at a drug and alcohol treatment center. The psychopharmacologist who saw her had confirmed my diagnosis of addiction to cocaine and recommended an outpatient group program. He also suggested a medication to decrease her craving. But she was so horrified by the possibility of having to attend a program for drug addicts that she did not do drugs for several days. Today, she told me that she was better. But was she? Was it possible to permanently scare someone out of a chronic addiction? I thought she was either overly optimistic or the victim of her own misplaced hopes.

Of course, I applauded her accomplishment of not using drugs for several days. But I added that there was still work to do before she could claim to be clean. "How can you say that?" she screamed? She felt I mischaracterized her current "recreational" drug use as the remnant of a former addiction and said that now she mainly did drugs with her boyfriend. I asked if there were times when she was together with him when they were not high, and she said there were. I asked if there were times when they had sex and they were not high, and she said "yes." But when I asked when the last time was, she could not remember. "If you can't remember, it must have been a while ago." I said that perhaps her relationship was powered by drug use, and that this was probably not the healthiest MO for her and the relationship. She fell silent. "What do you think?" I demurred. Still no answer. Finally, she said I was being too critical. I said I was concerned for her and was trying to help her do better than just survive long term.

I waited, and her follow-up surprised me. Her affect brightened, and she said that I was "telling it like it is." She confessed that she had known all of this already, even discussed it with her boyfriend, but that they each had reasons for evading the truth. She was afraid that total withdrawal would be painful, and he liked sex when he was high. She said they were in a kind of pact, except here they swapped out death for a stimulating denial. "But you're not giving me any room to lie, either to myself or to you." So, she had to acknowledge the truth, to meet my truth-telling with hers because she felt shaken by the candor of my approach. Sometimes, therapists have to put patients' evasions on display so that they cannot – logically or in good conscience – deny them. The truth has to be so plain that any further evasion would call into question their desire for a future, or at least for self-preservation as they go about an ordinary day.

I suppose that Irene could have walked out, but she chose not to walk out on herself. When we are confronted with the truth, handed to us from someone we respect, we are embarrassed to blow it off. She knew that I knew about her and, as it were, she came clean.

Psychodynamic psychiatrists may believe that insight and understanding are routes to a patient's getting better. No doubt these are useful approaches, and even essential to personal growth and change. But other approaches should be integrated into what we do. For example, a drug or alcohol issue may need interventions that we cannot provide in our office. At times, a person may need to be hospitalized and require a team approach in an inpatient setting. Or another service such as Alcoholics Anonymous (AA) may be helpful. The truth is that we are sometimes limited in being able to help a patient get better, and it is important to know those limitations so that other professionals and caretakers can help.

The truth hurts

Psychotherapists are often selective concerning the patients they treat. For example, I tend not to work with patients who are psychotic or an acute danger to themselves or others. Partly, this has to do with my past experience and managing risk in my practice. Also, I prefer patients that I think I can help more using fewer medication-based approaches.

Mr. Saddington has been a disappointment because, while I thought I could help him, he has not improved. In some ways, he may even be getting worse. After he was scammed out of his life savings, he presented in a depressed state with a recently diagnosed medical condition and in need of psychiatric care. He responded in a limited way to an antidepressant and is now on track in terms of his diet and exercise. But he is not doing much to dig himself out of his financial morass – the cause of his depression in the first place. If he is to survive, and I mean that quite literally, he has to find a job.

Previously, he had been a high-powered attorney, but he gave that up 15 years ago. Since then, his work history has been sporadic, and he has been ambivalent toward finding employment. Our conversations raise issues concerning self-worth and his resentment regarding his need to work, but for all my probing he remains unmotivated. My efforts at career counselling fared little better. After what seemed like helpful suggestions, followed by cajoling, I finally spoke frankly to him: "Look, you won't be able to pay your rent if this keeps up, you won't be able to afford treatment, and you will end up hating yourself."

I prefer not to be confrontational, but I am frequently the only person in a patient's life who both sees the situation and is willing to tell them the truth. At some point, a therapist knows that unless he or she can startle the patient into action, there is little anyone can do. So, I told Mr. Saddington that he could find work and save himself, or regret it. It was his choice.

He did what no other patient has ever done to me before. He stood up and walked out of my office in the middle of his session. Obviously, I had struck a nerve. But the outcome was precisely opposite what happened with Lynn. Whereas she found the truth inescapable, and a reason to seek further help, Mr. Saddington couldn't stand the truth. In both cases, I had taken something of a risk in confronting these patients, but with Mr. Saddington I felt that I had no choice. In Lynn's case, I felt that the situation had reached a point where confrontation could do the most good, but with Mr. Saddington there were no other good options to weigh. Unfortunately, the truth just made him angry and walk away. Rather than realize that he was erasing his future, he chose to foreclose any thought of it.

Did I feel like I had failed, that maybe – with no apparent choices left – I should just have stayed quiet and let *him* discover the solution in time? No, because I felt that he would not discover it, however long we kept talking. I felt that if I strung him along in therapy, listening to him complain but having nothing further to offer, my own integrity would have suffered in claiming his few last dollars. I told the truth in a kind of pitch to help save a patient, but also to consider my own professionalism. I had no way to know that Mr. Saddington would be dramatic in that way, but, when I found out, there wasn't much left to say. I took a risk that severed the relationship. He had more choice than I did.

Tact and timing are important in our work. If we say too much too soon, we can lose a patient. If we say too little too late, that doesn't help either. It can be a delicate balance between telling the truth – at least as we see it – and having enough humility for some doubt. Generally, as long as we're coming from a good place of care and support, a patient knows and appreciates that we are trying to help.

Getting better

Mary has been my patient for eight years. During this time, her actor husband has lived off her, refusing to get a serious job. Today, she spoke about finally confronting him on not making any tangible contribution to their relationship. He said that if she could not accept him, then he would leave. This outraged her, and she said so. He was stunned by her calling him out on his laziness and by her confidence and directness in addressing the issue. She had finally pierced his self-regard, and he resented it.

She had found her voice at least in that moment. She said what was on her mind.

During our session, Mary reflected on her personal journey in psychotherapy, which is an aspect of the process of personal growth for many people. She said, "When I first came into therapy, I was upset and angry but had no idea what it was about. Then, I could put more of what I was upset and angry about into words. But I could not say them to the people I felt those emotions toward. I literally had to write them down. Eventually, I could voice my thoughts and feelings to the people I had those emotions toward." I complimented her on the excellent summary of how the process works – or, at least, how it should work and how it worked for her. She articulated how finding the truth is part of it, but being able to speak is another, equally difficult part. In Mary's case, she found the will to speak to the person who needed to hear her, whom she was afraid would bolt when she spoke.

Finding the power to speak truthfully, when it entails a risk, depends on developing one's sense of self. Mary had had to rebuild her self-esteem in the face of her husband's enormous, almost impenetrable self-regard. She had measured herself against him, and it was only when she found his self-regard ludicrous, even bizarre, that she was able to better construct her own self-regard. My point to her was that the ability to speak the truth is contingent and requires a degree of self-knowledge and respect. You cannot cower before someone and then expect to say what is on your mind. You need confidence in what you have to say and confidence enough to say it without fear. Mary knew that if her husband did walk out, she would survive, maybe even prosper. Would she be able to apply her new self-confidence universally, to everyone whom she wanted to confront? Probably not, but she could at least speak to her husband, who until this point had held her off just by affecting to be above reproach.

Mary knew that she still had further to go. She told me about an incident with her mother from over the weekend. Apart from the clutter of standing resentments, she felt that her mother was paying too much attention to her sister, Mary's aunt, and not enough attention to Mary. Her emotions seemed disproportionate to her mother's distraction, and I said so. She agreed and went on to discuss how, as a child, she had felt unprotected by her mother. Her father was an alcoholic and could be brutal when he was out of control. So, while it seemed at the time that Mary's mother was not protecting her, she now saw the situation more for what it was: her mother was weak and ineffectual. She was intimidated by her husband the way Mary had been by hers. The recognition was stunning for her. Mary forgave her mother and said that she would tell her. It would be painful, but she felt she had to be honest about her misperception.

I think Mary had gotten on a roll with truth. Once she discovered that telling the truth made her feel better – or at least left her unscathed – she felt compelled to be honest with everyone whom she had previously eluded. This was more than I had expected. Sometimes therapy addresses a specific situation – in Mary's case, the relationship with her husband – and we do not anticipate the ramifications. But Mary finally took the therapy into her own hands, so there is no telling how she will follow through with it.

In the course of therapy, a person often finds their own voice. This may be in terms of how they are able to act in the world, but it may literally be about being able to speak truth to power or to loved ones. It can also be having the quiet confidence to say less and listen more.

Good reasons

Mr. Sterling has clearly dropped out of treatment. Last week, he missed his appointment and failed to call. I called during his appointment time but was told by his administrator (whom he still sees) that he was in a meeting. I left a message on his cell phone, but still didn't hear back. I gave him a final call midweek, but it was pointless. I think I shouldn't have to chase a patient whom I know I can help – except that he doesn't share my view. Worst of all, I feel stranded. It's one thing when a patient's treatment remains unresolved (we're accustomed to that), but quite another when that irresolution applies to you.

There's the usual tangle of explanations: he got bored, he disliked being dependent, he is just taking a break. I blame myself, him, the circumstances. It's a bit draining. I want closure. The truth. Probably I shouldn't take one patient's whims that seriously, but I am trained to think about motives, causes — whatever comprises intrapsychic phenomena. I really can't help myself. I want to initiate Mr. Sterling's treatment again just to find out why he left it. Of course, the irony is funny and makes me reflect on the therapist's dilemma: we offer intangibles (self-knowledge? honesty? peace of mind?) that can seem like a mirage and make us seem self-important to patients distracted by the very ills we set out to cure.

Mr. Sterling needs treatment. He could be a disaster waiting to happen. The woman he is involved with has Borderline Personality Disorder, has drug and alcohol problems, and claims she was previously raped. If she feels hurt or desperate, she could turn on him, blaming him irrationally, ruining his professional and personal life. Her presence has already turned him into a sneak, forcing him into risky behaviors that force him into risky rationales. When patients start lying to themselves to sustain behaviors they know are unsustainable, they're in trouble. Though he is obviously not focused on the gravity of his situation — if he were, he would have stayed in therapy — the fact that he is now smoking a pack a day should tell him something. Still, he is not an acute danger to himself or others, so I am limited in terms of how I can intervene.

I think about our relative situations. I want to know what happened between us, while he wants nothing to happen between us. I am looking for the truth — for closure — while he has fled the possibility. So, the tables are turned: I want for myself what therapy can offer, but the patient does not. The ironies of our situation make a little O. Henry story, shuttling between our respective perches on an inverted ladder, exposing my needs when *his* should be the focus. But therapists often see literary possibilities in the course of treatment, winding (or unwinding) toward its denouement. In our heads, our interpretation is "creative nonfiction," based in truth that did not start as a narrative but irresistibly became one. As we compare ourselves and our patients — which this journal has done throughout the year — we quietly think "Oh well, maybe I lost a patient, but there is a shape to the story, there *is* a story which is itself, perhaps, of some value." In other words, the truth is in the shape of the story that emerged ... I suppose I can live with that.

And yet, Mr. Sterling was a good patient — bright, articulate, likable. He is responsible and could have afforded my fee. If someone like that seeks my help, the assumption is that he first made inquiries. So, I feel that I disappointed him. The last time I saw Mr. Sterling, I was hopeful. We talked in terms of "investing" in his personal well-being, language whose long-term implications he understood. But this story (which now it is) is becoming an endless one, so enough said.

Distraction

I have been seeing Mr. Adman for a complaint that he identified as "ADD." I am suspicious when a patient presents his own diagnosis, but he said that another psychiatrist confirmed Attention Deficit Disorder, which today is a frequently diagnosed – perhaps overdiagnosed – condition.

Mr. Adman is a Hollywood-type from Los Angeles. He described having trouble functioning at his high-powered job. Currently, he is responsible for producing a major motion picture and is missing deadlines. He is easily distractible and spends hours researching various peripheral subjects rather than attending to the film's immediate needs. As the other psychiatrist noted, he met the formal criteria for ADD and, based on this diagnosis, was prescribed Adderall, an amphetamine that helps the condition but is also a controlled substance prone to abuse.

But pills only treat symptoms. I was looking for the cause. Significantly, Mr. Adman's problem began years earlier when his mother developed breast cancer. This simple fact had been missed by prior consultants. He had a complex relationship with his mother and was fixated on her possible death. He went back and forth between not wanting to lose her and feeling that finally he could be independent. The ambivalence was paralyzing. He felt guilty, ashamed – and relieved – in quick succession, as he thought about what might come next.

I concluded that what seemed like a clear-cut symptom of a psychiatric condition actually had significant psychodynamic underpinnings. His distractibility was a compromise formation of an underlying psychological conflict. The idea of losing his mother – dealing with that psychological reality – was too difficult and painful for him to bear. So, he turned his attention to distractions. Or, rather, his attention became choppy, as one distraction followed the next.

As we spoke about the etiology of his condition, he acknowledged what I had thought was true. He felt that the only way past his gnawing ambivalence was to stop *trying* to get past it. In other words, he had to develop an enhanced commitment to what he was doing, and he had to believe that he could carry it to completion "on time and within budget." He had to elevate his belief into a kind of personal truth that would block lesser, interfering projects. Of course, it's hard to change one's thought patterns, the mental habits of years. But in the end, he wanted to be true to his own possibilities, so he set out to be.

The Diagnostic and Statistical Manual of Mental Disorders (DSM), which is used to make diagnoses in mental health, sets out criteria for various disorders. If someone meets the symptoms on the checklist for a condition, then he or she has the condition. The text is useful for informing treatments. But it is not the sum total of human psychopathology. Attentional issues, for example, present in many conditions beside ADD (though you might conclude that someone has ADD if they display attentional issues). Depression, anxiety, and PTSD, among other conditions, all have an attentional component. Issues with sleep, motivation, and obsessional thinking are common to many psychiatric conditions. The therapist has to get a real sense of what someone is struggling with overall (i.e., the underlying truth about the condition) in order to best provide help. Otherwise, the therapist is just treating the symptoms and not serving the person.

Family politics

Shortly before Thanksgiving, I had a session with Fran and another with her niece, Mary. The family usually met at Fran's house for the holidays. But this year it was impossible, since Fran was living with Mary's mother, who could no longer function independently. So, the holiday parties moved to Mary's mother's house – exposing some simmering friction. When Fran went to greet her family as they arrived, Mary took offense since it was her mother's house and she was hosting the meal. She called Fran's gesture "pushy," and Fran responded by calling Mary childish and obnoxious. The two stared stonily at dinner, and nobody felt relaxed.

I heard the story from both sides. Mary disliked Fran's rebuke because she saw herself as justifiably in charge – after all, it was Mary's mother's house and Mary had grown up in it. "Fran was just another guest, but she can't adjust to that after running the parties all those years." She saw Mary as trying to co-opt her affair. But Fran saw Mary as petulant and controlling, unwilling to recognize that Fran was running everything for Mary's mother now. "Mary's mother *wants* me to run things. It's the new normal." According to Fran, her greeting just reflected current reality. So, both had their own perspectives, and both could invoke history. As I thought about each, I realized that behind the rationales that they offered there were personal struggles, which crystallized in the seemingly innocuous act of welcoming relatives – really, why should anyone care? They cared because they were not competing with other so much as trying to define themselves. Fran was struggling to retain the mantle of matriarch, which gave her a sense of importance. Mary felt insecure about her position as her mother's eventual heir, who would exercise real authority in the family. Each would react against any threat to their positions, which just happened to come from each other.

After explaining Mary to Fran and vice versa, I could see each of them soften. Each understood why the other felt threatened and realized that there was no personal animus. This was important and allowed them to focus on what both of them shared. They both loved Mary's mother, and the last thing they wanted was to upset her. There would be no messy scenes going forward. Instead, they agreed to a compromise, so that next year they would both greet everyone (oddly enough, this simple solution had not previously occurred to them).

My takeaway from this resolution is that where both sides honestly feel that they are in the right, it is important that they share — that is, carefully consider — each other's truths. If both sides come at the situation willing to think beyond themselves, they will appreciate the other's position — not flat out deny it — and find a way for both truths to coexist. Truth is not necessarily a zero-sum game. One person's truth can share the same space with another's. The parties just need to devise a method to accommodate both.

> *Unless you are treating a couple or a whole family, you don't get to hear all sides of the story. This limits your perspective. You should have as broad a perspective as possible in order to get near the truth. Sometimes the person you're listening to can fill in gaps or describe another person's perspective, but often they have their own biases and blind spots. Therapists do as well. There are the facts of the matter — what actually happened — and the underlying truths about them which can be harder to deduce. I generally assume that I don't have the full picture. I have a healthy sense of doubt. That makes for a more balanced perspective, but it also means I approach the truth asymptotically.*

Insight

There was an article in today's *Science Times* about insight-oriented therapies and whether they are useful in treating psychiatric conditions. It included examples of patients with substance abuse and weight issues, both of which I consider appropriate for insight-oriented psychotherapy. However, whether or not a *condition* is generally amenable to this approach does not mean that using it will benefit any particular individual. Moreover, even if a patient does benefit, the results may be insignificant or transient. In the end, not very much may change, and other therapies may become necessary as time passes and the results are assessed. The patient's disposition toward therapy is often the ultimate desideratum.

I was reminded recently of the essential fragility of "insight" by the inconclusive outcome in a patient whom I have been treating. David is a 30-year-old who works in the arts. He dropped out of college several years ago and never returned. He lives on his own in a rented studio and subsists from month to month doing odd jobs. It's a definite comedown. His father is a successful businessman who sent David to an elite private high school — until David dropped out after he was caught cheating. He did not need to cheat to do well on an exam but seemed to get a thrill out of doing so.

David was in an analytic treatment for years with a senior colleague, whose work I respect. He had what he describes as a good therapeutic experience. He became more honest, became more comfortable socially, and developed a sense of humor. However, in terms of finding some direction, he went nowhere. He seemed stuck in a mildly rebellious adolescent mode of which even he had grown weary. I was struck by how much insight he had into himself and how little of it he had applied. So, when I asked why he had now come to see me, I expected some slacker response like "My father is paying for it." But, instead, he said he knew about insight-oriented therapy and had asked his family to pay for a few sessions to see if he could learn anything.

Over the next few weeks, he spoke about his family, his love of taking risks for their own sake, and his interest in several possible professions without being committed to any of them. "I really know who I am, and I don't like getting trapped by stuff. It's okay, really." I told him that coming to see me was, perhaps, just another exercise in not getting trapped (i.e., in keeping one foot out the door while resisting any sort of psychic commitment). I said that coming to me was part of a pattern that he didn't feel like breaking, just another detour to nowhere that he vaguely enjoyed. I emphasized the vagueness, which I said seemed to be a defining character trait.

He did not get angry, and he was not insulted. He actually agreed and said that my situating him so starkly was illuminating, and that he wouldn't like someone who fit that description. "You almost make me want to stay in therapy since, if you keep talking, I might get to dislike myself even more and maybe I will do something constructive." He kept coming – I guess his father kept paying – and he kept agreeing with my assessments. A few times, he used the word "truth," saying "I guess I needed a dose of truth" and "if the truth hurts, then I am waiting to scream."

But then he stopped coming. Sometimes we collect truths about ourselves. We post them like stamps in an album and look at them. But we choose not to do anything with them. We do not deny them, and we do not actively resist the consequences of applying them. We just do not think about them, and they become little artifacts that we revisit sometimes out of boredom with our boredom. I think that was David. He could understand his problems, acknowledge that therapy had provided real insight into his situation, and then just shrug. He didn't care enough about himself to re-create himself. I thought we were getting somewhere, but insight is useless when someone skips past it on his way to nowhere.

There is a significant difference between achieving insight and understanding and actually changing your life. It is not like a lightbulb goes on in your head and then everything changes. You have to apply what you learn and then practice it. It's like exercise and getting in shape. You have to work at it. I'm reminded of the joke about how many psychiatrists it takes to change a lightbulb. Answer: One, but the lightbulb has to want to change.

Believing in dreams

Today I saw Monique, a 50-year-old woman who grew up in Europe amidst the remnants of Old World privilege. She had trained as a lawyer, but chose marriage over legal practice. She met her husband while he was in medical school. They moved to the U.S. with the idea that he would be certified in his specialty, and then she would go back for an LL.M. as a means to pass the bar exam. However, her husband could not complete his certification, and she had to earn a living. She worked as a paralegal at a grueling pace late into the evening. She had no time for an LL.M., except maybe at night. But her nights were already taken. Then her husband developed cancer. The tumor was treatable but left him disabled. Monique remained committed to their relationship. She tried to have a child but miscarried.

The years passed, and Monique now found herself living alone. Her husband was living in Eastern Europe, the only place he could find employment as a doctor. There was no prospect of his returning to join her. She found herself caring for her elderly father, who had emigrated to the U.S. and was now in an assisted living facility. It was a struggle for Monique to pay her bills each month. She had little savings or economic security. She had not taken a vacation for two years. She was exhausted and depressed.

I felt for her. She was a nice person with a good work ethic. She had made what seemed like good choices – coming to America to pursue opportunity and staying with her husband through his illness – but life had not worked out the way it should have. I wondered if she had once had fantasies that ultimately misled her. She acknowledged that when she was younger, she dreamed of marriage, children, and a nice house. She thought that her life would be continuous with the comfort she had always had, provided she made no big mistakes. Of course, these were not fantasies, just reasonable aspirations for someone of her class. But then I saw what went wrong. The inflection point was coming to the U.S., assuming that her husband could take up his career, and that she, ultimately, could take up hers. She and her husband had been hooked on the American Dream. They believed it. It seemed like fact – it seemed real – and not dreamlike at all for people with good educations and the will to work. They never contemplated that there would be serious barriers to entry to high-powered careers. So now the future seemed limited, even bleak. She felt demoralized and asked if I could help.

I hesitated. I thought perhaps I should send her to a clinic for low-fee treatment. But I was concerned about the quality of care. I also wondered how much of a difference a weekly therapy session might make. How do you tell someone that what seemed real and true may still be for some people but not for them? We tend to construct our truths out of dreams that seem plausible – so much so, that we follow those constructions until they turn back into dreams and then disappear. Monique was looking for a reason to think that she could retrieve the person that she always thought she would be. But with each succeeding year, the prospect receded. She hesitated joining her husband in

Eastern Europe because that represented her letting go forever of aspirations that brought her here and had seemed so achievable. She still saw them as a kind of truth. At some point, she probably won't. But dreams die hard when they seem like truth.

Further Reading

Berne, Eric. *Games People Play: The Basic Handbook of Transactional Analysis.* New York: Grove Press, 1964.
Brafman, Ori, and Rom Brafman. *Sway: The Irresistible Pull of Irrational Behavior.* New York: The Doubleday Publishing Group, 2008.
Brooks, David. *The Social Animal.* New York: Random House, 2012.
DeSteno, David. *The Truth About Trust: How It Determines Success in Life, Love, Learning, and More.* New York: Penguin Books, 2014.
Doidge, Norman. *The Brain That Changes Itself: Stories of Personal Triumph From the Frontiers of Brain Science.* New York: Viking Press, 2007.
Duckworth, Angela. *Grit: The Power of Passion and Perseverance.* New York: Scribner, 2016.
Duhigg, Charles. *The Power of Habit: Why We Do What We Do in Life and Business.* New York: Random House, 2012.
Eagleman, David. *Incognito: The Secret Lives of the Brain.* New York: Pantheon Books, 2011.
Ellis, Albert. *Reason and Emotion in Psychotherapy.* Secaucus, NJ: Lyle Stuart, 1962.
Gilbert, Daniel. *Stumbling on Happiness.* New York: Vintage Books, 2007.
Gladwell, Malcolm. *Blink: The Power of Thinking Without Thinking.* New York: Little, Brown and Company, 2005.
Haidt, Jonathan. *The Happiness Hypothesis: Finding Modern Truth in Ancient Wisdom.* New York: Basic Books, 2006.
Sullivan, Harry Stack. *The Interpersonal Theory of Psychiatry.* New York: William A. White Psychiatric Foundation, 1953.

8 Love and healing

Healing involves the idea of making whole or restoring to health. It is in effect a kind of cure. Sometimes when a bone heals correctly, it is stronger than before where it was broken. In psychology, there are identifiable factors that help to strengthen a person and make them better and more whole. These are sometimes referred to as resilience factors: Hope and realistic optimism, determination or grit, a good moral compass and/or religious beliefs, taking care of oneself, learning from mistakes, flexibility and adaptability, friends and family or other social supports, and gratitude. When these are present, one is more likely to do better. When some are not, it is possible to work on them. After all, a chain is only as strong as its weakest link. The philosopher Nietzsche said that "what doesn't kill me makes me stronger."

Love is a source of healing. It is underappreciated – and so often underutilized – as a factor in psychotherapy. This may be because it is seen as unscientific and emotional. Yet anyone one who loves or has been loved knows its power as a catalyst for change. Here I'm not talking about falling in love, although that combination of fantasy and friction can be transforming as well. I mean love in terms of deep understanding and empathy for another person. Love helps a person recognize possibilities in him- or herself that he or she would have been blind to; it helps them accept their flaws and work on them; and it helps them find strengths they never knew they had.

Need

Fran began her session by asking how my vacation had been. I appreciated her asking but did not want to focus on my activities. It seemed that she understood. Sometimes when treating an elderly person, I may share myself a bit more as a way of connecting, and I could see why she wanted to talk about me. In effect, my vacation displaced other issues touching how I was helping her, and she didn't want to feel like a patient or someone who needed help. Small talk tends to make patients feel like we're just "friends," talking about stuff, rather than in a professional relationship where it is my role to help.

Like so many times when you're caught off guard, I only realized later how I could have defused Fran's polite but firm inquiry. Probably, I should have responded innocuously ("Oh, it was nice"), signalling that I understood what lay behind the seemingly innocent question but, that if we got down to business, she'd see that we were moving in the right direction. Instead, however, I was too dismissive. I said that we should just pick up where we left off before my vacation – in effect, that my vacation did not matter to our relationship and that our relationship was fine. Patients are sensitive to shades in meaning, and Fran understood that I had told her that I was unwilling to talk about Us in another context. She changed the subject. She said that she missed her subway stop on the way to see me and noted that this was unusual. She mentioned running late to begin with. I asked her what she made of it, and she said she felt agitated. Then she said she had felt "in need" this past week. I saw where this was going, and that she was making another attempt to raise my vacation – or, rather, the issue of how my presence in her life affects her sense of progress toward healing.

Fran was surprised at how unsettling she had found my absence. During that period, she had received glowing reviews in local media on the 25th anniversary of a center she had founded for troubled teenagers. The Board was a group of accomplished adults who respected and admired her. But no praise could allay her sense that she was alone and unloved. As we spoke, she pointed to one of her grandchildren who is mildly learning disabled. "His parents love him and I love him, but I'm just fine and who loves me? Who has ever loved me?" She contrasted her own childhood to her grandchild's. When she was growing up, she felt left out because she was tomboyish and awkward. She saw her sister, who was prettier, as privileged and specially treated. She had even wondered if she was adopted, and at one point rummaged through her father's papers looking for her birth certificate. Apparently, I was now one of a string of people whom, she concluded, did not love her, and I had shown it by first going away and then, at least in her experience, refusing to talk about the effect of my absence.

We discussed how my being away had stirred up feelings of loss and, most immediately, her fear that I was on a continuum of people who should care about her but did not. She acknowledged feeling that I had left her – even though every patient gets plenty of notice – and she shuttled back and forth between complaints concerning my vacation and being unloved as a child. She supposed that missing her subway stop was an expression of anger because, by leaving me waiting, I would wonder whether she loved *me*. (When patients are their own therapists, their interpretations often reflect how they would like things to be.) I answered that because I did not have her background, I had not associated her being late with any failure in our relationship. "Maybe you were just late," I demurred.

Again, however, this was the wrong response, since she heard it as me saying that I took her for granted. I realized that much as she had turned to me for professional help, she could not separate herself from needing my reassurance that I was personally invested in providing that help. She wanted me to love her in the sense of caring for her, never leaving her, and always being there as someone who did not put himself first. When we do not get what we need early on, we rarely make up for it fully, and keep making demands on people to supply what they are often in no position to supply. Even, and maybe especially therapists. I realized that we would have to examine this issue, since it did bear on our relationship and on my ability to credibly offer her help.

We will need to redefine love and its relationship to healing in our relationship. I do care about Fran, and she knows that ... just not in the unqualified sense that would go beyond any professional relationship and might even be unprofessional. Patients sometimes want us to behave unprofessionally and assume the roles of parents, siblings, lovers, or friends who never fulfilled their needs. When patients are extremely needy, they can make extreme demands without any thought to how they are derailing a proper professional relationship and, hence, the possibility of long-term healing. Often, they want short-term assurances, right now. And sometimes it's helpful to give that to them. I am not sure whether Fran is capable at the moment of seeing how her demands are interfering with her progress, but if we talk more about her past and examine its influence, I think she will come around. Talk therapy is founded on the idea that as patients come to understand their past, they will adjust their lives to help counteract its worst effects.

> Sometimes grief continues not just because a spouse was lost but because love was missing early on. The person grieves for the absence of that love during the marriage. Franz Alexander, a psychoanalyst, coined the term "corrective emotional experience" to describe an emotional experience with another person that is healing where an initial relationship failed. He thought it was of secondary importance if the experience took place in treatment and a transferential relationship or in some other relationship. This view did not make him popular with the psychoanalytic community, but, I think, any caring and loving relationships can be healing.

Myself

I woke up startled last night after a bad dream. I was a patient at the hospital where I have an academic appointment and had been admitted for psychiatric observation. My colleagues seemed familiar – I knew their names – but our relationships had changed. I could not release myself and had to sign a form when they released me.

The dream must have reflected the previous day, when a patient needed me to fill out a form for the second time regarding his psychological fitness to return to work. I had filled it out once before, but the HR office that needed it claimed that it had never arrived.

I knew what this patient had gone through and sensed what it must have felt like. For weeks, he had been disturbed, with serious lapses that made work impossible. Both times, when I signed the form, I had felt some trepidation about his stability. But I decided to certify him because I felt that returning to work would be an enormous boost and that he wanted desperately not to let anyone down.

I wondered why I identified with this patient in the dream. Did I feel that I needed to prove *myself* to my colleagues? I often feel that because they emphasize academic work – peer-reviewed books and articles – they consider my mostly clinical work as not up to theirs. I worry whether they think I became a professor under the Ancien Regime at my hospital, when you didn't have to publish as much to get promoted. But then I realized that, in the dream, *they* had signed my release. They had certified that I was okay, and so they must have known that I help my patients. Moreover, since "they" were actually me – the dream's author – I understood that while I could not sign myself out of the dream hospital, in effect I could do so in real life. That is, I could say with sufficient evidence that I was competent. What a relief!

The dream reflected a sense, I think, that I worry too much what my colleagues think because my work differs somewhat from theirs. But it's good work. This realization was a moment of clarity, even healing, and an affirmation that my position justified a reasonable level of self-esteem among my distinguished peers. Any such feeling was not vain, just okay and permissible.

Life among highfliers is hard. We compete with them, whether we will it or not, and thus we compete with our notions of how we should measure up. They may not even share our notions, but we still enforce them. Unlike loving another person – a spouse, a child – without qualification, we qualify our love of ourselves. We hold ourselves up to some standard that becomes a moving target. "Okay, you wrote an article, but what about another one – look at your officemate who just grinds them out." In the dream, I encountered myself in this unforgiving gyre and forgave myself for being good at what I do. I allowed myself to understand that I was a valued member of the hospital community.

It's easy to doubt who we are and to look outside for better models. But part of becoming better, I think, is when we can understand and accept our own value without constantly having to reaffirm it. Of course, it is natural to strive and to seek praise. But that's different from discounting what we have already done and what we continue to do. As I thought about my dream, I realized that we are sometimes surprised by how valuable we really are, and how our peers would likely agree, notwithstanding our fears.

In a way, that came as good news though, obviously, in some part of my mind I knew it all along.

> *In terms of being resilient, it helps to have a belief system or moral compass that does not depend on others' praise or approval. It is important to enjoy the respect of colleagues and peers, but their praise should not determine how we feel about ourselves. We should let conscience be our guide, and we should feel good about doing what's right.*

Loss

Fran was so upset yesterday, which was surprising since she is doing much better. She has reclaimed many aspects of her life and has even developed new activities. She recently published a book and is working on a poetry collection. She is tutoring several students. She is participating more in family activities and is involved in writing grant proposals for the community center she founded.

But today was the anniversary of her husband's death, and Fran was grieving. She talked about not having him, rather than reminiscing about their good times. I tried to lift her up without leaving an impression that I did not appreciate the depth of her loss after 50 years of marriage. Delicately, I observed that in some ways he was still present in her life. She thought about him constantly.

She had brought a card from her husband to show me, which she found while going through some old papers. He had handwritten a Shakespearian sonnet which began, "When to the sessions of sweet silent thought/ I summon up remembrance of things past/ I sigh the lack of many a thing I sought/ And with old woes new wail my dear Time's waste." She asked me to read it to her, and afterward we both felt moved. It seemed to speak of regret and to anticipate how one of them would feel when the other passed away.

She recited other examples of how, indeed, he still resided with her. But I wondered if all that emotion would be too much for her to bear since she knew that he was not coming back – and of course that thought had depressed her. Regret over the loss of love can be tempered with recollections of all the good times, but it can also pitch into reverse, becoming a morbid preoccupation. I wanted to encourage her to take comfort in the good times she had shared with her husband, but not to get lost in longing for what was irrecoverable. Like so much in therapy, I wanted Fran to find the right balance, which is hard to locate when someone may go too far in one direction because the other one causes such pain.

Love and healing

I got an e-mail from her the next day, which reminded me of the closing couplet of the sonnet, "But if the while I think on thee, dear friend/ All losses are restored and sorrows end." I did not want to contradict Shakespeare, but I did, and suggested to Fran that too much coddling of her husband's memory was perhaps not her best choice. It would lead to inevitable letdowns and keep her from making the best life she could now. It is hard to say "now" to someone full of sadness regarding the past and who willingly keeps dragging the past into the present as a painkiller. The next time I see Fran, I will perhaps be less comforting, less a version of the past. I plan to tell her that working on her life requires letting go, gently but decisively – not entirely, but sufficiently. She will know when that is.

Family and friends can be a great help when dealing with the loss of a loved one. Of course, we strive to be self-reliant, but as the poet John Donne said, "No main is an island." People don't do as well recovering from a loss when they are lonely or isolated. Psychotherapists try to be there for the people that we work with – responsive to their needs while helping them to better understand themselves.

Not getting it

Tom was a good candidate for therapy. The first couple of times we met, he seemed bright, verbal, and motivated to get better. He did not have any exotic, intransigent condition but was depressed over his stalled career and because his wife had divorced him. These were major issues, but still garden variety concerns that people deal with successfully all the time. Frequently, in fact, they go together where, as in his case, the spouse has the more impressive career and the other party becomes needier and more sensitive to perceived slights. I thought we could work on his issues and, if he could gain more confidence at work, he would be less resentful of his former wife and more interested in moving on.

Tom blamed himself for not living up to his wife's expectations. When they married, both were fresh out of grad school – he had an MA in physics and an MBA, and she was a veterinarian. They both worked hard and seemed destined to succeed, but Tom remained a mid-career number cruncher. His wife, however, developed a thriving practice in a local mall and threw herself into it. Her career became her life and, as Tom sees it, she had no time left for the marriage. He tried to be supportive and was committed to the marriage, but she got annoyed when he suggested that they go out more and finally she left him. He was terribly hurt, since he genuinely loved her and felt that he had failed. "Maybe if I just hadn't said anything, she would have stayed." He kept recurring to their shared experiences and felt that he had blown the chance to have a fulfilling life like his parents had.

Nonetheless, during our first few sessions, we seemed to be making progress. He understood that his wife was driven – far more so than he – and that the breakup was at least as much her fault as his. Probably, more so. There was a conflict in professional styles, and I suggested that he would feel better about himself if he could procure a promotion. We talked about how he got along with his boss and whether switching to another department (e.g., from accounting to sales) might open up new opportunities. He felt his wife's success had damaged his self-esteem, and while I saw it more in terms of his own psychology, I wondered aloud whether maybe now it was his turn. If he did gain more confidence, I also thought he'd have an easier time finding someone new and perhaps better suited to his desire for achieving a work-life balance.

But then he called to say that he was not remaining in treatment with me. I encouraged him to talk about why, but he just said that I didn't understand him and that he didn't think we were a good fit. Finally, he said that I was more concerned about his career than with helping him grieve for his marriage.

I knew what he meant. I had acted on the belief that someone so capable should be more successful, and I offered practical suggestions for getting out of his professional trough. I knew that he wanted to find love again, but thought that success would put him in the right frame of mind to start dating. But oh, did I misread him. He resented that I "promoted" practical considerations over helping to cope with sadness. He had wanted me to say that losing a person that you love is devastating, and that I would take time to grieve with him. He didn't want my help so much as my sympathy or, rather, he saw sympathy as the best help I could give him. He really didn't want a therapist, so much as a friend (or maybe a therapist who was first a friend).

In a funny way, though, I was trying to be a friend – sort of. I thought that talking about his career was a *mano a mano* type thing, the sort of approach that one man would offer another when his spirits were down but his prospects could improve by adopting some practical measures. But I misjudged Tom, and I misjudged the situation. Sometimes, when we are emotionally traumatized, the world seems to recede. Nothing else matters. We can't just turn on a dime and say "Okay, here's a good way to tackle the situation." We feel paralyzed by grief and we don't even want to try to get past it. I should have realized that Tom might be in this state and should have waited a while before addressing his career.

Being a therapist sometimes requires holding back. Just waiting. Love takes a long time to stop hurting us once it *has* hurt us. In such cases, healing takes time. I should have remembered.

If we have meaningful work, it can bolster our resilience. It helps to buffer loss, for example, when a relationship does not work out. It gives us a sense of purpose and direction. It also provides connection with other people and allows us to contribute to their lives.

Mothers

I thought about Mrs. Downe this morning, which is unusual because our next appointment is not until the following week. Probably, I associated the stories she tells of own her mother with memories that I have of mine. I am going to see my mother in a couple of hours, so I must have mothers on the brain. In fact, the more you think about everyone's mothers, and put all the stories together, the more they converge into a single image with common traits. You say "Mother," and everyone gets the idea – even animals (to the extent that animals have ideas). This is one reason why there is so much cross-species research about mothering – in mammals, anyway, the primal pull of a crying baby (a bat, a seal, a dog) will attract mothers of another species (a deer, a human). It's instinctive, the evolutionary product of millions of years.

When a patient starts talking about his or her mother, there is already a framework. Every mother is different, of course, but the bond is inescapable. As a therapist, you start from that assumption and then listen to how that bond has been warped, frayed, mishandled, treasured, or resented ... but never dismissed or forgotten. Frequently, female patients will begin talking about themselves as mothers and then segue into being mothered. They want to make comparisons, showing how they live up to their mothers' expectations or – where the relationship was problematic or even bad – how they are much better with their own children. During her last session, Mrs. Downe talked about her child, whom she did not send for tutoring for his preschool exam. She commented, "I didn't want to pressure him, and he still got a 95." In other words, her methods were vindicated, and her own mother was proud.

She went on to discuss her relationship with her mother, a Holocaust survivor. Mrs. Downe's mother, who was forced to flee Europe as a young girl, had lost her parents in a concentration camp. She was left emotionally scarred but was able to marry and have children. However, when many years later her husband abandoned her, she became depressed and turned to the adult Mrs. Downe for comfort. Their relationship became complicated by the role reversal. Her mother's emotional reliance felt stifling, since Mrs. Downe's own children made emotional demands as well. Was she neglecting them? She wasn't sure, but she felt that her family pattern had been disrupted and that no one could rely on her anymore. "I'm spreading myself too thin," she complained. Mrs. Downe worried because her husband complained of an "intrusion." She was put in the painful position of defending her mother – whom she loved – even as she was starting to resent her. She felt caught between competing obligations. She could not explain it all to her mother whom, she knew, would just withdraw into silence and become even more depressed. The net result was that she was worn out, trying to be everything to everyone.

It's difficult to distance oneself from one's mother when love competes with preserving one's personal space. So, I told Mrs. Downe that in the last stages of their lives, parents can become consuming and that her predicament was not unusual. I suggested that she help her mother find outlets – there must be women's groups, with similarly situated older women, at the local Jewish center or synagogue. Maybe her mother could learn a new language or take up something else that requires time and attention. The point is that without confronting and hurting her mother, Mrs. Downe should begin drawing boundaries. We do not have to limit our love for someone in order to keep ourselves intact. We just have to keep ourselves intact. No one owes anyone their life. The trick is to live out this principle gracefully, so that any resulting hurt is minimized. Mrs. Downe's mother may not understand all at once, but she will get the idea and realize that pulling back somewhat will be best for everyone.

I indicated to Mrs. Downe that her mother has been slow to heal and that – to a degree – Mrs. Downe has been complicit. Now, after some years and much stress, it is time for Mrs. Downe to acknowledge her role in her mother's exclusive reliance on her. That would be the first step in her mother's healing. It might also be a next step in Mrs. Downe's healing from internal conflicts and the conflicts in her family. She said it would be hard, and I replied that love can be reshaped without being diminished. She said she would try.

> *As a parent ages, he or she may become more dependent on the child, and the child has to be there in unaccustomed ways for the parent. This may help the parent – even at this late stage – come more into his own as an adult and even learn important lessons about love and care.*

Letting go

Jake came to see me today, upset about his dying father. He had spent the weekend with his father at the hospital, just talking. No further treatment was now possible.

Terminal illness is hard for any patient to face. But in addition to trouble breathing, Jake's father was depressed. He had requested to be only lightly sedated and, as he looked back over his life, he felt that it had been a failure. He had hoped to become a professional, but never did. Family obligations intervened. He had wanted to stand out in the community, but had led a modest life. Jake, on the other hand, was a successful lawyer. His wife was in finance.

During his hospital visits, Jake told his father that he had a reputation as a very decent, caring man. He thanked his father for how much he had helped him – just by example – to become a hard-working, respected professional. It sounded kind, but I was surprised. During our earlier sessions, Jake had said he and his father had not been close while he was growing up and he viewed his father as a poor role model – someone who never tried to become much because he fundamentally didn't know how. He felt that while his father never stood in his way, he never made an effort to provide either moral support or practical guidance.

But today he did not get into his dim view of his father's accomplishments, either as a professional or as a father. He said that at the hospital, he wanted to help his father let go, to feel that he had done well by his community and his family. He wanted to help bolster his self-esteem, even though it hardly mattered in any practical sense. He wanted his father to feel proud. He told him that he had not been a failure because what really mattered was that people loved him. He said that he loved him, which he did albeit with a clear eye on their so-so relationship.

As we spoke, I suggested to Jake that while his words were intended to help his father in his last days, they would also have a rebound effect. That is, in helping his father get past his depression and achieve some composure, Jake was also helping himself. Jake could feel good about what he had said, and about letting go – however briefly – of any residual resentments. The fact is that Jake *had* achieved success, and his father had not prevented it. He had just been kind of a cipher, mainly because he lacked the capacity to be much more. Were these sufficient grounds to bear a grudge, let alone to allow an old man to let go of life without his son's reassurance? As the end approached, Jake acknowledged that they were not. Ultimately, he had to let go of his father in the right frame of mind, just as his father had to let go in a frame of mind that was best for him. By helping with the one, Jake could achieve the other.

Sometimes, love is defined most clearly in its last moments. All the excrescences fall away, and we see a relationship for how it could have been. Jake's relationship with his father was never great, but it could have been better had Jake not carried around so much resentment. When he acknowledged his burden and ceased to let it prevent him from acting with kindness, he realized that his relationship with his father could have been better all along. But at least, in the end, he retrieved it. He achieved a kind of clarification which, in effect, was healing. Jake said that he could never have been at peace if, even at the end, he had acted as if his father had failed him. He said that his father's peace would be the starting place for his feeling better about himself.

It is harder to make peace with someone after they're gone. So, if you can reconcile differences with loved ones while they're around, that helps. Letting go of strong negative emotions can lead to greater healing. Forgiveness helps to lessen feelings of loss.

Former patients

This year, several former patients got back in touch with me. These people had previously been in treatment for some time, and we had developed good working relationships. I was glad to hear from them.

Iris, the painter, e-mailed to say that she was okay. She was raising a child, earning a living, and pursuing new relationships. Mr. Young, a successful businessman, called to wish me a happy holiday. He had become even more successful, though it seemed that settling down into committed relationship still eluded him, even in his 50s.

Both these patients' treatments ended before I felt they were completed. They may have known this on some level, and their getting back in contact could have left open the possibility of resuming sometime later. There is a classical psychoanalytic ideal that when a treatment is over, there should be no further contact between analyst and analysand. But this complete break rarely occurs because many patients remain close by. We may even come in contact with them during the course of our professional lives.

It is part of human nature to want to stay in touch and to continue a relationship in which we are invested. There is, in fact, scientific evidence that human beings have evolved to hear and understand speech because, basically, we communicate. Talking is part of our nature and fundamental to forming attachments. I would suggest that once we have formed a relationship through psychotherapy, it matters to how we proceed through life – "we" meaning both therapist and patient. This is not to elevate the importance of therapy, but just to say that what happens over the course of treatment resonates beyond it. It leaves an imprint. When treatment ends, we lose only the immediate connection. Having been part of each other's lives, psychotherapist and patient remain part of each other's memories. In this sense, learning on the one hand and healing on the other are open-ended. Memory affects how we think, feel, and act.

I like the idea of patients returning because I feel that healing occurs depending on the context, and that what may not have worked in prior years may actually work now. We bring the past into every session, and yet every session is a different opportunity just because it occurs at a different time. The past is a foundation to build on. If you read the Sunday *New York Times*, there are sometimes stories about relationships coming to life again after 30 or 40 years, divorces, children, and retirements. There are stories about people remarrying after a bitter split. I'm not surprised. Memories catch up with us. They drive us. Circumstances change, and memories seem like steadying forces – "Look, there is still some 'there' there, and you can work with it." Thus, when a patient returns, it is, in part, because they need the sense of possibility that is embedded in good memories – just like those old sweethearts who find their way back to each other. Memory is not just backward looking, though it surely is. It provides a basis for looking ahead. It allows us to formulate a plausible future that is already partly in place.

When these patients got in touch, I thought about how continuity is the basis of healing. We want to feel that we are not static creatures, but moving in a direction toward the next good experience. I saw these patients' getting in touch, therefore, as affirmative. They were not signalling that they were needy so much as that they were in a new place and open to being in newer ones. The idea of continuity was, in itself, healing.

> *Learning is ongoing, especially with regard to oneself. Gains made at one time may need to be reexamined at another. That's okay. It shows strength and open-mindedness, not weakness. Mistakes can be a reservoir of life lessons. As Oscar Wilde famously said, "Experience is what all of us call our mistakes." Sometimes what we learn is oriented toward insight and understanding, but sometimes it's based in acquiring new knowledge and applying it. Having the knowledge necessary to make choices is important for personal growth.*

Effort

Mr. White, an accountant in his late 30s, is curiously sheepish for someone in practice for 15 years. When we first met, I joked "Well, you're not Ben Affleck from *The Accountant*," and he acknowledged that he'd heard that joke before. With every retelling, I expect, it had become less funny.

Not surprisingly, Mr. White was having trouble with women. After a couple of dates, they seemed bored and drifted away. His social life was at a standstill, he said, and he was too shy to resuscitate it online or in bars. At work, he also felt stymied. He was conscientious, but so was everyone and he did not stand out. He worked at a prestigious accounting firm where his colleagues were more assertive, had more impressive degrees, and were better connected professionally. The senior partners had let him know that there was no room for advancement at the firm.

But Mr. White could be persistent. When he failed the CPA exam the first and second times, he kept studying until he passed. He applied the same commitment to his social life. Though he lacked the courage for online dating, he attended several singles events. "It's funny," he observed, "but WNYC is turning into a dating service." (I kept that information handy for some other patients.) Nonetheless, he had to acknowledge that application alone was not enough – which he knew anyway, and which had brought him here – so we decided to work on his confidence. We practiced confidence. I even role-played, which felt curious when I thought about it ... but therapists do inventive things to help their patients. We discussed how he could introduce himself, the interests he could express, and how to ask for a woman's number. We discussed dating etiquette. I suggested that he avoid canned jokes and try to seem spontaneous.

I confess that I wondered, as I taught Dating 101 to this grown man, how I could keep from feeling a snarky macho superiority. Even as a therapist, it's still natural for one man to compare his success with women to another man's

... and I had been a success. Now I was happily married. Nonetheless, psychotherapists *should* distance themselves from private musings concerning their relative sexual prowess. Or, at least, we should appear to distance ourselves. During my sessions with Mr. White, I maintained a disinterested, by-the-book persona and hoped he wouldn't pick up my lapse into thinking "Why is this guy so out of it?" Later on (i.e., now, while I am writing this up), I realize that awkwardness around the opposite sex is not just the product of insufficient practice. At its most treatable, it's a lack of confidence, fear, or discomfort with oneself which practice can ameliorate. I approached Mr. White as frightened, and envisioned his healing (if that term is appropriate to learning how to date) as accustoming him to the notion that women are just people. They want to be interested in what a man has to say. They want to think that he could keep them interested. That is, they value conversation, and they like men who can engage in it adroitly.

Since Mr. White had seen women avidly talking to men at the events he attended, he was inclined to agree. So, we began clearing away his social inhibitions by demystifying women. But there was still the question of actual sex. What should happen once you talk with a woman? Suppose you like each other? Mr. White was reluctant to become further involved because he equated physicality with causing a woman physical pain. The possibility turned him off from making even tentative moves. When I asked how he had come by such ideas, he said only that he viewed women as castrated men who could no more enjoy intercourse with a man than he could. I said that the idea was curiously medieval and, I realized, Mr. White knew almost nothing about women's anatomies. I thought to bring out an old anatomy book that I hadn't used in ages and explained the sexes' respective reproductive equipment. I imagined saying, "You see, it has evolved over thousands of years so that people want to reproduce – it's overwhelmingly mutual because it's designed to be pleasurable." But I kept silent so as not to make him feel more inexperienced and uncomfortable.

In one sense, Mr. White was a Visitor, one of those people from another planet who have to get used to Earth. Did he really think those things? Yes. Would our talking about them make a difference? The proper question, I think, is whether it *could* make a difference as Mr. White accommodates to the planet he lives on. Part of healing is getting to first base. If Mr. White can allow himself to attempt intimacy, and if the effect is positive, then he could be on his way. But he could get short-circuited – or, rather, he could short-circuit himself – if he gives in to fear or frightens or bewilders the woman. That could initiate a viscious cycle that could be hard to reverse. We focused, therefore, on physical and sexual self-confidence as well as its verbal counterpart. I pointed out that progress comes in stages, like healing a wound, and that if he felt good about himself when he took a woman's hand or put his arm around her, he would at least be on his way.

When I was riffling through that old anatomy book after Mr. White left, I looked up the healing process – that is, how a wound is repaired. There are four main stages, each with a fancy medical name. The first, haemostasis, stops the bleeding. I thought, in a metaphorical leap, that we had gotten there. But as the text indicated, failure at any stage can slow or even stop the process. Inflammation was necessary since, as the second stage, it enabled certain specialized cells to cart away all the debris. Too much inflammation, however, and the healing is stalled. Every stage is delicately calibrated. In Mr. White's case, would the process follow the course that it should or collapse on itself? I was not sure, but thought that I might need to have confidence in the psychotherapeutic process to hope that he would make progress. That is, I want to believe that therapy can help someone so radically out of step with his peers and with the stages of normal human development.

We will continue to talk. I don't want to project too much self-confidence, since that could encourage him to be overconfident in himself. It's difficult for a therapist to believe that a patient is making progress, or could make progress, and not spread congratulations all around. I will show that I am pleased when he is, but still be relatively reticent. When there is a real, undeniable breakthrough (if there is), I will quietly cheer for him (and for therapy).

When a person presents for treatment, their relationship history is critically important. If someone is into adulthood and has never had a relationship for more than a year, you wonder why that is. There may be issues with intimacy or trust. While the therapist is not judgmental in these situations, there may still be implications for treatment.

When an issue with intimacy or trust comes up in treatment, does that mean the patient may be more apt to bolt from the therapeutic relationship? If I think that is the case, I might even make a comment on the front end: "You know, I notice that when issues come up in relationships for you, you tend to leave. Psychotherapy is a relationship. Rather than suddenly stop or drop out of treatment, it would be good when something comes up – which is inevitable – to talk about it with me. That might help you do better in other relationships as well."

In either case, it is important to try. Determination or grit helps to overcome adversity. Sometimes this relates to a professional accomplishment like becoming a doctor or writing a book. But it also applies to relationships. As the saying goes, "If at first you don't succeed ..." When you feel hopeless about a situation, trying can often make a difference. For someone who is depressed or going through a serious medical treatment like chemotherapy, getting out of bed or making a meal can be an accomplishment. For an exceedingly shy person, going on a date or making a new friend can seem like a heroic act. The point is that it's important to take that first step.

An affair

Mr. Sterling missed a couple of sessions after his initial consultation. I thought he was avoiding further discussion of his affair. He said he was just busy preparing for a conference.

He was embarrassed by continuing the relationship, and felt awful about it, but also felt powerless *not* to continue. He insisted that he loved his wife but could not get past his desire for this other woman. He did not see himself with her long term and knew that at some point he would break it off. But he needed to pursue it for now.

I felt I had to deal with the reality of the situation – an intractable affair – even as we delved deeper into Mr. Sterling's desires and fantasies. In fact, his deep motivations were as much "reality" as was his reluctance to stop seeing the woman. He had not even asked for help to stop seeing her, but only for help with how he felt about it. This often occurs with guilt feelings – we want them eased or erased so that we can get over what is causing the guilt. I told him that this deferral, for that is what it was, could not go on indefinitely, and I used a medical example to illustrate: "It's like if you see a patient with a benign tumour. You know that if he continues to ignore it, he will end up with a more serious problem requiring more radical surgery. You tell him that but he continues anyway." He understood and said he would consider it however he proceeded.

I did not want to be critical or judgemental, but I also felt that he was not acting in his best interest. After all, he *knew* that he would end the affair but just wanted more time. He just could not bring himself to set any limits. I suspected that whatever I said would not make an immediate difference. But if we kept talking, perhaps he would come to realize that he was playing games with himself, *gambling* with when the situation finally required more radical surgery. No one wants to feel that they are turning themselves into a loser. On the bright side, he said that talking with me was helping him to feel more confident. Perhaps he was looking for courage to go through with a breakup and further courage to withstand the loss. I wanted him to get past the guilt, which was a symptom of sorts, and focus on the endurance that amounted to a cure.

There was more than an ounce of prevention needed for this cure. Several pounds, in fact, and Mr. Sterling would have to do the heavy lifting of dealing with the loss. If I can coach him to see the point of the effort, however, we will have begun. But still, there is also the concomitant risk. Psychotherapy gives patients an "out," a way of telling themselves that they are addressing the problem – and that everyone knows how long therapy takes. The patient can share his feelings, listen to the therapist, and keep right on keeping on with his behavior. Therapy potentially provides, at least for a while, the ultimate rationalization. All the patient has to do – if he wants to look himself in the eye – is to tell himself that he really is working on his issues. They're just hard. Everyone knows that he can't expect to make a change right away.

But this is a conundrum. If I question a patient's honesty, I could discourage him, especially if he is at least partially committed to change *sometime* during the course of therapy. I can't, of course, call him a liar and say he is using me. So sometimes I just listen in earnest and hope for the best. They might just quit and play the same game with someone else.

The most I can do is trust my own judgment. If, finally, I think the patient is on a protracted trip to Denial, I will try to rein him in. I will challenge him to try harder, to shift the balance between trying to change and procrastination. I will try to get on his self-deluding wavelength and point out its perils. Maybe he will respect my perspicacity for figuring his game out. Maybe that will move him.

We tend not to give up something that we like unless we have to. Letting go of an affair, for example, can seem like a heroic endeavor – like Sisyphus pushing that huge boulder up the hill, only to have it roll down again. But we have to have hope and maintain a realistic optimism. Sometimes, a person may seem stuck in place, and no insight or understanding will change anything. But then unexpectedly something does. It's a bit like someone chiselling at a block of ice. A little chip here, a little chip there. But then suddenly with one more tap, the whole block shatters.

There is a saying, "Dom spiro spero," where there's breath, there's hope. This does not apply just to someone on their deathbed. It is true for anyone going through hard times. So, it's important to have hope. In psychotherapy, I encourage hope and a realistic optimism in people as part of healing and getting stronger.

Love

Jeremy is a 25-year-old young man with a strapping physique and the nervous energy of someone with too much to do. He plays keyboard in a local band. He kayaks. When he lived on the West Coast, he surfed with a group of bravos who defied the "No Surfing After Dark" signs. Once he sparred with a shark. When he came to my office several months ago, he was depressed over a younger brother who had died from a heroin overdose. He blamed himself for what had happened and was performing poorly in college.

Jeremy and his brother Mark had had a fraught relationship. Mark was three years younger and liked to tag along – if he wasn't at band practice – when Jeremy was out with his pals. His presence annoyed Jeremy, who felt he had to apologize for Mark and, when the going got rough, keep an eye out for him to make sure he was okay. Once when his brother became bothersome and slowed Jeremy down, Jeremy hit him and broke his nose. When they got home, Mark protected Jeremy and said that he'd been hit on the nose when his surfboard overturned. He thought he was protecting Jeremy, but his lie backfired – his parents forbade both of them to go surfing for six months – even though Mark hadn't been surfing at all when Jeremy hit him. The tension between them increased. Without his brother to hang with, Mark got in with a bad crowd and started doing drugs. One night he came home high and collapsed on the couch mumbling about a home game where he had to play clarinet. Jeremy woke up, put a blanket on him, and went back to bed. Mark never woke up.

Jeremy felt that if he had tolerated his brother, or at least included him occasionally, Mark would not have died. "Mark loved me, and I just cared about myself and my friends. I was selfish, and couldn't even see what was happening." He drew a direct line between rejecting Mark and Mark's falling in with the wrong crowd. "My friends were rough, but they were clean." He thought if he had been attentive to the signs of overdose, he could have called an ambulance. He pondered what else he might have done differently. But the fact remained that his brother was tragically lost and that his own life would never be the same. He felt he would always dwell in the wake of his brother's death. "It was all so unnecessary."

Guilt is hard to expunge because there are always plausible alternative histories that proclaim endless variants on a theme of what-ifs. In Jeremy's case, suppose he had sometimes welcomed Mark when it would have been easy – say, when everyone was playing basketball or just having a party on the beach with the girls. Jeremy kept playing the scenarios over in his mind. He felt that his interminable guilt was Mark's revenge. He recognized that he was making himself suffer the way he had made Mark suffer. I wondered what to say but wasn't sure since what even makes sense to someone so deeply scarred, who keeps opening the wound? Jeremy's explanation of Mark's death – "Just blame me. I did it." – had just enough plausibility to sound convincing to someone who wants to convince himself of its plausibility.

For a while, we kept going in circles. I tried to ease into the subject by saying that Jeremy was not *only* to blame, since there were so many factors involved. But he said that even if he bore only some of the blame, that was still horrific. I had to agree and suggested that Jeremy might think about how he had loved his brother, and how he would never have threatened his life. I commented, "Perhaps you acted out of selfishness and were inattentive, but you also loved Mark." We started talking about love, and how he wouldn't feel so awful if he hadn't loved his brother deeply. The point was to refocus Jeremy's thoughts away from guilt to *why that guilt mattered to him*. If he could understand that his love for his brother was real, and that it had always been there, then he could in time understand that his actions were flawed but not so culpable that he should blame himself forever. His motivations were time limited, spur of the moment, and in no way denied the love for his brother which had always been there. We will keep talking.

Forgiving oneself and others is often a part of healing. It requires a love and care that recognizes our common humanity and reaches beyond ourselves. It means taking care of yourself and others, learning about yourself and others, applying those lessons, and pursuing a common journey.

So, in ending this journal, I come back to healing wounds. Everyone who walks in my door has some kind of wound. I can't sew them up. But what I can do is help them to heal naturally, to go through the long process of healing by casting back over events that still keep their wounds open – and by seeing those events in a new light, allow their wounds to finally close. The process can be daunting for me as well as for them. I get involved in their heads. But I knew it would be like this. It was like love: it was there all the time.

Further Reading

Angelou, Maya. *I Know Why the Caged Bird Sings.* New York: Random House, 1979.

Emerson, Ralph Waldo. *Essays: First and Second Series.* New York: Library of America, 1983.

Grosz, Stephen. *The Examined Life: How We Lose and Find Ourselves.* New York: W.W. Norton & Company, 2014.

Hesse, Herman. *Siddhartha.* New York: Bantam Books, 1951.

Howell, Elizabeth. *Trauma and Dissociation-Informed Psychotherapy: Relational Healing and the Therapeutic Connection.* New York: W.W. Norton & Company, 2020.

Kohon, Gregorio. *Concerning the Nature of Psychoanalysis: The Persistence of a Paradoxical Discourse.* London: Routledge, 2019.

Lear, Jonathan. *Love and Its Place in Nature: A Philosophical Interpretation of Freudian Psychoanalysis.* New York: Farrar, Straus and Giroux, 1990.

Lear, Jonathan. *Wisdom Won From Illness: Essays in Philosophy and Psychoanalysis.* Cambridge: Harvard University Press, 2017.

Pressman, Todd. *Deconstructing Anxiety: The Journey From Fear to Fulfillment.* London: Rowman & Littlefield, 2019.

Sacks, Oliver. *Awakenings.* New York: Vintage Books, 1973.

Sacks, Oliver. *The Man Who Mistook His Wife for a Hat.* New York: Simon & Schuster, 1985.

Salinger, J. D. *Franny and Zooey.* Boston: Little Brown, 1961.

Szasz, Thomas. *Pain and Pleasure: A Study of Bodily Feelings.* Syracuse, NY: Syracuse University Press, 1988.

Teyber, Edward and Faith Holmes Teyber. *Interpersonal Process in Therapy: An Integrative Model.* Boston: Cengage Learning, 2017.

Thoreau, Henry David. *Walden, Or, Life in the Woods.* London: J.M. Dent, 1908.

Winnicott, Donald. *The Child and the Outside World: Studies in Developing Relationships.* London: Tavistock Publications Limited, 1957.

Winnicott, Donald. *The Family and Individual Development.* London: Tavistock Publications Limited, 1965.

Reflections

Until just now, I had not read *Two Minds in a Mirror* from the beginning. When I finally did, and each of those short encounters segued into the next, I understood *Two Minds in a Mirror* as a shortened version of my career – a miniature reflection of my career, so to speak, with all the ups, downs, tangents, and loose ends of a therapist's professional life. So, carrying through the organizing metaphor of this book, it seemed appropriate to reflect on that reflection.

I would say that all my encounters with patients add up to an overriding conclusion: psychotherapy is never definitive. We are always discovering ourselves. But along that way, there are inflection points, takeaways that effect change and, ultimately, determine how we exist in the world. Not everyone changes for the better, but the possibility of self-discovery remains open. *Two Minds in a Mirror* stands for that proposition. Indeed, in psychotherapy, "change" is reciprocal, since as patients move toward greater self-discovery, so does the therapist. In these Reflections, I want to talk about some of what I have learned about myself over 25 years in practice, as well as what I have learned about the practice of therapy – as an art as much as a science.

I am going to acknowledge right here that unlike other practitioners with an M.D. after their names, psychotherapists still call upon art as much as (if not more than) science in order to heal their patients. Establishing a relationship with a patient – the key element in psychotherapy – *is* an art and depends on finding just the right way to encourage and sustain someone's trust. It depends on developing empathy which, in turn, depends on the therapist's self-knowledge. This is not science. It's based on a type of trained humanity that we then professionalize. When I entered the profession, I understood this, but now I have lived it for 25 years. My humanity is still in training, but it's not like a radiologist's continued training, or a thoracic surgeon's. One of my preoccupations in *Two Minds in a Mirror*, therefore, has been to show that the therapist's development and application of his art – his skills – is as difficult and consequential as that of other M.D.s. It's just that the skills are different.

Of course, while talk therapy is as much art as science, the field of psychotherapy now provides practitioners many more options than it did even

25 years ago. These options are based in science, and the "art" comes in when we decide whether to go the scientific route or, at least, combine science with continued talk therapy.

Through neuroscience and pharmacotherapy, we are much better at treating psychotic disorders, bipolar illness, refractory depression, and other conditions. We also have better treatments for personality disorders like borderline and narcissistic states. Of course, there's a long way to go. But we're much more on track and refined about our treatments. When we're able to help, we're more inclined to intervene in sensitive and appropriate situations. Moreover, it's not just through psychotherapy and psychopharmacology that people get better. There is greater awareness in mental health about how diet (through the microbiome and neurotransmitters in the ganglia of the gut) and exercise (through hormonal systems and endorphins) help to address mood and anxiety.

But, at this point, let's stay with the art, since it involves my personal discoveries, rather than the medications and protocols that most everyone in the profession has learned to adopt and apply. I used to listen at least twice as much as I talked, and I still do. However, what I now say is much more informed by my clinical and life experience: dating, marriage, children, losing loved ones, success, falling short, and outright trauma. I share myself and my own life as a way of developing trust and creating empathy. Such self-disclosures can also be instructive and useful to patients trying to find their own way. I am much more willing to provide practical advice based on my experience. In this regard, I have shared with patients my professional mistakes and personal shortcomings as well as examples of success.

What has surprised me is that establishing trust is not just important to the healing process – that's elemental – but that when mutual trust is not present or cannot be developed, it may be best to end the relationship. If I do not think someone is a good fit in that way for my practice (e.g, if we cannot trust each other), then I will refer them to a colleague. It only takes one problematic patient to hurt your reputation or standing in the community. So, I have become more self-protective, and now even model that for my patients. I think President Reagan was right to "trust but verify." I have worked hard to develop trust in my professional judgements and the confidence to act on them. I have become more frank with patients who are not working out and, most of the time, I think they appreciate that.

Nonetheless, I think I have become better at maintaining relationships with patients, not least because I have learned to be more empathetic. One interesting discovery is that empathy can be acquired. When I started practicing, empathy was not my greatest strength. I had to figure out how to resonate with other people's thoughts and feelings. While I always tried to have *their* concerns in mind, I learned to better calibrate my own life experiences with their issues so that, as we spoke, I could register our common humanity. Now when I speak, my comments reflect more of my life – as a person and as a clinician – as well as my patients' lives. I have learned to listen internally and externally simultaneously. It is not easy, but it is essential. I tell my patients that *they* can learn to become more empathetic as well.

Where you do establish an empathic, trusting relationship, you necessarily challenge the old idea of Psychiatrist as Authority which, in any case, has mostly fallen out of favour. Patients still recognize you as *an* authority, but they don't want you acting as an authority figure. They want a more interactive experience that, for the therapist, is less intrapsychic, less the prelude to some obiter dicta. Moreover, they may not see you as *just* a therapist. Thus, when I am sitting with a patient, I ask myself who I am to them and why they are telling me what they are telling me. Perhaps they see me as a father figure and are looking for some advice or guidance, or as a mother who may or may not have been there for them when they were growing up. Those relationships and associated feelings from the past can crystallize in psychotherapy, and there is an opportunity to look at them. Though I need to distinguish myself from whomever the patient sees me as, I have learned to seek out their perception and integrate it into the course of therapy. In this sense, the patient is the "authority," since the therapist cannot risk discounting the patient's perceptions — and any needs that flow from such perceptions.

As I am suggesting, my approach is no longer strictly, or in many cases, classically "Freudian," although in some ways it may be closer to how Freud actualy practiced. I still think that insight and understanding were crucial to greater mental health and happiness. And there's no question that in psychodynamic treatment, they are integral and even essential. But my model was a Freudian one of making the unconscious conscious and analyzing conflict to find more adaptive compromise formations. However, I now realize that there are other important ways of helping people. Useful information about the real world (e.g., social etiquette, interviewing techniques, how to keep to a budget) will make a difference. So, I am more apt to coach a patient about work and rehearse him or her in a social or family situation. I fill in blank spots. Also, promoting cognitive and behavioral changes can be enormously helpful. Looking at maladaptive patterns of thinking — such as the glass being half empty or things always not working out — and replacing them with more realistic ideas can lead to more positive perspectives. I intervene in ways that change patterns of behavior through family support, AA, religious, and other resources. My therapeutic approach has become more pragmatic and eclectic — whatever works. In pursuing the talking cure, I do not shy away from complementary approaches.

But precisely because I am willing to extend myself, I cannot always "be there" for patients and I am not their friend in the way that their real friends are. It is hard to draw the line because patients develop expectations and can feel hurt if you do not satisfy them. Helping patients understand unrealistic expectations is part of the art of therapy, which I have not entirely perfected. Nonetheless, I find that patients' feelings about themselves cannot, of course, be disentangled from the rest of their lives, and that it would be less than helpful to act as if clear distinctions could be drawn. Most patients understand the dilemma of drawing lines (even if they disagree with where to draw them), and welcome my broad-gauge help without imagining that I can be relied upon for advice on everything that occurs in their lives. Ideally, a person's own insight, understanding, and realistic assessment of his situation helps to inform good choices.

Some boundaries develop naturally when I acknowledge that "I don't know." Thus, while I start from the position that I can help someone discover his or her inner truths, in the end I sometimes can't. Sometimes, the memory of a traumatic experience will come to light, and the person feels better. He may feel freer to move forward with greater clarity, more confidence, and less guilt. But it's hard to know the truth because experiences from the past are literally re-membered, or put back together again. So, I will just say, "I'm not sure…," "You might consider…," or "What's known is…," and finally "I don't know." I feel wiser for saying I don't know.

I have found that admitting my lack of ultimate knowledge about someone does not undermine our relationship or even detract from their commitment to talk therapy. If anything, they welcome my honesty and willingness to continue searching for inner truths and plausible solutions. In our age of psychopharmacology, it's easy to forget the therapeutic power of a real relationship. Sometimes, as psychotherapists, we offer corrective emotional experiences to patients. This way of using ourselves is different from an interpretive approach. It's being there in a way for another person that a parent or perhaps another loved one was not or is not. We don't replace those people, but we try to offer the level of concern that they would (have) if they could (have). I've learned how care and kindness are therapeutic modalities. So, while my professional identity is that of a psychiatrist and psychoanalyst – a psychodynamic psychiatrist as I now call myself – my calling is closer to what is sometimes called a healer. I am a persistent healer, hanging in there for as long as it takes … provided the patient remains committed. While life for everyone appears to be speeding up, I offer a type of therapy that allows patients to slow down, get in touch with their feelings, and reflect on them in a safe place.

I have learned from my patients over the years: from their insight and understanding, their courage and resilience. As the stories in *Two Minds in a Mirror* demonstrate, I try to apply their gifts not only to clinical practice but also to my own life. Psychotherapy is a profoundly intersubjective experience. The experience continues to resonate with patient and therapist, almost as in a hall of mirrors. It becomes deeper with time – changes continue to occur – as I have tried to suggest in these reflections.

Perhaps the most important thing I have learned is that in practicing therapy, your own mind changes. You never stop reflecting on what you have said, seen, felt, done, thought, envisioned, and set out to try. As I said in the Introduction, if this book has a shape, it has the shape of my own mind. I might amend that to say my own mind … as I reflect on it all the time.

When I just wrote "all the time," I meant it literally. So, once I had thought about – and then described – what I had learned over the course of my career, I realized that I had also learned a lot just from writing this book. That is, the process of collecting and organizing these encounters made me think about the difference between what actually happened in a particular encounter and what I might (with hindsight) have done differently. Perhaps my patient would have benefited more, or more quickly. We can always do better. This left me wondering whether the patient ever saw what I, finally, came to see. It also left me wondering whether psychotherapy, because it is as much art as science, inclines therapists to second-guess themselves more often than other medical professionals do. Human nature is a lot less discrete than, say, bones or teeth.

It's sometimes hard to know what helps, if only because the patient and therapist may see things from very different perspectives. Should every patient undergo "training" to think like a therapist and have appropriate expectations? No, of course not.

When you write a book about psychotherapy, as in doing psychotherapy, you accept a kind of blurriness. Thus, while I chose subjects for each chapter, and slotted the stories into them, I realized that there could have been other subjects and that any given story might belong as much in one chapter as another. A story about Relationships might as easily belong in Truth and Doubt. However, this dilemma (if it was one) reminded me of something about therapy: every problem has a valence to other problems, so that you cannot just say, "I will treat this problem and the patient will get better." That would be simplistic. Even when someone comes in with depression or fear or an inability to form relationships, you are treating the whole person. These issues can all be connected. I come back to the need to listen. To take time. Without getting a sense of the person – not just the symptom – the therapist will not truly heal that person. Only books fall into nice, discrete subjects. People can't, don't, won't.

Finally, I want to reflect on writing this book collaboratively. Sandra Sherman is a lawyer, a former professor of English, and a perfectionist. We did not always agree. She would insist, I would bridle, and we would somehow find a way. I had to adjust to Sandra's very different way of thinking. She loves precision. I am comfortable with a level of clarity that has always seemed adequate to me. Sandra would sometimes say "Well, in my class..." as if I were her writing student. It was a joke, but with an edge. She once told me "Well, I've read all these stories, and people say a lot worse to you!" Okay. But I undeniably learned a lot about writing creative nonfiction, the process of applying the techniques of novel-writing to actual facts. These stories came alive because of that process. As with my patients, we developed an intense relationship, and I will carry what I've learned into relationships that I have yet to form. Beyond just writing this book, that may be what I really gained from our collaboration.

Once I chose the mirror as this book's organizing metaphor, I became even more interested in mirrors as literary/artistic subjects. Some of these I discuss in the Introduction. But they are endless. I'd like to focus on just one here which, I think, captures my experience in writing this book. In Alfred Lord Tennyson's

"The Lady of Shalott" (1832), a woman high up in a castle only views the world indirectly, as reflected in a mirror. Finally, however, she peeks out the window, sees the world first-hand, and the mirror cracks. She must descend into reality. As a psychotherapist, I think about my patients, spin theories about them, but I am under no pressure to produce an objective correlative of my relationships with them. I could, if I wished, live in solitude, a Park Avenue version of the Lady of Shalott.

What happened to change all this was that I looked at those diary entries and the mirror cracked – I had a glimpse of what I had done, hence of what might do, and then I had no choice. It was like one of those sudden, insight/ understanding moments that I describe in Chapter 6. I have learned enough from those moments in my practice to recognize that when they occur you follow them up. The result was *Two Minds in a Mirror* which reflects what I have learned as I move forward.

★★★★★★★★★★★★★★★★★★★★★★★★★★★★★

I wrote those last words in February 2020, just before we were all engulfed by the coronavirus. As the pandemic took hold, I reread this book yet again, on the assumption that what I had learned from interactions with my patients might apply to the new crisis that presented. I wasn't wrong. I still had to empathize when my patients were afraid and still had to help them understand that guilt is unproductive except insofar as we confront and deal with it. What was different was that now everything was more immediate and intense. Where previously someone was afraid, they were now terrified and utterly bewildered; if they had been guilty, they were now almost inconsolable. Everything had become more resonant, with higher stakes. I felt under enormous pressure to help people see that they were still in control of their lives – or at least elements that could still make a difference. This wasn't easy. My patients and I were no longer even in the same room, but on the phone, Zooming, or Skyping. The context, which in my case was an intimate but professional office, had given way to a vacuum in cyberspace.

But I am still here. We continue to talk. I wonder how my patients and I will emerge from this crisis. I expect that we will have a greater appreciation for maintaining connections with other human beings. There is reassurance in the quotidian when everything else – fear, guilt, grim statistics – seems to grow larger by the day. I think we will return to living our lives on a more nearly human scale.

Throughout this crisis, I sometimes asked: "Am I doing enough to help when people are dying throughout New York City?" I think that a lot of M.D.s not directly dealing – I should say duelling – with the virus, asked the same question. I finally decided that while I wasn't in the ER or on the wards, I was still near the front lines: the virus had caused so much mental distress, with knock-on physical effects like loss of sleep and appetite, that my intervention was part of the whole, integrated medical response. Many patients were suffering from a type of "double depression," where the effects of living through the pandemic – and finding it endlessly depressing – exacerbated earlier depressive tendencies that they had heretofore managed to control. Some needed medication. Some needed advice on diet and exercise. They were suffering and needed tangible help. The toll on me was real, and I tried to take my own advice on staying healthy and maintaining my ability to focus on each patient's needs.

We are not yet past this. Nor will we be for some time as we rethink everything from personal responsibility to the role that government should play in our lives. Thus, writing *Two Minds in a Mirror* was practice for how I can address the array of human emotions in a new, more questioning and uncertain time. If by rereading this book I was looking backward, I did so in part because I had to look ahead. We all need to toggle between what we have done and what remains to be done. Maybe that is one definition of resilience.

Index

Abelard and Eloise 27
acceptance 82–83
ADD; *see* Attention Deficit Disorder
Alcoholics Anonymous (AA) 131
Alexander, Franz 144
ambivalence, patient's 22, 50, 117
anger 24–25; disproportionate 24; externalizing 25; resentment 24
anxiety, source of 119
Ashbery, John 5
Attention Deficit Disorder (ADD) 102, 103, 135–7

Beck, Aaron 109
being deficient, sense of 26
being distracted 102–3
bipolar disorder 15
Breuer, Joseph 6, 75

Carroll, Lewis 2
case presentation, to colleagues 80–82
CBT; *see* cognitive and behavioral therapies; *see* Cognitive Behavioural Therapy
character 34–36; attachment to 35; definition 34
Chrichton, Michael 80
cognitive and behavioral therapies 33
Cognitive Behavioural Therapy (CBT) 110
cognitive dissonance 129
competitiveness 29
complications 99
connection: childish modes of forming 93; in psychotherapeutic relationship 78–79
cost of treatment 63–64
couch, for patients 75–77
couch-based treatment 75–77
countertransference 54, 57, 89
criticism, on poor response to therapy 55–57

defining moment 113–14
Diagnostic and Statistical Manual of Mental Disorders (DSM) 136
Diagnostic and Statistical Manual of Psychiatry (DSM V) 35
distraction 135–7
Donne, John 147
doubt 122; about own value 126; healthy sense of 138; truth and 123
dreams 94–95, 103–4, 145; believing in 140–1; truth and 123–4
dropping out of treatment 69–71; knowing the truth of 134–5

effort 153–5
emotional debt 60
empathy: definition 67; development of 73; meeting old friend 80–81; Narcissistic Personality Disorder and 71; in psychotherapeutic relationship 67; trusting relationship 83
"enactment," 57, 72
Erikson, Erik 37–38, 40, 62, 98
erotic feelings 87
erotomanic attachment, patient 31–32, 33
exposure therapy 33

face-to-face contact 75
facing reality 119–20
family: biology 20; history 19–21; during loss 147; meetings 64–66; mothers 149–50; politics 137–8
fantasies, patient 69–70
fear: of being cured 71; of being trapped 94
feeling of loss; *see* loss
feeling special 36, 38–40
forgiving, and healing 159
former patients 151–3

Freud, Sigmund 1–2, 6, 8, 16, 25, 38, 40, 75, 85, 87, 105, 123; Oedipal stage of development 42; views on dreams 94–95
Freudian slips 42–44
Friedberg, Ahron 18

getting engaged 96–97
Gladwell, Malcolm 64
grief 107, 109, 144
guilt, feelings of 10–13, 28, 37, 24, 60, 68, 70, 79, 92, 105–7, 117–18, 136, 156–58, 163, 165; Oedipal 81

healing 142; emotional scars 2; mirror as metaphor for 2–3; relationships in 4–5; self-scrutiny in 2
Heisenberg, Werner 122
honesty 124–5
"hypochondria" 84

identification 95–96
impediments: to love 90; to success 109
initial interview 67–69
insight 101, 138–9; being distracted 102–3; from dream 103–4
insight-oriented psychotherapy 23–24, 36, 73
interpersonal psychotherapy 28
Interpretation of Dreams 94
intimacy 97–98
"intrusion" 104

journal, keeping 7–8

late payments 58–59
leaving home 116–17
leaving things in clinic, patients 21–22
letting go, negative emotions 150–1
listening 10–11; breathing and 15; to negation 16–18; and reflection 15–16; as therapy 13–15
loss 146–7
love 157–8; impediments to 90; loss of 146; and money 59–61; relationship to healing 144; source of healing 142

making up 31–33
masturbation, therapist allusion to 120
"memories" 85
middle age, life during 61–63
Middlemarch 27
mirror: as metaphor for healing 2–3; as metaphor of mind 3; and objective reality 3

mirror neurons 80
missed appointments 49–52, 63
missing sessions 53
mistrust 42–44
mother, patient relationship 149–50
mother-child relationship 90–91
motivation, in therapeutic relationship 71–73, 118, 125–6
Murphy's Law 45–46
myself 144–6

name; *see* patient name
Narcissistic Personality Disorder 71
need 142–4
negation: listening to 16–18; to silence 17
negative emotions, letting go 150–1
"negative therapeutic reaction," 57, 72
negativistic relationship 118
neurotic conflicts 39
note-taking 11–12

obsession 127–8
Oedipus: Complex 105; guilt 81; Rex 105
overbooked patients 52–53

pain 23–24, 83–84
panic disorder 15
past: attachment to 90; develop distance towards 86; as memory 85; patient, therapist response to 89
patient history, taking 9–10, 14
patient name 18–20
patient-psychotherapist relationship 1, 4–5; transferential aspect of 76, 77
personal truth 122, 125
perspective 91
physical positions; *see* seating arrangements, in psychotherapy
precarious, feeling 28–29
Pride and Prejudice 27
problem, dealing with 117
psychoanalytic training 41–42
"psychodynamic psychiatry" 3
psychodynamic therapy 3–4, 85, 89, 162; ambivalence towards 50; Freud's advice on listening 8; goal of 35; mistakes in 54–55; observations in 54–55; transference in 88, 93; trust in 30–47; *see also* trust; use self as an example in 128–30
psychotherapeutic relationship: connection in 78–79; empathy and 67

quit treatment, patient 87–88

Rashomon problem 64
reflection 160–5; listening and 15–16
relative failure 62
resistance to therapy 44–5, 117–18, 119
risk management 45–7
Russell, Bertrand 83

sacrifices for therapy, patient's 55–57
Santayana, George 85
scheduling: error 52–55; problem 36–38
seating arrangements, in psychotherapy 73–77; couch in 75–77; relative proximity and 74
secret history 22–23
self-esteem 133
self-regard 133
sensitivity 114–16
separation 110–11
settling down, desire of 104–5
sex life, after marriage 120
siblings, patient's relationship 92–93
social life 153
Sontag, Susan 82
stuttering 92
suggestion 86
"suspension of disbelief" 31
symbiotic trust relationship 39
symptoms 105–7; treatment of 35–36

"talking cure," 1, 6
talk therapy: listening in 10–11; *see also* listening
terminal illness 150
Through the Looking Glass 2

tikkun olam 126
time and money 49–66; cancelled appointment to save, patient 49–52; cost of treatment 63–64; financial support from family 61–63; late payments 58–59; love and money 59–61; marital breakup 58; middle age, life during 61–63; patient's sacrifice for therapy 55–57; scheduling error 52–55; turning 50, 61–62
transference 4, 54, 57, 87, 88, 93; erotic 32, 87; father 84; maternal 83; relationships and 85
trauma 111–113
trust 30–47; and character 34–36; covert test by patient 32; mistrust 42–44; mutual 30–31; in oneself 47; psychoanalytic training and 41–42; regaining 37; and resistance to therapy 44–45; and white lie with patient 31–33; working 33
truth, in therapy 122–4; acknowledging 130–1; for closure of patient case 134–5; and doubt 123; getting better after telling 133–4; honesty and 124–5; hurts 131–3; personal 122, 125; psychic 123
Two Minds in a Mirror, 5, 160, 163, 165

understanding 101

Waiting for Godot 1
Wilde, Oscar 153
Winnicott, Donald 91, 128
work 26–27
"working trust" 33
"working through" 8